Promises to Keep

volume 2: from 1865

Promises to Keep

A portrayal of nonwhites in the United States

Bruce A. Glasrud and Alan M. Smith
California State College at Hayward

Rand McNally & Company Chicago

Second Printing, 1972

Preface

This book is designed to provide a series of collateral readings on the history of nonwhite Americans for students of United States history. Although many standard American history textbooks have recently been revised to correct their almost total neglect of these minorities, the result in most cases is a token appearance of dark-skinned characters in what is essentially a white man's story. The obvious need for materials treating nonwhites in American history courses has been met by a number of readers on specific minority groups. This book presents readings dealing with the history of all the major nonwhite groups that have played a part in the development of America.

The term "nonwhite" is difficult to define. In this work, we have included articles about Americans who have viewed themselves, or who have been viewed by the white majority, as distinct and different because of their skin color. The groups included—the Indians, blacks, Mexican-Americans, Chinese-Americans, Japanese-Americans, Filipino-Americans, and Puerto Ricans—differ greatly in their roles and experiences in American history, but all have encountered prejudice and difficulties on account of their skin color.

The articles which compose this volume are arranged under six chronological headings covering American history from the founding of Jamestown to the present. In each historical period there is an article concerning the nonwhite groups in American society at that particular time; there are also several articles which cover the relationships among nonwhite groups. The articles are the work of scholarly students of America, most of them historians, writing during the past thirty years. The authors vary in their focuses and points of view, but all are concerned with the interaction between the nonwhite minorities and the white majority in the United States. In most cases, the articles have been edited for the sake of brevity, but citations of sources have been retained and introductory material has been supplied to place the essays in a larger context.

We hope that these readings will aid students of American history in discovering the richness and diversity of the peoples of the United States and in understanding the origins of the racial problems which still plague the nation.

We wish to thank three people for their help in developing this volume: Richard J. Orsi for his suggestion of potential selections, Ann S. Jablin, our editor at Rand McNally, for her careful reading of the manuscript, and Pearlene V. Glasrud for her incisive and instructive comments as the work progressed.

Bruce A. Glasrud
Alan M. Smith

Hayward, California

Table of Contents

NOTE: Solid line type refers to contents of this volume.
Screened type refers to contents in companion volume.

Selected Bibliography

Index

Part I
Introduction

Introduction

Nonwhites in the United States comprise a substantial minority whose experience and life style differ significantly from that of the white majority. White Americans developed a social system in which race, color, and culture were important distinguishing criteria. With these factors as broad indicators of status in society, red, yellow, brown, or black skin marked a man as inferior in the eyes of the white majority and set limits on the extent to which he could share in the benefits of an expanding and upwardly mobile society.

As did the various white ethnic groups, nonwhites arrived in substantial blocs at specific junctures in the national development. There has been an increase in the population of nonwhites, although until recently Native Americans, called Indians because of a well-known mistake, were an exception. The population of Native Americans had declined as a result of incessant warfare, and in the process they lost much of their land, heritage, and livelihood. The first nonwhites to immigrate to North America were blacks from Africa who began to populate the continent at the same time as the Europeans since they were imported as slaves for profit-seeking whites. Even after the abolition of slavery, blacks faced a harsh caste system which severely regulated their lives.

The incorporation of other nonwhite groups awaited the mid-nineteenth century when the United States waged war against Mexico, conquered vast stretches of territory, and added to its population former citizens of her southern neighbor. Other Mexicans entered the United States as impoverished agricultural and industrial workers in the twentieth century, and, because of barriers created by language, culture, religion, and alien status, they were easily exploited.

Beginning in 1848, Chinese also entered the United States. They sought gold to take back to China; but racial and cultural differences again precluded equitable treatment, and they became poorly paid laborers. When some were able to achieve success despite the obstacles, alarmed whites brought about the enactment of the Chinese Exclusion Act. Other Orientals, Japanese, Filipinos, and Koreans, trailed the Chinese to the United States. Recently, additional minorities including Hawaiians, Eskimos, Puerto Ricans, and lesser numbers from Southeast Asia, India, and the Middle East have migrated to the United States.

Relations among the nonwhites varied with the predicament of each group. Often they competed with one another for the few menial positions or favors offered to minorities. At other times they joined forces against the white majority in a bid for privileges that were denied them. Some nonwhites strove for acceptance by the majority, which meant adopting white values, but usually they were restricted to separate and unequal areas where they developed their own cultures and societies apart from those of the whites.

Three themes stand out in the history of nonwhites in the United States. First, nonwhites confronted total domination by the white majority. Their subjugation took the forms of slavery, war, annihilation, physical torture, cultural deprivation, economic restriction, political exclusion, geographical removal, and social ostracism. Second, segregation became a way of life as the paramount white society forced physical separation upon them. Whenever the nonwhites sought apartheid, the whites, fearful of collective action directed against them, took reluctant steps to modify legal segregation. But there have been few meaningful steps toward integration, and the result remains in the confinement of blacks in ghettos, Chinese in Chinatowns, Chicanos in barrios, and Indians on reservations. Third, nonwhites resisted white encroachments. Their defiance assumed overt and covert forms, often at the same time. Overt resistance included riots, revolts, warfare, and murder; covert resistance often hid behind smiles, good behavior, and the signing of treaties. But dislike of whites and the white dominated society was obvious, even to those whites who insisted that nonwhites were happy with their second-class status.

The United States, a nation which has prided itself on its equalitarian nature, is, in actuality, a heterogeneous society that exhibits major schisms between the groups which comprise it. The tensions of American society are particularly apparent between the dominant white majority and the various nonwhite minorities. The nonwhites, subjugated, segregated, and defiant, remain a challenge to the nation's capacities for providing the promise of equality to all its citizens.

Milton M. Gordon,
"Assimilation in America: Theory and Reality"

Accounts of the manner in which immigrants or minority groups become, or fail to become, "Americanized" too often portray the myths, rather than the realities, of that process. Milton M. Gordon, in "Assimilation in America," asserts that Americans have used three concepts to explain both what has happened and what should happen to immigrants and the manner in which newcomers have interacted with the dominant society: (1) Anglo-conformity, (2) the melting pot, and (3) cultural pluralism. Although cultural pluralism is the most accurate of the three, none are apt descriptions of assimilation; rather, Gordon concludes, the phrase "structural pluralism" better interprets the American experience. In the United States acculturation which stresses secondary and impersonal relationships takes place, but structural assimilation which emphasizes primary and personal relationships is often lacking. For racial minorities, however, even acculturation has been limited. Instead, nonwhites have established separate communities within the prevailing white society.

Assimilation in America:
Theory and Reality

Milton M. Gordon

Three ideologies or conceptual models have competed for attention
on the American scene as explanations of the way in which a nation,
in the beginning largely white, Anglo-Saxon, and Protestant, has
absorbed over 41 million immigrants and their descendants from
variegated sources and welded them into the contemporary American
people. These ideologies are Anglo-conformity, the melting pot, and
cultural pluralism. They have served at various times, and often
simultaneously, as explanations of what has happened—descriptive
models—and of what should happen—goal models. Not infrequently
they have been used in such a fashion that it is difficult to tell which
of these two usages the writer has had in mind. In fact, one of the
more remarkable omissions in the history of American intellectual
thought is the relative lack of close analytical attention given to the
theory of immigrant adjustment in the United States by its social
scientists.

The result has been that this field of discussion—an overridingly

Abridged from Milton M. Gordon, "Assimilation in America: Theory and
Reality," *Daedalus*, XC (1961), pp. 163–185. Reprinted by permission of
Daedalus, Journal of the American Academy of Arts and Sciences, Boston, Mass.,
Spring 1961, *Ethnic Groups in American Life*. Some footnotes have been re-
numbered.

important one since it has significant implications for the more familiar problems of prejudice, discrimination, and majority-minority group relations generally—has been largely preempted by laymen, representatives of belles lettres, philosophers, and apologists of various persuasions. Even from these sources the amount of attention devoted to ideologies of assimilation is hardly extensive. Consequently, the work of improving intergroup relations in America is carried out by dedicated professional agencies and individuals who deal as best they can with day-to-day problems of discriminatory behavior, but who for the most part are unable to relate their efforts to an adequate conceptual apparatus. Such an apparatus would, at one and the same time, accurately describe the present structure of American society with respect to its ethnic groups (I shall use the term "ethnic group" to refer to any racial, religious, or national origins collectively), and allow for a considered formulation of its assimilation or integration goals for the foreseeable future. One is reminded of Alice's distraught question in her travels in Wonderland: "Would you tell me, please, which way I ought to go from here?" "That depends a good deal," replied the Cat with irrefutable logic, "on where you want to get to."

The story of America's immigration can be quickly told for our present purposes. The white American population at the time of the Revolution was largely English and Protestant in origin, but had already absorbed substantial groups of Germans and Scotch-Irish and smaller contingents of Frenchmen, Dutchmen, Swedes, Swiss, South Irish, Poles, and a handful of migrants from other European nations. Catholics were represented in modest numbers, particularly in the middle colonies, and a small number of Jews were residents of the incipient nation. With the exception of the Quakers and a few missionaries, the colonists had generally treated the Indians and their cultures with contempt and hostility, driving them from the coastal plains and making the western frontier a bloody battleground where eternal vigilance was the price of survival.

Although the Negro at that time made up nearly one-fifth of the total population, his predominantly slave status, together with racial and cultural prejudice, barred him from serious consideration as an assimilable element of the society. And while many groups of European origin started out as determined ethnic enclaves, eventually, most historians believe, considerable ethnic intermixture within the white population took place. "People of different blood" [sic]—write two American historians about the colonial period, "English, Irish, German, Huguenot, Dutch, Swedish—mingled and intermarried with little thought of any difference."[1] In such a society, its people predominantly English, its white immigrants of other ethnic origins either English-speaking or derived largely from countries of northern and western Europe whose cultural divergences from the English were not great, and its dominant white population excluding by fiat the claims and considerations of welfare of the non-Caucasian minorities, the problem of assimilation understandably did not loom unduly large or complex.

The unfolding events of the next century and a half with increasing momentum dispelled the complacency which rested upon the relative simplicity of colonial and immediate post-Revolutionary conditions. The large-scale immigration to America of the famine-fleeing Irish, the Germans, and later the Scandinavians (along with additional Englishmen and other peoples of northern and western Europe) in the middle of the nineteenth century (the so-called "old immigration"), the emancipation of the Negro slaves and the problems created by post-Civil War reconstruction, the placing of the conquered Indian with his broken culture on government reservations, the arrival of the Oriental, first attracted by the discovery of gold and other opportunities in the West, and finally, beginning in the last quarter of the nineteenth century and continuing to the early 1920's, the swelling to proportions hitherto unimagined of the tide of immigration from the peasantries and "pales" of southern and eastern Europe—the Italians, Jews, and Slavs of the so-called "new immigration," fleeing the persecutions and industrial dislocations of the day—all these events constitute the background against which we may consider the rise of the theories of assimilation mentioned above. After a necessarily foreshortened description of each of these theories and their historical emergence, we shall suggest analytical distinctions designed to aid in clarifying the nature of the assimilation process, and then conclude by focusing on the American scene.

1. Allan Nevins and Henry Steele Commager, *America: The Story of a Free People* (Boston, Little, Brown, 1942), p. 58.

Anglo-Conformity

"Anglo-conformity"[2] is a broad term used to cover a variety of view-points about assimilation and immigration; they all assume the desirability of maintaining English institutions (as modified by the American Revolution), the English language, and English-oriented cultural patterns as dominant and standard in American life. However, bound up with this assumption are related attitudes. These may range from discredited notions about race and "Nordic" and "Aryan" racial superiority, together with the nativist political programs and exclusionist immigration policies which such notions entail, through an intermediate position of favoring immigration from northern and western Europe on amorphous, unreflective grounds ("They are more like us"), to a lack of opposition to any source of immigration, as long as these immigrants and their descendants duly adopt the standard Anglo-Saxon cultural patterns. There is by no means any necessary equation between Anglo-conformity and racist attitudes.

It is quite likely that "Anglo-conformity" in its more moderate aspects, however explicit its formulation, has been the most prevalent ideology of assimilation goals in America throughout the nation's history....

Anglo-conformity received its fullest expression in the so-called Americanization movement which gripped the nation during World War I. While "Americanization" in its various stages had more than one emphasis, it was essentially a consciously articulated movement to strip the immigrant of his native culture and attachments and make him over into an American along Anglo-Saxon lines—all this to be accomplished with great rapidity. To use an image of a later day, it was an attempt at "pressure-cooking assimilation." It had prewar antecedents, but it was during the height of the world conflict that federal agencies, state governments, municipalities, and a host of private organizations joined in the effort to persuade the immigrant to learn English, take out naturalization papers, buy war bonds, forget his former origins and culture, and give himself over to patriotic hysteria.

2. The phrase is the Coles's. See Stewart G. Cole and Mildred Wiese Cole, *Minorities and the American Promise* (New York, Harper & Brothers, 1954), ch. 6.

After the war and the "Red scare" which followed, the excesses of the Americanization movement subsided. In its place, however, came the restriction of immigration through federal law. Foiled at first by presidential vetoes, and later by the failure of the 1917 literacy test to halt the immigrant tide, the proponents of restriction finally put through in the early 1920's a series of acts culminating in the well-known national-origins formula for immigrant quotas which went into effect in 1929. Whatever the merits of a quantitative limit on the number of immigrants to be admitted to the United States, the provisions of the formula, which discriminated sharply against the countries of southern and eastern Europe, in effect institutionalized the assumptions of the rightful dominance of Anglo-Saxon patterns in the land. Reaffirmed with only slight modifications in the Mc-Carran-Walter Act of 1952, these laws, then, stand as a legal monument to the creed of Anglo-conformity and a telling reminder that this ideological system still has numerous and powerful adherents on the American scene.

The Melting Pot

While Anglo-conformity in various guises has probably been the most prevalent ideology of assimilation in the American historical experience, a competing viewpoint with more generous and idealistic overtones has had its adherents and exponents from the eighteenth century onward. Conditions in the virgin continent, it was clear, were modifying the institutions which the English colonists brought with them from the mother country. Arrivals from non-English homelands such as Germany, Sweden, and France were similarly exposed to this fresh environment. Was it not possible, then, to think of the evolving American society not as a slightly modified England but rather as a totally new blend, culturally and biologically, in which the stocks and folkways of Europe, figuratively speaking, were indiscriminately mixed in the political pot of the emerging nation and fused by the fires of American influence and interaction into a distinctly new type?

Such, at any rate, was the conception of the new society which motivated that eighteenth-century French-born writer and agriculturalist, J. Hector St. John Crèvecoeur, who, after many years of

American residence, published his reflections and observations in *Letters from an American Farmer*.[3] Who, he asks, is the American?

> He is either an European, or the descendant of an European, hence that strange mixture of blood, which you find in no other country. I could point out to you a family whose grandfather was an Englishman, whose wife was Dutch, whose son married a French woman, and whose present four sons have now four wives of different nations. He is an American, who leaving behind him all his ancient prejudices and manners, receives new ones from the new mode of life he has embraced, the new government he obeys, and the new rank he holds. He becomes an American by being received in the broad lap of our great *Alma Mater*. Here individuals of all nations are melted into a new race of men, whose labours and posterity will one day cause great changes in the world.

Some observers have interpreted the open-door policy on immigration of the first three-quarters of the nineteenth century as reflecting an underlying faith in the effectiveness of the American melting pot, in the belief "that all could be absorbed and that all could contribute to an emerging national character."[4] ...

... Around the turn of the [twentieth] century the melting-pot idea became embedded in the ideals of the age as one response to the immigrant receiving experience of the nation. Soon to be challenged by a new philosophy of group adjustment ... and always competing with the more pervasive adherence to Anglo-conformity, the melting-pot image, however, continued to draw a portion of the attention consciously directed toward this aspect of the American scene in the first half of the twentieth century. In the mid-1940's a sociologist who had carried out an investigation of intermarriage trends in New Haven, Connecticut, described a revised conception of the melting process in that city and suggested a basic modification of the theory

3. J. Hector St. John Crèvecoeur, *Letters from an American Farmer* (New York, Albert and Charles Boni, 1925; reprinted from the 1st edn., London, 1782), pp. 54–55.
4. Oscar Handlin, ed., *Immigration as a Factor in American History* (Englewood, Prentice-Hall, 1959), p. 146.

of that process. In New Haven, Ruby Jo Reeves Kennedy[5] reported from a study of intermarriages from 1870 to 1940 that there was a distinct tendency for the British-Americans, Germans, and Scandinavians to marry among themselves—that is, within a Protestant "pool"; for the Irish, Italians, and Poles to marry among themselves—a Catholic "pool"; and for the Jews to marry other Jews. In other words, intermarriage was taking place across lines of nationality background, but there was a strong tendency for it to stay confined within one or the other of the three major religious groups, Protestants, Catholics, and Jews. Thus, declared Mrs. Kennedy, the picture in New Haven resembled a "triple melting pot" based on religious divisions, rather than a "single melting pot." Her study indicated, she stated, that "while strict endogamy is loosening, religious endogamy is persisting and the future cleavages will be along religious lines rather than along nationality lines as in the past. If this is the case, then the traditional 'single-melting-pot' idea must be abandoned, and a new conception, which we term the 'triple-melting-pot' theory of American assimilation, will take its place as the true expression of what is happening to the various nationality groups in the United States."[6] The triple-melting-pot thesis was later taken up by the theologian Will Herberg and formed an important sociological frame of reference for his analysis of religious trends in American society, *Protestant-Catholic-Jew.*[7] But the triple-melting-pot hypothesis patently takes us into the realm of a society pluralistically conceived. We turn now to the rise of an ideology which attempts to justify such a conception.

Cultural Pluralism

Probably all the non-English immigrants who came to American shores in any significant numbers from colonial times onward—settling either in the forbidding wilderness, the lonely prairie, or in

5. Ruby J. Reeves Kennedy, "Single or Triple Melting-Pot? Intermarriage Trends in New Haven, 1870–1940," *American Journal of Sociology*, 1944, 49:331–339. See also her "Single or Triple Melting-Pot? Intermarriage in New Haven, 1870–1950," *ibid.*, 1952, 58:56–59.

6. *Ibid.*, "Single or Triple Melting-Pot? ... 1870–1940," p. 332 (author's italics omitted).

7. Will Herberg, *Protestant-Catholic-Jew* (Garden City, Doubleday, 1955).

some accessible urban slum—created ethnic enclaves and looked forward to the preservation of at least some of their native cultural patterns. Such a development, natural as breathing, was supported by the later accretion of friends, relatives, and countrymen seeking out oases of familiarity in a strange land, by the desire of the settlers to rebuild (necessarily in miniature) a society in which they could communicate in the familiar tongue and maintain familiar institutions, and, finally, by the necessity to band together for mutual aid and mutual protection against the uncertainties of a strange and frequently hostile environment. This was as true of the "old" immigrants as of the "new." In fact, some of the liberal intellectuals who fled to America from an inhospitable political climate in Germany in the 1830's, 1840's, and 1850's looked forward to the creation of an all-German state within the union, or, even more hopefully, to the eventual formation of a separate German nation, as soon as the expected dissolution of the union under the impact of the slavery controversy should have taken place.[8] Oscar Handlin, writing of the sons of Erin in mid-nineteenth-century Boston, recent refugees from famine and economic degradation in their homeland, points out: "Unable to participate in the normal associational affairs of the community, the Irish felt obliged to erect a society within a society, to act together in their own way. In every contact therefore the group, acting apart from other sections of the community, became intensely aware of its peculiar and exclusive identity."[9] Thus cultural pluralism was a fact in American society before it became a theory—a theory with explicit relevance for the nation as a whole, and articulated and discussed in the English-speaking circles of American intellectual life. . . .

The classic statement of the cultural pluralist position [appeared early in 1915 in two articles entitled] "Democracy versus the Melting-Pot." Their author was Horace Kallen, a Harvard-educated philos-

8. Nathan Glazer, "Ethnic Groups in America: From National Culture to Ideology," in Morroe Berger, Theodore Abel, and Charles H. Page, eds., *Freedom and Control in Modern Society* (New York, D. Van Nostrand, 1954), p. 161; Marcus Lee Hansen, *The Immigrant in American History* (Cambridge, Harvard University Press, 1940), pp. 129–140; John A. Hawgood, *The Tragedy of German-America* (New York, Putnam's, 1940), passim.

9. Oscar Handlin, *Boston's Immigrants* (Cambridge, Harvard University Press, 1959, rev. edn.), p. 176.

opher with a concern for the application of philosophy to societal affairs, and, as an American Jew, himself derivative of an ethnic background which was subject to the contemporary pressures for dissolution implicit in the "Americanization," or Anglo-conformity, and the melting-pot theories. In these articles Kallen vigorously rejected the usefulness of these theories as models of what was actually transpiring in American life or as ideals for the future. Rather he was impressed by the way in which the various ethnic groups in America were coincident with particular areas and regions, and with the tendency for each group to preserve its own language, religion, communal institutions, and ancestral culture. All the while, he pointed out, the immigrant has been learning to speak English as the language of general communication, and has participated in the overall economic and political life of the nation. These developments in which "the United States are in the process of becoming a federal state not merely as a union of geographical and administrative unities, but also as a cooperation of cultural diversities, as a federation or commonwealth of national cultures,"[10] the author argued, far from constituting a violation of historic American political principles, as the "Americanizers" claimed, actually represented the inevitable consequences of democratic ideals, since individuals are implicated in groups, and since democracy for the individual must by extension also mean democracy for his group.

The processes just described, however, as Kallen develops his argument, are far from having been thoroughly realized. They are menaced by "Americanization" programs, assumptions of Anglo-Saxon superiority, and misguided attempts to promote "racial" amalgamation. Thus America stands at a kind of cultural crossroads. It can attempt to impose by force an artificial, Anglo-Saxon oriented uniformity on its peoples, or it can consciously allow and encourage its ethnic groups to develop democratically, each emphasizing its particular cultural heritage. If the latter course is followed, as Kallen puts it at the close of his essay, then,[11]

10. Horace M. Kallen, "Democracy versus the Melting-Pot," *The Nation*, 18 and 25 February 1915; reprinted in his *Culture and Democracy in the United States*, Boni and Liveright, 1924; the quotation is on p. 116.
11. Kallen, *Culture and Democracy . . .*, p. 124.

The outlines of a possible great and truly democratic common-wealth become discernible. Its form would be that of the federal republic; its substance a democracy of nationalities, cooperating voluntarily and autonomously through common institutions in the enterprise of self-realization through the perfection of men according to their kind. The common language of the commonwealth, the language of its great tradition, would be English, but each nationality would have for its emotional and involuntary life its own peculiar dialect or speech, its own individual and inevitable esthetic and intellectual forms. The political and economic life of the commonwealth is a single unit and serves as the foundation and background for the realization of the distinctive individuality of each *nation* that composes it and of the pooling of these in a harmony above them all. Thus "American civilization" may come to mean the perfection of the cooperative harmonies of "European civilization"—the waste, the squalor and the distress of Europe being eliminated—a multiplicity in a unity, an orchestration of mankind.

... In the twentieth century, particularly since World War II, "cultural pluralism" has become a concept which has worked its way into the vocabulary and imagery of specialists in intergroup relations and leaders of ethnic communal groups. In view of this new pluralistic emphasis, some writers now prefer to speak of the "integration" of immigrants rather than of their "assimilation."[12] However, with a few exceptions,[13] no close analytical attention has been given either by social scientists or practitioners of intergroup relations to the meaning of cultural pluralism, its nature and relevance for a modern industrialized society, and its implications for problems of prejudice

12. See W. D. Borrie *et al., The Cultural Integration of Immigrants* (a survey based on the papers and proceedings of the UNESCO Conference in Havana, April 1956), Paris, UNESCO, 1959; and William S. Bernard. "The Integration of Immigrants in the United States" (mimeographed), one of the papers for this conference.

13. See particularly Milton M. Gordon, "Social Structure and Goals in Group Relations"; and Nathan Glazer, "Ethnic Groups in America; From National Culture to Ideology," both articles in Berger, Abel, and Page, *op. cit.*; S. N. Eisenstadt, *The Absorption of Immigrants* (London, Routledge and Kegan Paul, 1954); and W. D. Borrie *et al., ibid.*

and discrimination—a point to which we referred at the outset of this discussion.

Conclusions

In the remaining pages I can make only a few analytical comments which I shall apply in context to the American scene, historical and current. My view of the American situation will not be documented here, but may be considered as a series of hypotheses in which I shall attempt to outline the American assimilation process.

First of all, it must be realized that "assimilation" is a blanket term which in reality covers a multitude of subprocesses. The most crucial distinction is one often ignored—the distinction between what I have elsewhere called "behavioral assimilation" and "structural assimilation."[14] The first refers to the absorption of the cultural behavior patterns of the "host" society. (At the same time, there is frequently some modification of the cultural patterns of the immigrant-receiving country, as well.) There is a special term for this process of cultural modification or "behavioral assimilation"—namely, "acculturation." "Structural assimilation," on the other hand, refers to the entrance of the immigrants and their descendants into the social cliques, organizations, institutional activities, and general civic life of the receiving society. If this process takes place on a large enough scale, then a high frequency of intermarriage must result. A further distinction must be made between, on the one hand, those activities of the general civic life which involve earning a living, carrying out political responsibilities, and engaging in the instrumental affairs of the larger community, and, on the other hand, activities which create personal friendship patterns, frequent home intervisiting, communal worship, and communal recreation. The first type usually develops so-called "secondary relationships," which tend to be relatively impersonal and segmental; the latter type leads to "primary relationships," which are warm, intimate, and personal.

With these various distinctions in mind, we may then proceed.

Built on the base of the original immigrant "colony" but frequently extending into the life of successive generations, the characteristic ethnic group experience is this: within the ethnic group there devel-

14. Milton M. Gordon, "Social Structure and Goals in Group Relations," p. 151.

ops a network of organizations and informal social relationships which permits and encourages the members of the ethnic group to remain within the confines of the group for all of their primary relationships and some of their secondary relationships throughout all the stages of the life cycle. From the cradle in the sectarian hospital to the child's play group, the social clique in high school, the fraternity and religious center in college, the dating group within which he searches for a spouse, the marriage partner, the neighborhood of his residence, the church affiliation and the church clubs, the men's and the women's social and service organizations, the adult clique of "marrieds," the vacation resort, and then, as the age cycle nears completion, the rest home for the elderly and, finally, the sectarian cemetery—in all these activities and relationships which are close to the core of personality and selfhood—the member of the ethnic group may if he wishes follow a path which never takes him across the boundaries of his ethnic structural network.

The picture is made more complex by the existence of social class divisions which cut across ethnic group lines just as they do those of the white Protestant population in America. As each ethnic group which has been here for the requisite time has developed second, third, or in some cases, succeeding generations, it has produced a college-educated group which composes an upper middle class (and sometimes upper class, as well) segment of the larger groups. Such class divisions tend to restrict primary group relations even further, for although the ethnic-group member feels a general sense of identification with all the bearers of his ethnic heritage, he feels comfortable in intimate social relations only with those who also share his own class background or attainment.

In short, my point is that, while *behavioral assimilation* or acculturation has taken place in America to a considerable degree, *structural assimilation*, with some important exceptions, has not been extensive.[15] The exceptions are of two types. The first brings us back to the "triple-melting-pot" thesis of Ruby Jo Reeves Kennedy and Will Herberg. The "nationality" ethnic groups have tended to merge within each of the three major religious groups. This has been particularly true of the Protestant and Jewish communities. Those

15. See Erich Rosenthal, "Acculturation without Assimilation?" *American Journal of Sociology*, 1960, 66:275–288.

descendants of the "old" immigration of the nineteenth century, who were Protestant (many of the Germans and all the Scandinavians), have in considerable part gradually merged into the white Protestant "subsociety." Jews of Sephardic, German, and Eastern-European origins have similarly tended to come together in their communal life. The process of absorbing the various Catholic nationalities, such as the Italians, Poles, and French Canadians, into an American Catholic community hitherto dominated by the Irish has begun, although I do not believe that it is by any means close to completion. Racial and quasi-racial groups such as the Negroes, Indians, Mexican-Americans, and Puerto Ricans still retain their separate sociological structures. The outcome of all this in contemporary American life is thus pluralism—but it is more than "triple" and it is more accurately described as *structural pluralism* than as cultural pluralism, although some of the latter also remains.

My second exception refers to the social structures which implicate intellectuals. There is no space to develop the issue here, but I would argue that there is a social world or subsociety of the intellectuals in America in which true structural intermixture among persons of various ethnic backgrounds, including the religious, has markedly taken place.

My final point deals with the reasons for these developments. If structural assimilation has been retarded in America by religious and racial lines, we must ask why. The answer lies in the attitudes of both the majority and the minority groups and in the way these attitudes have interacted. A saying of the current day is, "It takes two to tango." To apply the analogy, there is no good reason to believe that white Protestant America has ever extended a firm and cordial invitation to its minorities to dance. Furthermore, the attitudes of the minority-group members themselves on the matter have been divided and ambiguous. Particularly for the minority religious groups, there is a certain logic in ethnic communality, since there is a commitment to the perpetuation of the religious ideology and since structural intermixture leads to intermarriage and the possible loss to the group of the intermarried family. Let us, then, examine the situation serially for various types of minorities.

With regard to the immigrant, in his characteristic numbers and socioeconomic background, structural assimilation was out of the question. He did not want it, and he had a positive need for the comfort of his own communal institutions. The native American, moreover, whatever the implications of his public pronouncements, had no intention of opening up his primary group life to entrance by these hordes of alien newcomers. The situation was a functionally complementary standoff.

The second generation found a much more complex situation. Many believed they heard the siren call of welcome to the social cliques, clubs, and institutions of white Protestant America. After all, it was simply a matter of learning American ways, was it not? Had they not grown up as Americans, and were they not culturally different from their parents, the "greenhorns"? Or perhaps an especially eager one reasoned (like the Jewish protagonist of Myron Kaufmann's novel, *Remember Me To God*, aspiring to membership in the prestigious club system of Harvard undergraduate social life) "If only I can go the last few steps in Ivy League manners and behavior, they will surely recognize that I am one of them and take me in." But, alas, Brooks Brothers suit notwithstanding, the doors of the fraternity house, the city men's club, and the country club were slammed in the face of the immigrant's offspring. That invitation was not really there in the first place; or, to the extent it was, in Joshua Fishman's phrase, it was a " 'look me over but don't touch me' invitation to the American minority group child."[16] And so the rebuffed one returned to the homelier but dependable comfort of the communal institutions of his ancestral group. There he found his fellows of the same generation who had never stirred from the home fires. Some of these had been too timid to stray; others were ethnic ideologists committed to the group's survival; still others had never really believed in the authenticity of the siren call or were simply too passive to do more than go along the familiar way. All could now join in the task that was well within the realm of the sociologically possible—the build-up of social institutions and organizations within the ethnic enclave, manned increasingly by members of the second generation and suitably separated by social class.

Those who had for a time ventured out gingerly or confidently, as the case might be, had been lured by the vision of an "American"

16. Joshua A. Fishman, "Childhood Indoctrination for Minority-Group Membership and the Quest for Minority-Group Biculturism in America," in Oscar Handlin, ed., *Group Life in America* (Cambridge, Harvard University Press, forthcoming).

social structure that was somehow larger than all subgroups and was ethnically neutral. Were they, too, not Americans? But they found to their dismay that at the primary group level a neutral American social structure was a mirage. What at a distance seemed to be a quasi-public edifice flying only the all-inclusive flag of American nationality turned out on closer inspection to be the clubhouse of a particular ethnic group—the white Anglo-Saxon Protestants, its operation shot through with the premises and expectations of its parental ethnicity. In these terms, the desirability of whatever invitation was grudgingly extended to those of other ethnic backgrounds could only become a considerably attenuated one.

With the racial minorities, there was not even the pretense of an invitation. Negroes, to take the most salient example, have for the most part been determinedly barred from the cliques, social clubs, and churches of white America. Consequently, with due allowance for internal class differences, they have constructed their own network of organizations and institutions, their own "social world." There are now many vested interests served by the preservation of this separate communal life, and doubtless many Negroes are psychologically comfortable in it, even though at the same time they keenly desire that discrimination in such areas as employment, education, housing, and public accommodations be eliminated. However, the ideological attachment of Negroes to their communal separation is not conspicuous. Their sense of identification with ancestral African national cultures is virtually nonexistent, although Pan-Africanism engages the interest of some intellectuals and although "black nationalist" and "black racist" fringe groups have recently made an appearance at the other end of the communal spectrum. As for their religion, they are either Protestant or Catholic (overwhelmingly the former). Thus, there are no "logical" ideological reasons for their separate communality; dual social structures are created solely by the dynamics of prejudice and discrimination, rather than being reinforced by the ideological commitments of the minority itself.

Structural assimilation, then, has turned out to be the rock on which the ships of Anglo-conformity and the melting pot have foundered. To understand that behavioral assimilation (or acculturation) without massive structural intermingling in primary relationships has been the dominant motif in the American experience of creating and developing a nation out of diverse peoples is to comprehend the most essential sociological fact of that experience. It is against the background of "structural pluralism" that strategies of strengthening intergroup harmony, reducing ethnic discrimination and prejudice, and maintaining the rights of both those who stay within and those who venture beyond their ethnic boundaries must be thoughtfully devised.

NOTE:

Parts II, III and IV (pages 23-186) appear in Volume 1, To 1865

Part V
Divided We Stand,
1865-1900

Divided We Stand, 1865–1900

During the decades following the Civil War, white Americans sought to mend the nation's sectional wounds. White reunion was accomplished, at least on a political level, and the country enjoyed a spectacular growth of industrialism accompanied by the rapid development of cities, urban problems, and strife between capital and labor. The advances in the quality of life which were secured by at least a part of the white society were withheld from the nonwhite minorities. In a capitalist society which found its theoretical justification in the doctrine of "survival of the fittest," nonwhites were ruthlessly exploited and cast aside as unfit for economic competition. An age dedicated to "hard-headed" notions of progress had little sympathy for underdogs and scorned proposals for social reform as "sentimentality." White racism was dignified by a cult of Anglo-Saxonism which assumed the inferiority of nonwhite peoples. For America's nonwhites these were bitter years which brought a new form of servitude to blacks, exclusion to the Chinese, and loss of land and culture to the Indians and Mexican-Americans.

The harsh realities of the postwar years made a mockery of the promise of freedom and equality to black Americans. The "radical reconstruction" of southern society proved to be superficial and ephemeral. The guarantees of equality in civil rights, including that of the ballot, were systematically eroded by the aggressive opposition of white southerners and the growing indifference of the federal government as epitomized by the withdrawal of federal troops from the South in 1877. State governments controlled by white "conservatives" enacted legislation which insured that blacks would remain politically and economically powerless. Most southern blacks became sharecroppers, enslaved in a new kind of debt bondage which tied them to the land. Even those who escaped to the cities were relegated to the least skilled and lowest paying jobs by a system of racially biased economic competition.

Competition between the races for jobs and wealth also helped to determine the fate of the Chinese-American in the late nineteenth century. The Burlingame Treaty of 1868 between the United States and China guaranteed the right of free migration between the two countries, but as larger numbers of Orientals entered the United States, prejudice against them grew among whites. Excoriation of their contract labor system as a new form of slavery, bitterness toward their strikebreaking activities, envy of their economic success, and contempt for their culture made the Chinese the target of racist politics in California which soon spread to the rest of the nation. By 1876, both national parties had taken a stand against the Orientals, and in 1882 the political agitation produced the first of a series of laws which effectively excluded further Chinese immigration until 1943.

Following the Civil War, the United States army turned its attention from the defeated South to the Great Plains where the American Indian was making his last stand in defense of his traditional way of life. During the 1870s scattered tribes of Kiowas, Comanches, Arapahoes, Cheyennes, Sioux, Utes, Nez-Percés, and Modocs resisted the attempts of the government to confine them to reservations, but the cavalry, assisted by such technological aids as railroads and Gatling guns, eventually eliminated all opposition. Indian submission constituted a surrender of land and culture. The government's Indian program envisoned the "civilizing" of the red man, a concept which involved the substitution of Christianity for native religions, of private property for communal life, and of white values for red heritage. Idealistic in its conception, white America's program was a disaster for the red man. Under the Dawes Severalty Act of 1887, Indians were forced to accept the allotment of small farms from the government, a process which brought forth an amazing display of white chicanery and resulted in the red man's loss of almost all his useful land. Programs of education and Christianization accomplished little more than the degradation of Indian culture. In effect, white victory over the American Indian presaged the virtual destruction of a people.

Mexican-Americans also found themselves struggling against overwhelming odds for their survival as a people. The inhabitants of the lands taken from Mexico in 1848 were the victims of white progress. In the years after the Civil War, white Americans poured westward into the states of Texas and California and the Colorado, New Mexico, and Arizona territories. Vicious racial hatred and armed conflict marked the relationship between whites and Mexican-Americans as the latter struggled, often unsuccessfully, to preserve their land, culture, and political rights. Even in New Mexico, where the Mexican-Americans remained a majority during the nineteenth century, the white newcomers successfully manipulated the political machinery of the territory for their own advantage.

At the end of the nineteenth century, Theodore Roosevelt sang the praises of Anglo-Saxon Americans for their victory over Spain, noting that "in every instance ... expansion has taken place because the race was a great race," while popular novelist Jack London wrote disparagingly of, "dark pigmented things, the half castes, the mongrel bloods, and the dregs of long conquered races." The jubilation over the nation's coming of age as an international power was a celebration of white power. The nation's nonwhite minorities, routed and despised, were barred from the hopeful exultation with which white America looked to the new century.

Ralph K. Andrist,
"Ghost Dance and Gatling Guns"

The end of the Civil War signaled the closing chapter in the history
of intermittent warfare which marked the relationship between
whites and Indians in the United States. The last Indian resistance
to the steady loss of land and the ravaging of their culture transpired
during the 1880s on the Great Plains. In "Ghost Dance and
Gatling Guns," Ralph K. Andrist recounts the final Indian uprising,
that of the Sioux in the Dakota Territory. Driven to desperation
by the deceitful practices of the United States government, some
of the Sioux sought to renew their strength through the mystical
ghost dance religion. Attempts to prohibit ghost dancing led to
a series of minor hostilities between Sioux warriors and the United
States cavalry. The shameful episode ended with the massacre of
almost three hundred Indians, the majority of them women
and children, at Wounded Knee in 1890. The "battle" of Wounded
Knee, which occurred in the same year that the Census Bureau
announced the disappearance of the frontier, stands as a tragic
symbol of the final Indian capitulation to the superior armed
force of the white society.

Ghost Dance and Gatling Guns

Ralph K. Andrist

...Civilization was blotting out the last remnants of the old ways of life everywhere in the West, and in few places more thoroughly than on the Great Plains. There were still great spaces where a man could raise his eyes and still see nothing but grass and horizon— there are even today, although one must search well to find them— but with each passing year the open plain was giving way to cattle herds, sod shanties, plowed fields, and the sky-pointing towers of windmills.

Nothing did more to break up the open character of the plains than barbed wire. Fencing had been one of the unsolvable problems of living in a treeless country until Joseph F. Glidden of De Kalb, Illinois devised a wire fence with barbs for use around his own farm. It worked so well he started a small factory in 1874 with five boys stringing barbs on wires; by 1880 he had a huge factory in De Kalb with 202 machines turning out 600 miles of fencing every ten hours. As fast as it was produced, this barbed wire was being strung over land where herds of buffalo had grazed less than ten years before....

Abridged from "Ghost Dance and Gatling Guns," pp. 330–354. Reprinted with permission of the Macmillan Company from *The Long Death: The Last Days of the Plains Indians* by Ralph K. Andrist. Copyright © 1964 by Ralph K. Andrist.

The last remnant of the great, brown living blanket that had once grazed the plains from Canada to Texas was now concentrated in Montana, and, to a lesser extent, in northwestern Dakota Territory. And there the professional hunters went to work with a skill that had been drawn fine with several years of practice. The grass to the north of the herd was burned over to discourage the beasts from migrating northward into Canada. The buffalo, surrounded on all sides, were helpless before the hunters, whose equipment now included telescopic sights. A hunter could lie, with his gun on a good rest, and wipe out a small herd from a distance; all he had to do was to keep knocking down the animal that became nervous and tried to lead the herd away.

The northern herd was much smaller than the huge masses of buffalo that had ranged in the south. It melted away under the guns of experts who seldom wasted a shot or spoiled a hide; the clumsy amateurs of the early days in Kansas who wasted more than they marketed were missing. "I saw buffaloes lying dead on the prairie so thick that one could hardly see the ground," a hunter described the scene created by the industrious killers along the Little Missouri in the winter of 1881–82. "A man could have walked for twenty miles upon their carcasses." . . .

There had been a time when it was an article of faith that the civilizing of the Plains Indians would follow close on the annihilation of the buffalo—and a civilized Indian was universally understood to mean one who had given up everything of his own culture and had become an imitation white man. Once the buffalo were gone, it had been believed, the Indian would be forced to give up his roaming ways and settle down to feed and clothe himself by the sweat of his brow as a farmer, a herdsman, or a laborer. There were a couple of things wrong with this theory. One was that the former nomadic tribes had no experience in farming, and although the government promised implements, seeds, and instruction every time a treaty was made, it produced precious little that was tangible.

What was even more to the point was that almost all tribes, former farming peoples from the east and from the tall-grass prairie as well as the one-time horse-and-buffalo tribes, had been put on land that could by no means be called the best. Dohesan, a Kiowa chief, remarked acidly that if the President was so eager to have Indians raise corn, he should have given them land that would grow corn.

But even yet the land greed of the settlers was not satisfied. The biggest prize remaining was Indian Territory, the last piece of the old and forgotten permanent Indian Country. In the beginning, it had been the land of the Five Civilized Tribes until the government had taken the western half away from them on the thin pretext that it was punishing them for treason during the Civil War; the vacated western part was used as a dumping ground for unwanted tribes that were in the way of the tide of settlement elsewhere.... However, after the other tribes had been brought in, a large tract of land in the center of Indian Territory remained empty. These "Unassigned Lands" began to be irresistible to settlers as early as 1879, and organizations of land-seekers, who came to be called "Boomers," persistently moved in and were ejected by troops. When they transferred their efforts to Washington and began speaking the loud, clear language of votes, Congress listened and soon opened the Unassigned Lands to white settlement. The result was one of the most fantastic episodes in American history, when a pistol shot at high noon on April 22, 1889 set off tens of thousands of men and a good number of women from the Kansas border by wagon, horseback, railroad train (a line ran south through the lands), and even on foot to stake out claims.

Before night, the entire Unassigned Lands, almost two million acres, had been claimed and entire cities had been platted. Once the camel's head was in the tent, the rest of the beast quickly followed. The next year, the entire western half of Indian Territory, along with the Panhandle to the west, which was part of no state or territory, was organized into the Territory of Oklahoma. The Indian reservations were sold during the next several years and the land opened to settlers some of it by land rushes, some by lotteries. The eastern half of the former Indian Territory, the lands of the Five Civilized Tribes, continued to bear the old name for a few years more. Then the tribes, although they were operating as strong, effective nations with their laws and governments, were coerced into giving up their free existence. The result was the extinguishment of the last part of Indian Territory, which was merged with Oklahoma Territory.

...A great deal of other Indian land was taken in smaller bites, a nibbling away by "adjusting" reservation boundaries. Scores of such changes were made during the decade of the 1880's by simple presidential decree. Some of these adjustments, let the truth be said, were for increased efficiency in administration and two or three did correct minor injustices, but most of them seemed to end up leaving the Indians with less territory, or edging them onto land that was more rocky, sandy, or hilly.

There were few ways in which these were good years for Indians. Hunger was often with them; deprived of most ways of obtaining their own food, they had to depend overmuch on the annuities that were usually late in arriving and short in amount. Children were often virtually kidnaped to be sent away to boarding school, or sometimes rations were withheld from parents who refused to let their youngsters be taken. Disease was prevalent, fostered by malnutrition and exposure. Even the fact of being an Indian was a cause for shame as both agents and missionaries often tried to root out symbols of the old culture: tribal dances, Indian clothing, even the traditional way the men wore their hair.

In a time of misery and hopelessness, people who can see no way out of their troubles and woes are prone to look to some higher power for help, and the voice that now spoke to the unhappy Indians came from Nevada, from a messiah named Wovoka. This young man—he was about thirty-five—was a Paiute; he had never been outside the narrow limits of mountain-girt Mason Valley (about fifty miles southeast of Reno). When his father died when he was a young boy, he had been taken in by the family of a rancher named Dave Wilson, and so had come to be called Jack Wilson by all the whites in the valley (he had, several years before becoming famous, adopted the name of his grandfather, Kwohitsauq or "Big Rumbling Belly," which is undoubtedly a perfectly good Paiute name, but mercifully did not replace his boyhood name, Wovoka or "Cutter," in general use).

Wovoka received his inspiration from on high in 1888 during an eclipse which occurred while he was ill with a severe fever. The event, which he considered supernatural—"the sun died"—had a powerful effect on a mind disordered by fever. He was taken up into heaven where he not only saw God in a long white robe but all the people who had died in the past, now forever young and happy and engaged in their old sports and pursuits. God directed Wovoka to go back and teach his people to put aside war and love each other, and that they must also live in peace with the white men.

But the heart of the revelations was that the earth was to be regenerated and returned to the Indians, including all the dead of the past who would come back in all the beauty and strength of their youth. The Indians were given a special ceremonial dance, which required five successive nights to complete; the oftener they performed the dance, the more they would hasten the coming of the millennial future.

Wovoka, whose beliefs were a strange blend of Indian religion and the Christian theology he had learned from the Wilson family, apparently never claimed to be other than a prophet, although he had received certain small powers from God, such as songs by which he could produce fog, snow, a shower or a hard rain, or sunshine (once he had offered, for an annual fee, to keep Nevada supplied with rain but was ignored, a short-sighted act by a state which can use a great deal more precipitation). But rain-making and such were minor matters; it was the vision of the return of the Indians' old days of glory that won him his following as soon as he began preaching his doctrine. His own people, the Paiutes, danced, and soon Paiutes went out as missionaries to spread the new gospel to the tribes beyond the mountain valleys.

And the tribes, in their unhappiness, listened eagerly, because here was exactly what they wanted to hear. The Arapahoes and Cheyennes, both northern and southern, the Bannocks, Sioux, Shoshones, Utes and other tribes sent delegates to talk to the messiah; they returned full of wonders to start the dance—which the whites had named the Ghost Dance because it was to help bring back the dead—among their own tribesmen.

The Ghost Dance religion spread over most of the West, with the exception of the Columbia River country and much of the Southwest. Each tribe practiced it with its own variations, just as there are differences of liturgy among Christian denominations, but all believed in the same basic thing: the world made young again and returned to the Indians, with the dead come back to enjoy the good life. As they danced to bring the new day nearer, the excess of their emotions sent many of them into trances in which they saw visions—and this appears to be much of the hold it had over many of them, almost like a narcotic—and from their visions they built most of the simple, chanting songs which they used in subsequent dances. . . .

There was one place where the Ghost Dance did take on a slight martial note. Among the Sioux, where the new religion happened to coincide with a number of causes of unrest, "Ghost shirts" magically impervious to white men's bullets were worn, at first only in the dance, but later beneath the outer garments at other times.

The catalogue of misery and despair of the Sioux had grown very long by 1890. There was of course, the passing of the buffalo and the growing scarcity of deer and other game which deprived them of food and clothing, and except for what the poor land of their reservation would produce, put them at the mercy of government annuities. Then, only the year before, they had been separated from more of their land. About one-third of the Great Sioux Reservation had been lost when the Black Hills and adjacent regions were taken from the Indians during the Sioux War. A few years later, settlers in the Black Hills were demanding a corridor to eastern Dakota so they would not have to cross the reservation. They finally got their passage in 1889; it carved out the heart of the remaining reservation, cutting it in two and taking half its area, an opening sixty miles wide—no danger of rubbing elbows against Indian land on either side as they went down that alleyway. The remaining land was divided into five reservations.

The Sioux had been assured they would continue to receive the same rations after giving up so much of their lands, but immediately after the agreement had been approved, Congress cut the beef ration by 2,000,000 pounds at Rosebud Reservation, by 1,000,000 pounds at Pine Ridge, and by lesser amounts at the other three reservations. When the agent at Pine Ridge informed the Indian Bureau in April, 1890 that the monthly beef issue was only 205,000 pounds when agreements with the Sioux called for 470,400, he received the helpful answer that it was better to give half rations all year than to give three-quarters or full rations for a few months and none for the rest of the year. However, this was one case where the Indian Office was not much to blame. The fault rested with Congress which then, as ever, economized in the wrong places.

In both 1889 and 1890, severe outbreaks of measles, influenza, and whooping cough caused many deaths. Agency physicians blamed the high death rate on the poor physical condition of the Indians due to hunger. Whatever the cause, it greatly increased the mood of gloom and hopelessness affecting the Sioux. So did poor harvests and drought.

Into this unhappy situation, in March of 1890, came a group of returning Sioux who had been sent the previous autumn to visit the messiah and learn about the new religion. The stories they brought back were wonderful indeed. Wovoka had come to earth in a cloud of smoke to talk to them, and had shown them nail marks on his hands and feet; the very next spring he was going to wipe out the white men for being so wicked to him at his first coming to earth. When they were returning home, they had come on an encampment of the dead of their tribe and had visited with old friends for some time. On continuing their journey, they found a herd of buffalo (these buffalo had apparently returned from the dead for the occasion, too), and had killed one and feasted on its meat; head, hoofs, and tail were left lying as Wovoka had instructed them, and as they walked off, had reassembled into a new buffalo. This appears to be the most outrageous kind of fabrication, but many visitors to Wovoka came back with tales no less fantastic; apparently in their extremely suggestible state of mind the difference between reality and illusion all but disappeared. . . .

But while the Ghost Dance religion was promising a glorious hereafter, the present was looking more and more grim. Agent Gallagher, who had earlier written the Indian Bureau that his charges at Pine Ridge were getting less than half the beef they were supposed to, was writing more letters as the summer wore on, reporting that the Indians were suffering from hunger. The Bureau received warnings from other sources as well that the Sioux were becoming increasingly restive, but no more food arrived, and in the summer the Pine Ridge Indians rebelled and refused to accept the half-ration. They eventually took it—they had not much choice—but Gallagher decided his job was a hopeless one and resigned.

He was replaced in early October by one D. F. Royer. Few men less qualified have held the post, even in a service known for the general sorry level of its appointees. He was described as "destitute of any of those qualities by which he could justly lay claim to the position—experience, force of character, courage and sound judgment." The Indians quickly took his measure and dubbed him Lakota Kokipa-Koshkala, "Young-man-afraid-of-the-Sioux." From the first he had no control over his Indians; before he had been there a week he had stood by helplessly while a handful of them had released a prisoner from the jail. Before two weeks were up he was reporting that more than half his six thousand Indians were dancing, and that he was afraid troops would be needed because the situation was entirely beyond the control of the Indian police at his disposal.

The Sioux were dancing at the other four reservations, too, but the agents there, better endowed than Royer with judgment and courage, remained calm and tried to stop the dancing, though with only partial success. The fervor with which the Sioux were accepting the Ghost Dance religion was a measure of their need of it.

Agent Royer became more and more frightened by the strange chanting and dancing going on a few miles from his agency. He wrote to the Indian Bureau on October 30, saying that the situation could be saved only by the arrival of six hundred or seven hundred troops; within a week he was sending daily telegrams asking for permission to come to Washington to explain, but was told that the place of an agent during a crisis was at his post. At last, on November 15, he was directed to report the situation to the commander of Fort Robinson in northern Nebraska, the nearest Army post. Royer, by now in a state of near-panic, had sent off a message saying that the Sioux were wild and out of their heads, and that at least a thousand soldiers were needed to cope with the situation. But Royer was not speaking completely from hysteria, for the agent at adjoining Rosebud Reservation reported that his Indians were so engrossed in their dancing as to be beyond the control of himself and his police.

The old formality was observed, of transferring jurisdiction over the Sioux from the Interior to the War Department. The Army at once began moving units into the region, most of them into the area around the Pine Ridge agency, until within a matter of days it had almost three thousand men in the field. On the appearance of the troops, a large number of the Sioux, almost two thousand, living on Pine Ridge and Rosebud reservations fled to an area called the Bad Lands on the western edge of Pine Ridge, a place of hills, canyons, and weirdly eroded tablelands which provided a hiding place where an army might not find them. Within a short time, as more refugees joined them, their numbers increased to at least three thousand. The escaped Indians, some of them rebellious but most only frightened, were declared to be hostiles, although the last thing most of them wanted was to engage in hostilities with Army forces. The movement to the Bad Lands had been almost entirely a stampede caused by panic at the appearance of the soldiers.

Things became quieter on the reservations with so many troops around. Most of the Ghost Dancing ended or was reduced to a much smaller scale; the main centers where it continued were at the camp of Sitting Bull on Grand River in Standing Rock reservation, northernmost of the five reserves, and at the camp of a chief named Big Foot on the Cheyenne River. The Indian Bureau, feeling that it should get some use out of all the troops on hand, asked its agents to submit lists of trouble-makers who should be arrested and removed, with the help of the military if necessary. Among them, four of the agents produced a total of about fifteen names. The fifth agent was Royer; all by himself he came up with a list of sixty-four which was a "conservative estimate" and to which no one paid any attention.

As it turned out, most of the men honored by being included on the list were in the Bad Lands at the moment, but the one considered the most potentially dangerous of them all, Sitting Bull, was within easy reach. There is not much doubt that the great medicine man was a center of mischief during most of the time since he had reached the agreement with the government that had let him return from Canada in 1881. Except for joining Buffalo Bill Cody's Wild West show for a season and touring the country, he had remained on or near the reservation, brooding on the past and feeding his hate of white men. Toward the last he refused even to come in to the agency. He was a matter of concern to the authorities because he was a rallying point for all conservative and dissident elements among the Sioux. When the Army took control of the Sioux reservations, it moved quickly to arrest the famous medicine man, and as its deputy it called on William F. Cody. It was believed that Cody had a great deal of influence over Sitting Bull, supposedly the result of friendship engendered by shared experiences in show business, and he was given authority to reach surrender terms with the Sioux leader or, failing that, to arrest him and bring him in by force. Cody arrived at Fort Yates on November 28, but the scheme was called off when Agent James McLaughlin of Standing Rock heard of it and urgently protested.

Wait until the weather got colder, said McLaughlin. Then Sitting Bull and his band would not be so likely to bolt and join the hostiles in the Bad Lands. McLaughlin also felt that the arrest should be made by his own Indian police, who were trained, dependable men, and not as liable to arouse opposition as white soldiers. The agent got his way; the arrest was deferred until December 12 when orders came to Colonel Drum commanding Fort Yates to make arrangements with

McLaughlin to take Sitting Bull in. The two decided to arrest the famous chief on the twentieth, when most of the Indians would be at the agency collecting their annuities and Sitting Bull would have few potential defenders.

But on the afternoon of the fourteenth, a messenger came from the Indian school near Sitting Bull's camp, saying that Sitting Bull had just received an invitation to come to Pine Ridge because God was about to appear there. The medicine man was even then making preparations for the trip, the informant said.

It was then sundown, but McLaughlin and Colonel Drum made plans to arrest Sitting Bull the next morning. The agent already had police watching the Sioux leader's camp; more were assembled by hard-riding couriers until forty-three men, under the command of Lieutenant Bull Head, approached the camp at daybreak. Two troops of cavalry, about one hundred men, with a Hotchkiss gun (a rapid-fire gun that shot two-inch explosive shells), rode more than thirty miles from the fort during the night to be within supporting distance of the police.

Indian police had been first authorized by Congress in 1878, and eventually they were used on a majority of reservations, although to varying extents. Those on the Sioux reservation were, in general, well-trained men with excellent morale. But Agent McLaughlin had miscalculated in thinking that an arrest by them would be less offensive to Sitting Bull than one by white soldiers. For the police represented the most progressive element among the Sioux, those who had accepted the white man's way completely. Sitting Bull and those around him were the most conservative element; the medicine man himself was an apostle of the good old days and looked with scorn on all Indians who cooperated with the white authorities.

At dawn on December 15, these two opposed forces confronted each other. The police surrounded Sitting Bull's house; then Lieutenant Bull Head and several others entered to find the prophet asleep on the floor. When he was awakened and told he was a prisoner, Sitting Bull agreed rather mildly to go with them to the agency, but as his followers began to gather outside, calling on him to resist, he started to berate the police for breaking into his house and waking him. When his seventeen-year-old son, Crow Foot, taunted him as a coward, he abruptly refused to go, and called on his people to rescue him.

By that time, the police outside had been backed up against the house wall by more than a hundred threatening men, and as Sitting Bull was brought outside and the police attempted to clear a path, one of the followers shot Bull Head in the side. The police lieutenant was walking beside Sitting Bull; as he sagged, mortally wounded, he turned and shot the Sioux Chief in the side as another policeman, Red Tomahawk, behind Sitting Bull, shot the leader through the head. The entire situation exploded into a deadly, close-quarter combat, in which the training of the police more than made up for the difference in numbers. They drove their attackers off and held the house until the cavalry came up to their relief about two hours later.

Six policemen were killed or fatally wounded, while their assailants lost eight, including Sitting Bull and his son, Crow Foot. Sitting Bull died in his fifty-sixth year, a great man, not only a valiant fighting leader, but a famous prophet and medicine man. In the end, however, the gift of prophesy faded; during his last years his visions were increasingly of the past. . . .

Except for the few military units engaged in controlling potential trouble-makers in the north, the great body of troops was operating against the Indians in the Bad Lands. Almost three thousand of them were there, under the immediate command of General John R. Brooke, although General Miles was in over-all command. It was the general strategy of the two men to avoid bloodshed if at all possible, and Brooke had thrown a strong wall of troops to the north and west of the hostiles' stronghold. With these he maintained a steady pressure which gradually forced the Indians toward the east and Pine Ridge agency.

Most of the Indians were weary and cold and ready to give up anyway; some of them never had had any real chip on their shoulder but had fled only from fear. Along with military pressure, General Brooke got word to the Indians that he would protect their rights as far as he was able, and this helped swing the balance toward surrender, even though the Sioux had scant faith left in the government. The hostiles began moving in, and on December 27, the entire body left the Bad Lands to go to the agency. There had not been a single battle except for a fight between hostiles and Cheyenne scouts; the only engagements between troops and Sioux were two or three very minor skirmishes. But the book had not yet been closed on the uprising, if such it can be called.

Big Foot and his people, fleeing south, had nothing on their minds except to get away from soldiers. They passed very near several ranches without committing any depredations, and once went directly through a pasture without taking even one of the horses or cattle there. At the edge of the Bad Lands, they sent scouts to make contact with the Indians camped in the stronghold, but no answers were received to their signals for the hostiles had already gone and were on their way to the agency. It was then, on December 28, as the band was proceeding along the edge of the Bad Lands, that it was intercepted by Major S. M. Whitside with four troops of the 7th Cavalry, about two hundred men.

Big foot was ill, too sick with pneumonia to ride on a horse, and was being carried on a travois. He got to his feet, had a white flag raised, and asked for a parley. Whitside refused, insisting on nothing other than unconditional surrender, and the Sioux chief, with only about one hundred cold and hungry warriors, was in no position to resist even if he had been of a mind to. The band was conducted by the cavalry to a place called Wounded Knee which was only a post office and a few scattered Indian houses near Wounded Knee Creek. There they went into camp as directed by Major Whitside, while the cavalry set up its tents nearby.

General Brooke, when informed of the capture, sent Colonel George A. Forsyth, commander of the 7th Cavalry, with four more troops of the regiment to reinforce the guard around the Sioux. A company of scouts also joined the guard, and a battery of four Hotchkiss guns, making a total of 470 men to keep a watch over about 340 Indians, of whom only 106 were warriors. . . .

The next morning, December 29, Forsyth made ready to disarm the Sioux. Their lodges had been set up on a flat piece of ground a short distance west of Wounded Knee Creek, which there flows approximately north. Just south of the tepees, a dry ravine running from west to east opens into the creek; to the north of the camp was a slight hill on which the four Hotchkiss guns were posted, and trained directly on the camp. On all sides of the camp, soldiers were stationed, both mounted and on foot. The Sioux had hoisted a white flag in the center of their camp as an indication of their peaceful intentions and a guarantee of safety.

At about eight o'clock the warriors came out of their lodges and sat on the ground in a semicircle. They were instructed to go, about a score at a time, into their tepees, and return with their weapons. The first twenty went, and came back with only two guns. The officers conferred. It was plain that this method was not going to produce the guns. Troops stationed by the council ring were ordered to move up to within ten yards of the seated warriors, and other enlisted men were detailed to search the tepees. It is exactly at this point that the situation began to get out of hand—and it is hard not to blame Forsyth, who approved the action, for letting it get out of control.

The soldiers acted like bully-boys, overturning beds and other lodge furnishings, shoving aside the women who protested loudly and tried to bar their way. The Sioux men were becoming greatly agitated at the sounds of strife from their tepees and the voices of their women, especially since they did not know what was going on. Most of them had knives under their blankets, and were approaching a state of mind when they were ready to use them. In the midst of this tense situation, a medicine man, Yellow Bird, walked about, blowing an eagle-bone whistle, and calling on the men to resist because, as he reminded them, they were invulnerable to bullets because of the Ghost shirts they wore. The officers did not understand Sioux; the dangerous trend of Yellow Bird's exhortations passed them by.

The search was completed and produced about forty guns, most of them antiquated and worn pieces. But one weapon they did not find, for the good reason that it was being carried under his blanket by a young Indian, name unknown but probably Black Fox, who was described by a Sioux witness to the event, later testifying in Washington, as "a crazy man, a young man of very bad influence and in fact a nobody...." But for a brief moment he was a very important somebody as he pulled out the gun and fired into the line of soldiers, killing one of them.

The line of troops replied instantly with a volley at point-blank range, killing possibly as many as half the warriors. The rest of the Sioux men threw off their blankets and drew their knives or, in some cases, pulled out old-fashioned war clubs, and grappled with the soldiers in hand-to-hand fighting. At almost the same instant, the Hotchkiss guns on the hills opened fire on the camp, pouring their two-inch explosive shells at the rate of nearly fifty a minute into the women and children gathered there. This, too, must be weighed when the question of whether Forsyth showed good judgment is considered.

Afterward, it was pointed out in his defense that he had separated women and children from warriors during the search for arms, to prevent just such a thing as did occur. Nevertheless, the Hotchkiss guns on the hill were trained from the beginning on the camp where there were women and children only, and if Forsyth did not know this, he should have.

The murderous fire was augmented by the weapons of the outer cordon of troops who surrounded the entire camp; they began shooting, killing many Indians who attempted to flee. Within a matter of minutes, some two hundred Indians and sixty soldiers lay dead or wounded, and many of the tepees had been ripped apart by explosive shells and were burning above helpless wounded. A good number of the soldier casualties appear to have been victims of their own comrades' bullets since troops were firing from four sides with rather blind enthusiasm.

The 7th Cavalry had a splendid record, but all witnesses agree that from the moment it opened fire, it ceased to be a military unit and became a mass of infuriated men intent only on butchery. Women and children attempted to escape by running up the dry ravine, but were pursued and slaughtered—there is no other word—by hundreds of maddened soldiers, while shells from the Hotchkiss guns, which had been moved to permit them to sweep the ravine, continued to burst among them. The line of bodies was afterward found to extend for more than two miles from the camp—and they were all women and children. A few survivors eventually found shelter in brushy gullies here and there, and their pursuers had scouts call out that women and children could come out of their hiding place because they had nothing to fear (one wonders how these Sioux scouts could have found the stomach to stay at their work); some small boys crept out and were surrounded by soldiers who then butchered them. Nothing Indian that lived was safe; the four-year-old son of Yellow Bird, the medicine man, was playing with his pony when the shooting began. "My father ran and fell down and the blood came out of his mouth," he said, "and then a soldier put his gun up to my white pony's nose and shot him, and then I ran and a policeman got me." ...

No one knows how many Indians died on that miserable field, because by the time anyone could count the bodies, some had already been removed. But the number was very close to three hundred, about two-thirds of them women and children. The sound of the firing had been heard very clearly at Pine Ridge agency, almost twenty miles away, and in time survivors reached the agency with their stories and their wounds. Some of the Indians who had come in from the Bad Lands to surrender rode out to Wounded Knee, where they found the troops scattered about the field, hunting down the few refugees. The Sioux attacked the cavalrymen, driving them in toward the center, where the troopers collected their dead and wounded, as well as about fifty Indian prisoners, almost all wounded, and then marched through to the agency....

The effect of the massacre on other Indians was immediate. Those camped at Pine Ridge agency, who had just come in from the Bad Lands to surrender, went hostile again. They attacked the agency itself, they attacked small troop detachments and wagon trains, and they killed one unfortunate herder near the agency who thereby gained the distinction of being the one white civilian slain in all the uprising. These Indians, even with the provocations they had, had somehow lost the will to fight after so many years of going down bloody for lost causes. Their attacks were half-hearted, and after their first anger had burned out, many of them began looking for ways to break away from the main hostile band.

General Miles moved his headquarters to Pine Ridge agency, and followed his former strategy of trying to avoid armed clashes; a cordon of troops was thrown around the hostiles again, and they were nudged and pushed toward the agency. It was over, for good and all, on January 16, 1891, when the hostiles surrendered. General Miles had them set up their tepees, 724 in all, just west of the agency, and from the Army's commissary supplies he issued beef, coffee, and sugar. It was their first full meal in several weeks.

So, abruptly, the history of the Indian wars of the West ends around cooking fires with hungry Sioux gnawing on ribs of grass-fed beef. There is very little epilogue. The Ghost Dance died at Wounded Knee, as far as the Sioux were concerned. When the Ghost shirts proved as impotent as everything else they had ever put their faith in, they quickly dropped the entire religion of the Ghost Dance. Skepticism proved to be as contagious as the first enthusiasm, and other tribes throughout the West soon followed suit. Although some tribes continued to dance for a year or two, final disillusionment set in when the bright world peopled by friends from the past and covered with restored buffalo herds did not appear as Wovoka had promised. The dance became a game for children, where it was remembered at all.

There was never any more fighting by Indians after the uprising on the Sioux reservations. The strength of the tribes everywhere was gone. They were broken up; apathy, hopelessness, hunger, and disease became their constant companions. Nor had the rapacity of their white neighbors lessened, for they have since lost three-fifths of the land they still possessed shortly before Wounded Knee—and what they have managed to keep is largely sand or rock that no white man has considered worth taking from them.

It is not completely coincidence that the Sioux who fell at Wounded Knee died at the close of the same year in which the Superintendent of the Census announced that the frontier, until then a dominant fact of American life, had ceased to exist. The Indian of the Old West was a creature of the other side of the frontier, the dwindling side, and when it finally pinched out, there was no place left for him. He became in truth the Vanishing American, and it was a long time before any bright spots began to appear on his future. There still are not anywhere near enough of them.

But that is another story entirely. This one began on the Great Plains, when uncounted buffalo grazed over grass that had never been marked by wagon wheels, where the great tribes fought and hunted, secure in their own strength. It has ended, after many years, broken promises, and tragedies, at the edge of a mass grave in Dakota. Indians have gone down many paths to defeat, along many ways filled with pain and heartbreak, but none so much so as this long, last trail.

John Hope Franklin,
"History of Racial Segregation in the United States"

The Civil War brought a legal end to the institution of slavery in
the United States. The Emancipation Proclamation, the Thirteenth,
Fourteenth, and Fifteenth Amendments, and the Civil Rights
Act of 1875 seemed to promise a status of equality under the law
to all Americans. Yet the steady refusal of the white majority to
recognize the principle of legal equality made a hollow mockery of
the constitutional protections provided for black Americans.
Supreme Court decisions, economic pressures, and violence were
used by the white majority to relegate the black minority to second
class citizenship. State legislation enforcing discriminatory
treatment of black citizens, particularly in the South, was also an
important part of the process. In the following article, John Hope
Franklin, a distinguished black historian, traces the "History of
Racial Segregation in the United States." He demonstrates that
during the late nineteenth and early twentieth centuries, southern
state legislatures borrowed from practices defining the status of
free blacks in the antebellum period and created a system of racial
apartheid which prohibited contact between blacks and whites.

History of Racial Segregation in the United States

John Hope Franklin

The enactment of state segregation statutes is a relatively recent phenomenon in the history of race relations in the United States. Of course there had been numerous segregation practices and some segregation statutes for many years, even before the nineteenth century. But it was not until the final quarter of the nineteenth century that states began to evolve a systematic program of legally separating whites and Negroes in every possible area of activity. And it was not until the twentieth century that these laws became a major apparatus for keeping the Negro "in his place." They were both comprehensive and generally acceptable, because they received their inspiration from a persistent and tenacious assumption of the innate inferiority of the Negro and because they had their roots deep in the ante-bellum period.[1]

Abridged from John Hope Franklin, "History of Racial Segregation in the United States," *The Annals,* CCCIV (1956), pp. 1–9. Reprinted by permission of the author and The American Academy of Political and Social Science. Some footnotes have been renumbered.

1. For an illuminating discussion of the assumptions of the inferiority of the Negro see Guion Griffis Johnson, "The Ideology of White Supremacy, 1876–1910," in Fletcher M. Green (Ed.), *Essays in Southern History Presented to Joseph Grégoire de Roulhac Hamilton* (Chapel Hill: University of North Carolina Press, 1949), pp. 124–56.

For centuries many Northerners and Southerners subscribed to the view that Negroes were of a permanently inferior type. As slavery came to be concentrated in the Southern states and as that section became conspicuous by the tenacity with which it held on to slavery, it built its defenses of the institution along lines of the inferiority of the Negro. A whole body of thought was set forth to demonstrate that "the faculties of the Negro, as compared with those of the Saxon, qualified him for a state of servitude and made him unfit for the enjoyment of freedom."[2] Slavery was, therefore, the natural lot of the Negro; and any efforts to elevate him to the status of freedom and equality were manifestly in opposition to the laws of nature and of God.

The slaveholder's task of keeping the Negro slave in his place was complicated by the presence of several hundred thousand Negroes who were not slaves, although they can hardly be described as wholly free. So that they would not constitute a threat to the slave regime, free Negroes were denied the full rights and privileges of citizens. They enjoyed no equality in the courts, their right to assemble was denied, their movements were circumscribed, and education was withheld. Their miserable plight caused them to be unfavorably compared with slaves and confirmed the views of many that Negroes could not profit by freedom. They were regarded as the "very drones and pests of society," pariahs of the land, and an incubus on the body politic.

Outside the South free Negroes fared only slightly better. White Christians began to segregate them in the churches in the first decade of the national period, and Negroes in Philadelphia and New York City withdrew rather than accept this humiliation. As early as 1787 a white philanthropic organization opened a separate school for Negroes in New York City. In 1820 the city of Boston established a Negro elementary school. Separate schools became the practice throughout the North. When Charles Sumner challenged the constitutionality of segregated schools in Massachusetts in 1849, his posi-

2. William S. Jenkins, *Pro-Slavery Thought in the Old South* (Chapel Hill: University of North Carolina Press, 1935), p. 243. See also Albert T. Bledsoe, "Liberty and Slavery, or Slavery in the Light of Moral and Political Philosophy," and Samuel C. Cartwright, "Slavery in the Light of Ethnology," in E. N. Elliott, *Cotton is King, and Pro-Slavery Arguments* (Augusta, Ga.: Pritchard, Abbott and Loomis, 1860), pp. 271–458, 691–728.

tion was bitterly opposed; and it was not until 1855 that the legislature of that state abolished them. Meanwhile numerous acts of violence in urban communities underscored Northern hostility to free Negroes. Between 1830 and 1840 anti-Negro riots occurred in Utica, Palmyra, New York City, and Philadelphia.

These ante-bellum experiences with free Negroes proved invaluable in the period following the close of the Civil War. In 1865 white Southerners were not "caught short" in facing the problem of the freedmen. From their point of view the former slaves simply augmented the group of free Negroes that they already regarded as "the most ignorant... vicious, impoverished, and degraded population of this country."[3] Thus, the whites merely applied to the former slaves the principles and practices that had guided them in their relations with ante-bellum free Negroes. The latter had subsisted somewhere in the hazy zone between slavery and freedom. To concede the freedmen this "place" was regarded by white Southerners as generous, the Emancipation Proclamation and the Reconstruction amendments to the contrary notwithstanding....

As the ex-Confederates proceeded to restore order in their war-torn communities, they took little cognizance of the implications of the Emancipation Proclamation and the proposed Thirteenth Amendment. The major assumptions of the slave regime, the cornerstone of which was the permanent inferiority of the Negro, were still so powerful as to be controlling in most matters involving Negroes. While making some concessions, such as the competency of Negroes to testify in the courts, they nullified almost every semblance of freedom with numerous proscriptive laws. Mississippi legislators passed laws forbidding Negroes to rent or lease lands except in incorporated towns. They also enacted a law requiring every Negro, after January 1, 1866, to carry on his person written evidence that he had a home and an occupation. Louisiana forbade Negroes to move about in certain parishes or to be out at night without special permits. North Carolina extended to the freedmen the same privileges, burdens, and disabilities that had previously applied to free persons of color.

That the races should be kept apart, except where the whites were clearly in a superior role, was an important feature of most codes.

3. From a statement by Howell Cobb, quoted in Jenkins, *ibid.* (note 2 *supra*), p. 246.

Louisiana required that every Negro be in the regular service of some white person who was held responsible for his conduct. Mississippi forbade employees of railroads to permit Negroes to ride in first-class cars with white persons, except in the case of Negroes or mulattoes, "traveling with their mistress, in the capacity of maids." Many states provided that if Negro offenders could not pay their fines they were to be hired out to "any white person" who would pay the fines and costs and take the convicts for the shortest period of time.

Negroes were not indifferent to the process by which their former masters and their associates were nullifying the gains of the war. While they displayed no spirit of vindictiveness against those who had held them in slavery, they manifested a firm determination to secure the rights to which they, as free men, were entitled.[4] The better educated and the more articulate among them assumed the leadership in expressing apprehension regarding the developments that were pushing them back toward slavery. They were especially concerned about the numerous acts of violence perpetrated against the freedmen, the burning of their schools and churches, and the economic proscriptions to which they were subjected. In Harrisburg, Pittsburgh, Indianapolis, and Cleveland they met in conventions and solicited the support of their Northern fellows in the effort to attain first-class citizenship. In Alexandria, Norfolk, Raleigh, Charleston, and other Southern communities they met, exchanged views, and addressed appeals to Southerners, Northerners, and federal officials. These supplications fell on deaf ears in the South, but they contributed to the increasing awareness elsewhere that the victory at Appomattox was empty.

The ex-Confederates looked upon the lenient Reconstruction policies of Lincoln and Johnson, which gave them virtual autonomy in every phase of life, as a normal concession to a section which was right on all the basic points in the dispute that led to the war. In the North, however, many people viewed the policy of leniency with skepticism from the outset; and congressional leaders made no secret of the fact that they regarded the resultant Presidential actions as unwise and improper, if not actually illegal. The first significant asser-

4. On the point of the absence of vindictiveness among Negroes see Francis B. Simkins, "New Viewpoints of Southern Reconstruction," *Journal of Southern History*, Vol. 5 (February 1939), pp. 49–61.

tion of their own prerogatives was the passage of the Freedmen's Bureau Bill in March 1865, which called for an extensive program of relief and rehabilitation in the South.

The Bureau's establishment of schools for the former slaves and its attempt to protect them in their relations with white employers were especially obnoxious to the white Southerners. They were loud in their condemnation of both these features of the Bureau's program, calling them incendiary, radical, and political. They realized all too well the adverse effect that a successful prosecution of the program would have on the continued subordination of Negroes. The attempts of whites to drive out teachers of Negroes and to assert their authority over their employees were well calculated to subvert the program of complete emancipation and to preserve the old relationships between Negroes and whites.

The findings of the Joint Committee on Reconstruction, established by Congress in 1865, convinced a majority of congressional members that federal intervention was necessary to salvage the victory over the South. The committee was of the opinion that there was in the South "no general disposition to place the colored race ...upon terms even of civil equality" and that no semblance of order could be maintained without the interposition of federal authority.[5] In accordance with the recommendation of the Joint Committee, Congress proceeded to enact a civil rights measure, to submit the Fourteenth Amendment to the states, and to pass a series of laws placing the reconstruction of the former Confederate states under congressional control.

The Civil Rights Act that became law on April 9, 1866, defined citizenship so as to include Negroes. Senator Lyman Trumbull of Illinois said that the purpose of the bill was to destroy the discrimination against the Negro in the laws of Southern states and to make effective the Thirteenth Amendment.[6] White Southerners were, of course, outraged that Congress should undertake to guarantee the equality of Negroes, especially since the law had been enacted in the absence of representatives from the former Confederate states. As

---

5. *Report of the Joint Committee on Reconstruction, at the First Session Thirty-ninth Congress* (Washington: Government Printing Office, 1866), p. xvii.

6. Horace Edgar Flack, *The Adoption of the Fourteenth Amendment* (Baltimore, Md.: The Johns Hopkins Press, 1908), p. 21.

a matter of fact, fear that at some later date a majority of Congress or a federal court would strike down the Civil Rights Act was an important motivation for writing the provisions of the act into the Fourteenth Amendment.[7]

During the debates on the resolution that was to become the Fourteenth Amendment the question arose as to whether the proposed amendment protected Negroes against discrimination and segregation. There was no agreement, but proponents of the amendment were optimistic regarding its effect. In supporting the amendment, Senator Jacob M. Howard of Michigan said that the equal protection clause "abolishes all class legislation in the states and does away with the injustice of subjecting one caste of persons to a code not applicable to another." Representative John Bingham of Ohio declared that the amendment would protect "by national law the privileges and immunities of all the citizens of the Republic and the inborn rights of every person within its jurisdiction whenever the same shall be abridged or denied by the unconstitutional acts of any state."[8]

Neither the Fourteenth Amendment nor the radical legislation embodied in congressional Reconstruction was sufficient to protect the Negro in his political and civil rights. Southern resistance was stiff and effective, while efforts at enforcement left much to be desired. Once they recovered from the initial staggering blow of Radical Reconstruction legislation the ex-Confederates grimly went about the task of nullifying it in every possible way. By violence, intimidation, and ingenious schemes of economic pressure, by increased participation in political affairs, they began to "redeem" their state governments. Neither the Fifteenth Amendment nor the Ku Klux Klan Acts could stem the tide. In one state after another, between 1870 and 1877, they were successful; and as they took over the Southern state governments, they began to enact laws to separate Negroes and whites.

Congress, against the bitter opposition of the ex-Confederates who were taking over the seats the Radicals had occupied, made one final

7. *Ibid.*, pp. 75–87, and Benjamin B. Kendrick, *The Journal of the Joint Committee of Fifteen on Reconstruction* (New York: Columbia University Press, 1914), pp. 267–69.

8. *Congressional Globe*, Thirty-ninth Congress, First Session (Washington: F. and J. Rivas, 1866), pp. 2459, 2766.

effort to prevent the destruction of the rights of Negroes. Between 1871 and 1875 it devoted much attention to various proposals for a comprehensive national civil rights bill. While the act that was passed in 1875 omitted the provision of earlier drafts requiring the admission of persons regardless of race to all public schools, it declared that all persons, regardless of race or color, should be entitled to the full and equal enjoyment of the accommodations, advantages, facilities, and privileges of inns, public conveyances, theaters, and other places of public amusement. In its scope and in its provisions for enforcement it far surpassed anything that had ever been done in the area of protecting the civil rights of Negroes.

Although the Southern whites viewed the Act of 1875 with utter contempt and violated it with impunity, they were not entirely comfortable so long as it was on the statute books. They found it impossible, therefore, to restrain their elation when the Supreme Court declared the act unconstitutional in 1883. When the decision was announced during a performance at the Atlanta Opera House, the audience broke into "such a thunder of applause . . . as was never before heard within the walls of the opera house."[9] An Arkansas newspaper expressed hearty agreement with the majority of the Court when it said, "Society is a law unto itself, which in matters social in their nature overrides the statutes. Against its decrees the written law is powerless."[10]

Before the momentous decision in the Civil Rights Cases in 1883 segregation by statutes was confined to a relatively few but highly important areas. In many states, for example, the laws against intermarriage preceded the Civil War by many years.[11] Although they were omitted from some state codes during Reconstruction, there was no wholesale repeal of them, and they remained in effect in many parts of the North as well as in the South.[12] The practice of maintaining separate schools for white and Negro children was well established in the North before the Civil War; and in the South if

9. Atlanta *Constitution*, October 16, 1883.

10. Little Rock *Daily Arkansas Gazette*, October 19, 1883.

11. Intermarriage was prohibited in Arkansas in 1838; in Louisiana in 1810. For a discussion of these statutes see Charles S. Mangum, *The Legal Status of the Negro* (Chapel Hill: University of North Carolina Press, 1940), pp. 236–73.

12. Gilbert Thomas Stephenson, *Race Distinctions in American Law* (New York: D. Appleton and Company, 1910), pp. 78–101.

ex-Confederates provided schools for Negro children at all they were of course separate. Although the Radicals made some attempts to break down segregated schools during their brief period of control, they met with little success.[13] In the military services Negroes had almost always been segregated, and the Civil War did much to strengthen the practice.

The decision in the Civil Rights Cases was an important stimulus to the enactment of segregation statutes. It gave the assurance the South wanted that the federal government would not intervene to protect the civil rights of Negroes. The decision coincided, moreover, with a series of political and intellectual developments that greatly accelerated the program of segregation. In the eighties several Southern governments were embarrassed by financial scandals, and some of them outstripped the Reconstruction governments in defalcations and pilfering.[14] Meanwhile, the agrarian unrest induced by widespread economic distress frightened the conservatives and forced them to adopt extreme measures in order to regain the leadership which in some states they had temporarily lost to white and Negro Populists. Distressed by the possibility of a strong new party composed of white and Negro farmers and workers, they dominated the Negro vote where they could and expressed grave fears of "Negro domination" where they could not. Thus, the magical formula of white supremacy, "applied without stint and without any of the old reservations of paternalism, without deference to any lingering resistance of Northern Liberalism, or any fear of further check from a defunct Southern Populism," gained ascendancy in the final decade of the nineteenth century.[15]

These were the years that witnessed the effective constitutional disfranchisement of Negroes by such devices as understanding clauses, grandfather clauses, and good conduct clauses. They also saw the

13. Francis B. Simkins and Robert H. Woody, *South Carolina During Reconstruction* (Chapel Hill: University of North Carolina Press, 1932), pp. 439–42, and T. Harry Williams, "The Louisiana Unification Movement of 1873," *Journal of Southern History*, Vol. 11 (August 1945), p. 362.

14. C. Vann Woodward, *Origins of the New South, 1877–1914* (Baton Rouge: Louisiana State University Press, 1951), pp. 67–70.

15. C. Vann Woodward, *The Strange Career of Jim Crow* (New York: Oxford University Press, 1955), p. 65.

launching of an intensive propaganda campaign of white supremacy, negrophobia, and race chauvinism, supported by a sensational and irresponsible press that carried lurid stories of alleged Negro bestiality. New waves of violence broke out, with increased lynchings of Negroes, unspeakable atrocities against them, and race riots. Concurrently, and at a "higher level," the literary and scientific leaders of the South wrote numerous tracts and books designed to "prove" the inhumanity of the Negro.[16] In this climate segregation took a giant step toward a fully developed white supremacy apparatus.

In the decade after the Civil War few laws were enacted demanding segregation. The first state segregation statutes were those of Mississippi and Florida in 1865, requiring segregation on public carriers. Texas followed in 1866, but five years later repealed the act. The Tennessee law of 1881, sometimes referred to as the first Jim Crow law, directed railroad companies to provide separate cars or portions of cars for first-class Negro passengers, instead of relegating them to second-class accommodations as had been the custom. There were only two votes against the measure in the House and one in the Senate.

In the ensuing twenty years separation of Negroes and whites on public carriers became a favorite preoccupation of Southern legislators. By 1892 six other Southern states had joined the ranks—Texas, Louisiana, Alabama, Arkansas, Georgia, and Kentucky. In some states, however, opposition had been bitter. In Louisiana, for example, a Negro representative declared that the law would humiliate Negroes and "make them appear before the world as a treacherous and a dangerous class of people."[17] In Arkansas a Negro member of the House sought to ridicule the bill's supporters by insisting that if whites did not want to associate with Negroes there should be laws to divide the streets and sidewalks so that Negroes could go on one side and white people on the other. "He would like to see an end put to

16. See the books by Thomas Dixon, notably *The Leopard's Spots: A Romance of the White Man's Burden—1865-1900* (New York: Doubleday, Page & Company, 1902); Charles Carroll, *"The Negro a Beast,"* or, *"In the Image of God"* . . . (St. Louis, Mo.: American Book and Bible House, 1900); and Robert W. Shufeldt, *The Negro, A Menace to American Civilization* (Boston: R. G. Badger, 1907).

17. *Louisiana House Journal, Second Session, 1890*, pp. 202–203.

all intercourse between white and colored people by day, and especially by night."[18]

With the pattern firmly established in a number of Southern states and the pressure for segregation growing, the other Southern states followed before the end of the century. South Carolina passed its law segregating Negroes and whites on railroads in 1898; North Carolina, Virginia, and Maryland soon after. When Oklahoma entered the Union in 1907 segregation had already been provided for.

By this time laws were being extended to cover all activities related to transportation. In 1888 the railroad commission of Mississippi was authorized to designate separate waiting rooms for Negroes and whites. By 1893 the railroad companies, on their own initiative, were doing the same thing in South Carolina, and in 1906 the state required separation of the races in all station restaurants and eating houses. Ultimately, legislation covered steamboats, buses, and other forms of transportation.

The first decade of the twentieth century witnessed the enactment of a wide variety of segregation statutes. Georgia had required separation of the races on streetcars as early as 1891. It was between 1901 and 1907, however, that North Carolina, Virginia, Louisiana, Arkansas, South Carolina, Tennessee, Mississippi, Maryland, Florida, and Oklahoma followed suit. Ordinances in Southern cities were even more specific than state laws. In 1906, for example, the city of Montgomery, Alabama, went so far as to insist that Negroes and whites use separate streetcars.

As the states assumed greater responsibility for the various wards of society they were careful to provide separate facilities for whites and Negroes. In 1875 Alabama made it unlawful for any jailer or sheriff to imprison white and Negro prisoners before conviction in the same apartments of the jail, if there were sufficient separate apartments, and ten years later prohibited the chaining of white and Negro convicts together or housing them together. In 1903 Arkansas directed that in the state penitentiary and in county jails, stockades, convict camps, and all other places where prisoners were confined, separate apartments should be provided and maintained for white and Negro prisoners. Within the next ten years most of the other Southern states had similar legislation. During the same period segre-

18. Little Rock Arkansas Gazette, February 14, 1891.

gation of white and Negro insane, feeble-minded, blind and deaf, paupers, tubercular patients, and juvenile delinquents was provided for.

In rounding out the system of legal segregation some states provided for the separation of whites and Negroes at work, at play, and at home. In 1915 South Carolina forbade textile factories to permit employees of different races to work together in the same room, or to use the same entrances, pay windows, exits, doorways, stairways, or windows at the same time, or the same lavatories, toilets, drinking-water buckets, pails, cups, dippers, or glasses at any time. In 1905 Georgia passed a law making illegal the use by Negroes and whites of the same park facilities; individuals were permitted to donate land for playground use only if they specified which race alone was to make use of it. Until 1940 Negroes and whites in Atlanta, Georgia, were not permitted to visit the municipal zoo at the same time. In 1929 Oklahoma authorized the Conservation Commission to segregate the races in the use of fishing, boating, and bathing facilities on lakes and streams under the supervision of the state. Arkansas enacted a law in 1935 requiring the separation of Negroes and whites at all race tracks and gaming establishments. Beginning in 1910 several cities, among them Baltimore, Atlanta, and Louisville, passed ordinances designating certain blocks, territories, and districts as Negro or white and forbidding members of one race to live in the area assigned to the other. Such zoning laws, however, were declared unconstitutional in 1917.

The supply of ideas for new ways to segregate whites and Negroes seemed inexhaustible. In 1915 Oklahoma authorized the Corporation Commission to order telephone companies to maintain separate booths for white and Negro patrons. North Carolina and Florida provided that textbooks used by the children of one race be kept separate from those used by children of the other race, despite the fact that both states have stringent rules covering fumigation of textbooks. In 1922 Mississippi forbade members of both races to ride in taxicabs at the same time unless the vehicle held more than seven passengers and was traveling from one city to another. New Orleans deemed it in the interest of the public welfare to enact an ordinance separating Negro and white prostitutes.

The law had created two worlds, so separate that communication between them was almost impossible. Separation bred suspicion and hatred, fostered rumors and misunderstanding, and created conditions that made extremely difficult any steps toward its reduction. Legal segregation was so complete that a Southern white minister was moved to remark that it "made of our eating and drinking, our buying and selling, our labor and housing, our rents, our railroads, our orphanages and prisons, our recreations, our very institutions of religion a problem of race as well as a problem of maintenance."[19]

Yet law was only one part of the mechanism keeping the races segregated. Numerous devices were employed to perpetuate segregation in housing, education, and places of public accommodation even in communities where civil rights statutes forbade such practices. Patriotic, labor, and business organizations kept alive the "Lost Cause" and all that it stood for, including the subordination of the Negro. Separate Bibles for oath taking in courts of law, separate doors for whites and Negroes, separate elevators and stairways, separate drinking fountains, and separate toilets existed even where the law did not require them. Finally, there was the individual assumption of responsibility for keeping Negroes in their place, such as the white man who placed a rod across the boat to segregate his Negro fishing companion while they ate lunch, and the archivist of a Southern state who cleared a room of manuscripts, ordered a special key, and assigned an attendant to serve a visiting Negro scholar who would otherwise have had to use the regular search room, from which he was not barred by law.[20]

By the middle of the twentieth century the pattern of segregation was as irregular as it was complex. Every conceivable form of segregation had been evolved, although one would have to visit many places to observe all the variations. The wall of segregation had become so formidable, so impenetrable, apparently, that the entire weight of the American tradition of equality and all the strength of the American constitutional system had to be brought to bear in order to make even the slightest crack in it.

19. Edgar Gardner Murphy, *The Basis of Ascendancy* (New York: Longmans, Green & Company, 1909), p. 138.

20. For numerous examples of the informal but tenacious practices of segregation see Charles S. Johnson, *Patterns of Negro Segregation* (New York: Harper and Brothers, 1943).

Leonard Pitt,
"Decline of the Californios:
The Second Generation, 1865–1890"

American society underwent a series of major changes after the
Civil War which included rapid industrialization, urbanization,
and westward migration. Leonard Pitt, in "Decline of the Californios:
The Second Generation, 1865–1890," analyzes the effect of these
changes on the descendents of the Mexicans who were incorporated
into the United States as a result of the Treaty of Guadalupe
Hidalgo. While many of the first generation maintained their
traditional culture under American rule, the second generation
saw their heritage succumb to the steady stream of Yankee
immigration to California. The Yankee invasion brought railroads,
cities, the imposition of alien laws, and the introduction of new
agricultural patterns; as a result, the Californios suffered loss of land,
decline in status, and eventual elimination from political influence.
By the end of the nineteenth century, the Californios were disappearing as a distinct group within society. A few men of Caucasian
lineage and inherited wealth were absorbed into the dominant
white society. The rest were relegated, along with more recent
Mexican immigrants, to the status of a despised minority.

Decline of the Californios:
The Second Generation, 1865–1890
Leonard Pitt

When the first railroad started running in southern California in November, 1869, shuttling back and forth from Los Angeles to San Pedro, vaqueros would gleefully race their horses against the locomotive. They won the short sprint, but of course lost in the long haul.[1] The results were symbolically quite meaningful, for the civilization represented by the locomotive was bearing down on them slowly but with irresistible force. In September, 1876, the Southern Pacific arrived from the north and in March, 1887, the first Santa Fe Railroad train snaked through the San Bernardino Mountains into Los Angeles. Thereafter, as many as three and four coach trains descended on the city each day, depositing in 1887 alone more than 120,000 tourists, health seekers, farmers, artisans, and businessmen.

These developments inaugurated southern California's first major

Abridged from Leonard Pitt, "The Second Generation, 1865–1890," *The Decline of the Californios: A History of the Spanish-Speaking Californians, 1846–1890*, pp. 249–276. Originally published by the University of California Press; reprinted by permission of The Regents of the University of California. Some footnotes have been renumbered.

1. Remi Nadeau, *The City Makers* (New York, 1948), p. 30.

land boom—"the most extravagant in American frontier experience"[2] —which sealed the coffin of the old California culture. Until the advent of the boom of the eighties, the embattled Californios were still fighting a desperate holding action in the south—forty years after the Mexican War, a generation removed from the gold rush, fifteen years beyond the Civil War and the great drought of the 1860's. Spanish conversation, adobe architecture, and traditional clothing, manners, and recreations had told the newest or most refractory gringo that, like it or not, he was in "foreign" territory and could not completely brush the "natives" aside. To all this the boom put an effective end.

Between 1865 and 1890 the second generation of Californios came to maturity: those persons who were only vaguely aware of the Arcadian period and the revolutions and wars that had engrossed their parents, but acutely conscious of the consolidation of the new order. The wellbeing of this generation greatly depended on the amount of land it might inherit. In the north, where the original estates had been checkered with settlers, alienated from their owners, or greatly reduced in size, the transmission of a viable rancho holding from father to son was a rare event indeed. And yet in the south, islands of rancho land remained intact, at least until the 1870's. They were sometimes large and contiguous, creating the effect of a vast chain or archipelago of rangeland stretching from the Tehachapis to the Mexican border.

By 1875, however, the southern rancho islands had shrunk and had lost their common boundaries. Family farms increased noticeably in their midst, and rails were approaching them from the north with the promise of commercial and real estate developments that would interfere with rancho supremacy.

From 1865 to 1885, miscellaneous ills beset the southern rancheros. At Santa Barbara their vaqueros had to crash through fences to secure access to grazing land, in a struggle reminiscent of the nester-cattleman conflict on the Great Plains.[3] In the San Fernando Valley, a ferocious Basque squatter, Miguel Leonis, armed a hundred fellow countrymen and Mexicans at Calabasas and clung to land by brute force, staving off both Yankees and Californians with better claims

2. Blake McKelvey, *The Urbanization of America, 1860–1915* (New Brunswick, 1963), p. 28. This chapter relies considerably on Glenn S. Dumke, *The Boom of the Eighties in Southern California* (San Marino, Calif., 1944).

3. Annie L. Morrison and John H. Haydon, *History of San Luis Obispo County and Environs . . .* (Los Angeles, 1917), pp. 81–85.

than his.[4] At Stockton, Major José Pico was arrested for alleged land-sale fraud concerning property in Baja California.[5] But the most chronic and incurable ills still concerned finances—high mortgage interest, costly litigation, low beef prices, and out-of-state competition for stockmen—and were compounded by the high living expenses of the more aristocratic rancheros. The financial troubles were severe enough to ruin Yankees, too—men with lower expenses, more flexible social values, and a keener sense of business tactics than the Californios'. For example, Abel Stearns, the south's wealthiest landowner, whose personal empire had incorporated the defunct Bandini estate, in turn was unable to prevent creditors from eating up his property after the drought.[6] . . .

The post-Civil War Yankee immigrants who acquired the subdivided ranchos . . . significantly altered the uses of the soil. For one thing, they introduced sheep in a big way, generally renting vacant rancho land for grazing purposes and simultaneously managing the ranchero's own stock; some land they bought outright. While the sheep craze lasted, it helped the Californios recoup their cattle losses.

The Americans also promoted agriculture, particularly wheat farming. Rancheros irrevocably wedded to pastoral agriculture could scarcely comprehend, much less use, the new farm techniques and never got into the swim of things. When Antonio María Lugo first saw a mowing machine, he lifted a bony finger and exclaimed in Spanish: "The Yankee is but one finger shy of the devil!"[7] The rancheros' sons and grandsons, however, did wield the devil's instruments. José M. Ramirez experimented with wheat as early as 1872; Rómulo Pico raised a crop near former Mission San Fernando in 1880; and in the same year C. Castro of Santa Clara shipped to San Francisco 400 tons of hay which he had grown on his 250-acre farm. Two years later Señores Olivera, Machado, Higuera, and M. Coronel planted the grain near La Ballona. Truck gardening also increased

4. Horace Bell, *On the Old West Coast: Being Further Reminiscences of a Ranger* (New York, 1930), p. 181ff.

5. San Jose *Pioneer and Historical Review*, Dec. 1, 1877.

6. John C. Hough, "Abel Stearns, 1848–1871," unpublished MS, ed. by John Caughey, p. 450.

7. Henry D. Barrows, "Don Antonio Maria Lugo: A Picturesque Character of California," Historical Society of Southern California *Annual Publications*, III (1893–1896), 32.

among the Spanish-speaking.[8] At Los Nietos, east of Los Angeles, more than 120 men ran farms in 1880, including scores of men with Spanish surnames who called themselves "farmer," "small farmer," or "farm laborer," depending on whether they had sons as helpers, worked for a Yankee, or worked for themselves. Few of the 120 owned much land, and several rented parcels or sharecropped on plots of from 15 to 75 acres.[9]

Rancheros and vaqueros uprooted by the drought or by poor finances had to take work they would ordinarily disdain. Able-bodied gentry of the lower and middle ranks went on a sheep-shearing circuit in the 1870's. Fifty or sixty strong—with silver trimmed bridles and stirrups, tooled leather saddles, broadcloth suits, ruffled shirts, dark sombreros—they rode from one sheep ranch to another looking for work. When hired, these original migratory laborers put away their finery and reappeared in brown overalls and red bandanas, ready for action. They supplied their own bedding and meals and stayed for a month or so at each stop.

The conversion to sheep provided only seasonal labor, however, lasting three to eight months in the year, and it generally made the vaquero a supernumerary. Majordomo Juan Canedo of Rancho Los Cerritos, a dignified person who understood but never deigned to speak English, grew melancholy as the cattle died and the place changed hands and became a sheep pasture. Yet he claimed that he "belonged" to the property when Jonathan Bixby bought it, and refused to leave. To Bixby's daughter he "looked like a bronze statue, with brown face, brown clothes, brown horse and infinite repose." Bixby's son comforted Juan on his deathbed and supported Juan's widow—to repay the old man, as the boy said, for having taught him horsemanship.[10]

Apart from agricultural work, California's Spanish-speaking lower class performed only one other main semiskilled job, mining. "By far the larger portion of work-people in California mines are Mexicans,"

8. El Demócrata (Los Angeles), Oct. 1882; H. S. Foote, Pen Pictures from the Garden of the World, or, Santa Clara County, California (Chicago, 1888), pp. 350, 488–489, La Crónica (Los Angeles), May 25, 1872.

9. United States Bureau of the Census, Tenth Census, 1880, Enumerator's Roll Book, Los Angeles County (microfilm).

10. Sarah Bixby-Smith, Adobe Days . . . (Cedar Rapids, Iowa, 1926), pp. 113–114, 126–127.

an expert observed in 1867.[11] Several hundred Mexican gold miners worked in Soledad Canyon in 1880. More important, until 1887 more than half of the world's mercury supply came from California, the greater proportion from the New Almadén Quicksilver Mine near Santa Clara. For this tedious and deadly work, employers rated the Mexicans "more adventurous than Cornishmen," who were generally reputed to be the world's best miners. Using techniques reminiscent of their ancestors three hundred years earlier, the 1,500 Mexicans at New Almadén clambered upward hundreds of feet, on groaning ladders, supporting 200-pound sacks of ore strapped to their foreheads and resting precariously on their backs. Above ground the smelters were often exposed to the fatal mercury fumes and died violently from it. Drinking, gambling, whoring, and murderous brawls erupted every payday, because, as one lady observer explained, New Almadén had "no advantages of church or school." A paternalistic management later organized a model company town, lining the streets with flowers and whitewashing the miners' cottages, until it became a sightseer's "must."[12] For some unaccountable reason, fashionably attired wedding parties came from San Jose to gape at the men emerging from the pithead.

The Spanish-speaking did not readily gravitate into newer industries. The oil refinery at Newhall had not a single Mexican hand in 1880. By then, Chinese hands harvested the fruit crops and did other menial jobs the Spanish-speaking might have hired out for previously. Southern California's most important new employer, the Southern Pacific Railroad, used Chinese gangs to bore the mammoth tunnel through the mountains and into the San Fernando Valley in 1875. Only on the last leg of the construction, from the valley to Los Angeles, did Mexicans and Indians join the work gangs, but the hundred railroad hands permanently employed at the downtown switching yard, a stone's throw from Sonoratown, came mainly from the eastern United States, not from Mexico or California.[13]

For many Spanish-American youths, California represented a place

11. J. Ross Browne, "Down in the Cinnabar Mines: A Visit to New Almadén in 1865," *Harper's Magazine*, XXI (Oct. 1865), 549.

12. Carrie Stevens Walter, quoted in Eugene T. Sawyer, *History of Santa Clara County, California* ... (Los Angeles, 1922), pp. 86–87.

13. U. S. Bureau of the Census, *op. cit.*

that had robbed them of their birthright, but had meanwhile provided innumerable opportunities to steal back parts of it. In any event, many of the disaffected still turned badmen. From 16 to 20 percent of San Quentin inmates from 1854 to 1865 were Mexicans or Californians[14]—a high figure in view of the relative numerical decline of the Spanish-speaking, even when correcting for Yankee prejudice in law enforcement. Mexicans engaged in numerous and brutal individual crimes, but their forte was highway robbery, stage holdups, and rustling, activities in which they continued to surpass all other nationalities, even after the gold rush. As late as 1875 the most notorious characters in the state still wore sombreros. . . .

Probably the last old-fashioned mob lynching in California of a person of Spanish-American background occurred in San Jose in 1877, when a pair of confessed murderers and robbers were snatched from the jail and strung from the Upper San Lorenzo Bridge.[15] As popular tribunals gave way to regular law enforcement, banditry in the old manner also declined; gold and livestock were now shipped more securely by railroad, and sheriffs' telegrams flashing up and down the state made a badman's escape more difficult.

A sheriff now could succeed without vigilante aid, particularly if, like Alameda Sheriff Harry Morse, archenemy of bandidos, he possessed perseverance to match their bravado. So closely did Morse hound bandidos that they took him for a demon. Between 1864 and 1874 he trailed Borjorques mercilessly (but never laid eyes on him); killed Norrate Ponce (although killing was not his specialty); captured Tejada; and simply strode up to Procopio in a San Francisco dance hall, laid a hand on the bandido's shoulder, calmly declared, "Procopio, you're my man," and took him to jail.[16] For sheer drama nothing surpassed his single-handed showdown with Juan Soto, whom he began tracking after the badman had robbed and killed a Suñol shopkeeper in January, 1871. With customary aplomb Morse hiked directly into Soto's mountain fastness south of Gilroy, masquerading as a weary and lost traveler. His disguise gained Morse easy entry into

14. California State Prison Directors, "Annual Report," in California Legislature, *Journals of 1860 Assembly* (Sacramento, 1861), App. 13, pp. 18–19; *1865–1866 Senate and Assembly* (Sacramento, 1866), App., p. 66.

15. *Pioneer and Historical Review*, May 5, 1877.

16. Charles Howard Shinn, *Graphic Description of Pacific Coast Outlaws* (Los Angeles, 1958), p. 64.

Soto's casa for "a rest." When the bandit and his crew discovered the ruse, they began shooting it out with the sheriff. A Mexican amazon momentarily pinioned Morse's arms, but he broke her grip and got safely outside. Finally the wounded Soto burst from the shack, "bareheaded, his long black hair streaming behind him, a cocked revolver in each hand," and flying suicidally at Morse. At this, the sheriff raised his rifle and shot Soto in the head.[17] . . .

After Juan Soto's death, only one important bandido remained at large—Tiburcio Vasquez, a Californio. A long and checkered career as cattle rustler, stage robber, and jailbird lay behind him when he engineered his final spree against the shopkeepers of Tres Pinos. A wanton killing aroused the authorities of several counties to weave a net around him. In a scenario-like episode appropriately played out near present-day Hollywood, a brigade of sheriffs and deputies tightened the net and caught Vasquez. Bound in irons, he seemed at close range as vicious and gallant as the Yankees had expected. When asked for the motives for his crimes, he recalled a boyhood scene in which he bade his mother good-bye and set out to avenge Yankee injustice—a touching and believable explanation, but altogether irrelevant to the judge and the jury that had him executed.[18] Bandido depredations soon subsided in California, partly as a function of Mexico's subsiding political turmoil. The archetypal California badman of the 1880's, Black Bart, wore a dark bowler instead of a sombrero.

Bandido Vasquez personified a major motif among the Spanish Americans in California—alienation of the second generation. Nevertheless, a good many of his contemporaries responded altogether differently to recent events by picking themselves up, resettling in the towns, and making a new life for themselves. In the town environment, the younger generation came in contact with new cultural influences and adjusted accordingly. Submergence of the Spanish-speaking thus entailed various possibilities: for some, an irrational armed resistance through crime; for a few, assimilation into the mainstream of Yankee culture; and for still others, assimilation into the Mexican community.

In the rural hamlets of Los Angeles County, a quarter of the in-

17. Joseph Henry Jackson, *Bad Company* (New York, 1949), pp. 264–267.

18. Ernest May, "Tiburcio Vasquez," *Historical Society of Southern California Quarterly*, XXIX (1947), 123–134.

habitants had Spanish surnames as late as 1880. Of course, in some townships Yankees reigned supreme. At Pasadena not one of the 392 occupants was Spanish American (the Chinese did all the menial labor); at Santa Ana only 4 of the 714 were Spanish-speaking; and at the beach suburb of Santa Monica, 7 of the 418. Elsewhere, on the other hand, Spanish Americans clustered so thickly as to alienate gringos. New Mexicans were still entrenched at isolated, self-contained, culturally preserved San Jose township. Also, near former mission San Juan Capistrano, there were 345 Spanish-speaking residents, as indigenous as the famous sparrows, born in California of California parents (some perhaps of neophyte Indian background); the remaining 31 residents were Europeans....

When a hamlet acquires a railroad, cheap labor, and slums, it is well launched toward cityhood. These requisites for maturity Los Angeles had attained by 1876. Nigger Alley, north of the plaza, had undergone the most striking change since epidemic smallpox had killed off so many Spanish Americans a decade earlier; excepting some French traders, every inhabitant was Chinese. This area was one of two slums. As the town updated itself, the neighborhood east and south of the plaza, as far east as the river and as far south as the railroad, remained a Mexican village and thus, by comparison, a slum. There the shops, saloons, brothels, and gambling dens crowded one another in overwhelming disarray. "Sonoratown" provided all the amusements, comforts, and vices of a ghetto except work, which lay in the better parts of town. The underworld of all nationalities gravitated to Sonoratown, and axe murders, shootings, beatings, and knifings commonly occurred there. Should the police seek an out-of-town villain, they knew where to look, perhaps at Francisco Carmona's disorderly house on Buena Vista Street. Gringo citizens once tried to close the place, but a judge dismissed their case as legally weak although morally sound.[19] Suddenly, about the time of the boom, Sonoratown became Chinatown and the Spanish-speaking went to live in other neighborhoods.

The Spanish-American town dwellers made a living chiefly as laborers, but also as farmers, broom makers, barbers, gamblers, butchers, zanjeros, miners, and shepherds. Women, too, worked. Those from better families often had had girlhood training in sewing and thus

19. Los Angeles *Times*, March 6, 10, 25, 1883. See also W. W. Robinson, *Los Angeles, from the Days of the Pueblo* ... (San Francisco, 1959), pp. 63–64.

became seamstresses; others became domestics; and some, prostitutes. Brothels sprang up even outside Sonoratown, as at the docks at Wilmington, where the Mexican-born Señora Paredez lived with two children and three women of Baja California and California; the census taker jotted her down as "Keeping House," and as an afterthought wryly added "of Ill Fame."[20] Indeed, the Spanish-speaking worked at anything to bring in "poco dinero"; they rated higher wages than the Chinese but lower than the Anglos.

The relative impersonality of town life was partly offset by the enveloping warmth of the family. The older the family and the longer its stay in California, the larger it was apt to be; small households denoted recent arrivals, sometimes of single Mexican men living in boarding houses. Californio families ran large in both town and country. Fifty-four-year-old Joaquín Sepúlveda and his wife had nine children, ranging in age from twenty to five years. Tomás Palomares, also in his fifties, lived at suburban San Jose township with his wife and ten children, the eldest twenty-two years and the youngest six months. Dwellings tended to be overcrowded with aged parents, grown and infant children, grandchildren, in-laws, nieces and nephews, boarders, and adopted orphans—all living under one roof, or next door, or down the street. Fifteen Reyeses stuck close together in two Main Street homes. In the household of Mr. and Mrs. Mott and their five children (a branch of the Sepúlveda family), eleven people lived under one roof, including Mrs. Mott's septuagenarian mother, a California-born servant, two sisters-in-law, and Mott's sister....

As Californio influence waned in Los Angeles, immigrant Mexicans assured the continuance of Spanish-American culture, which therefore never died. In San Francisco and other northern localities the Mexican community evolved independently of the native-born, but in Los Angeles it merged gradually and imperceptibly with them. The number of Mexicans slowly increased until they were ready to overtake the Californios, probably by the turn of the century. The Mexican community, moreover, attained a sense of respectability it formerly had lacked. As the memories of Manifest Destiny waned, Yankees thought better of Mexico and, at least for the record, had some good words for the sister republic—perhaps that it was finally "waking up" and "uniting with our country [in] the spread of civiliza-

20. U. S. Bureau of the Census, *op. cit.*

tion in the West."[21] Respectable Mexican patriotic organizations formed, disbanded, and re-formed, such as the Hispano-Americano Society of Los Angeles, dedicated to combating the "decadent" state of the community, the Mexican Progressive Society; the Juarez Patriotic Society (with a branch in San Juan Capistrano in 1872); and Botello's Cavalry and the Mexican Lancers, which appeared on festive occasions.[22] . . .

As part of the old-line community blended imperceptibly with the Mexicans, however, another merged into the dominant gringo culture. Thus, in a sense, the Californios were ground down between the upper and nether millstones of two immigrant groups.

The old upper class, particularly the Californios of Caucasian origin, continued to mingle with the new. . . .

If in olden days the dominant Mexican culture had transformed some Yankees into "Mexicanized gringos," now the new culture created a class of "gringoized Mexicans." This did not, however, represent a true blending of two cultures, but rather a triumph of the most aggressive and a defeat of the most recessive cultural characteristics. The socially prominent del Valle family of Los Angeles aspired toward, and in most respects attained, the status of the new "better classes." For all their old-fashioned fiestas at Camulos, their values looked to the present. Their personal mementos give this impression unmistakably. The family photograph album captures handsome dark faces, racially indistinguishable from most Anglo-Saxon ones. The album also contains the ordinary minutiae of the Gilded Age—society column notices, dance invitations, travel brochures, pressed flowers, flowered stationery, wedding and funeral notices, calling cards, school graduation programs, and illustrations of home furnishings and women's fashions. Except that many of the items relate to church or parochial-school functions, one can find scarcely any attributes of the older culture.[23]

Of all the battlefields on which the Spanish Americans fought a holding action to preserve their influence, they succeeded best on the

21. Los Angeles *Times*, Sept. 18, 1883.

22. Broadside in Coronel Collection, items 1563, 1568F, PC9, Los Angeles County Museum; La Crónica (Los Angeles), June 10, Nov. 2, 1872; Aug. 23, 1873.

23. Del Valle Collection, Los Angeles County Museum.

political one. A prestigious Spanish surname (especially when combined with a Caucasian face) remained a good entreé into public office, and many Spanish Americans used it successfully. Estevan Castro became a Monterey constable and later an assemblyman, although Don José Castro's other sons remained "without social standing"; Martin Aguirre became Los Angeles sheriff in 1885; Andrés Pico's son Ramon ran for state treasurer in 1875 (but lost); Andronico Sepúlveda served as Los Angeles county treasurer in 1873; Andrés Castillero sat in Congress in 1880; José G. Estudillo was state treasurer from 1875 to 1880; Santa Barbara's Angel G. Escandon served in the legislature from 1869 to 1874; and, following in the footsteps of his father, Manuel Coronel entered politics and served one term in the state legislature.[24]

Of all Spanish-speaking Californians, Romualdo Pacheco accomplished the most brilliant and unusual political stroke, by seating himself in the governor's chair. Born the son of a Santa Barbara army officer in 1831, young Romualdo received a superior Yankee schooling in the Sandwich Islands and came back with a head for figures; then he hired out as a supercargo on various trading vessels plying the California coast. After the Mexican War he managed his mother's rancho in San Luis Obispo and at the age of twenty-two (1853) won an assembly seat. He became state senator as a Democrat in 1858, and as a Union Democrat in 1862. After a stint in the Union Army in 1863, he changed party affiliation and gained election as Republican state treasurer, serving four years (and yielding that post to his kinsman, Ramón Pacheco). Except for Unionism, no particular political views clung to Romualdo's name, but his background made good press notices—he was an aristocratic native son, a ranchero, a bear fighter, a vigilante, a soldier, a sometime stockbroker, and the husband of an Anglo-Saxon woman. His popularity, the modest importance of the "Spanish" vote, and a desire to balance the ticket between two rival factions encouraged the Republican Party to nominate him for lieutenant governor in 1871. He came in during the Republican sweep of that year, serving routinely until 1875. In February, Governor Booth took an interim seat in the United States Senate and handed Pacheco the governorship for the balance of that year. Pacheco was

24. La Crónica (Los Angeles), March 12, 1873; El Demócrata (Los Angeles), Nov. 1, 1882.

little more than a figurehead in a caretaker government, but even so it gave the Spanish-speaking particular satisfaction to see their man in so exalted a position. The party managers thought better of re-nominating Pacheco, however, and upon leaving office he turned to selling stocks in San Francisco. Meanwhile, from 1878 to 1882, he served two terms in Washington as Santa Clara's congressman, and spent some of his declining years in Mexico and Texas.[25] ...

The Spanish-speaking leaders staved off complete annihilation for a remarkably long time, considering their early economic and numerical losses. Perhaps they could have accomplished more had they not iso-lated themselves from their own people as they entered "society" and abandoned their traditional ways. Perhaps, too, the ethos of the Gilded Age, which resisted social reform and encouraged political cynicism, prevented them from coping with the real social ills that beset the Spanish Americans. The greatest problem of the Spanish-speaking stemmed, however, from their loss of numbers, for which none of their leaders could provide a remedy. Although about 12,000 strong in Los Angeles by 1887, the Spanish-speaking constituted less than 10 percent of the total population, and too many of them were newcomers—ignorant, indifferent, or hostile to Yankee politics.

More or less suddenly, in the 1880's the Californians' political hold-ing action ceased. When Ignacio Sepúlveda retired from the bench, Romualdo Pacheco from Congress, and Antonio Coronel and Regi-naldo del Valle from active local politics, gringos replaced them. No younger brothers or sons duplicated the old Californios' prestige. The native-born leaders were left holding honorary chairmanships in this or that committee, but little else, and their community went leader-less.

In 1885 Los Angeles awaited the railroad spike-driving ceremony at Cajon Pass, promised for November, which would greatly promote the direct rail linkup with the East. The completion on September 16 of an intermediary rail hookup with Pasadena created only minor excitement; yet, because it coincided with Mexican Independence Day, it had symbolic meaning and called for a speech by a Spanish-American orator.[26] Not a Mexican, however, but Reginaldo del Valle,

---

25. Hubert Howe Bancroft, "Pioneer Register and Index," in *History of California* (San Francisco, 1886), IV, 764.
26. Los Angeles *Times*, Sept. 17, 1885.

was given the honor. In his own and his father's time, the San Gabriel Valley had burgeoned from an Indian hunting ground to a mission pasturage, then to a rancho empire, and was now sprouting farms, orchards, and towns. It turned out to be a notable September Sixteenth, although symbolically confusing; a Californian born in the American period paid tribute to Mexican liberty by speaking in English to a gringo crowd about Yankee progress. As expected, "The Little One" peppered his remarks with humorous anecdotes of the past thirty years, but the unfunny fact was that the same railroad he was commemorating would soon obliterate practically everything connected with the pastoral era, even his own political career.

The boom of the eighties contributed vastly to the ongoing process of "Americanization." The sheer volume of immigration brought to southern California the very transformations the northerners had witnessed a generation earlier. In two years or so the population of Los Angeles jumped 500 percent, automatically transforming the electorate into an Anglo-American one. The mores changed equally radically. The type of consumer goods advertised for sale, the tastes in food and dress, the prevalence of English over Spanish in daily and official conversation, the Gilded Age recreations, and the style of commerce—all changed rapidly and irreversibly. While describing the changing ethos of real estate promotion and commerce, Professor Glenn S. Dumke notes that "from 1888 onward, the southern counties were imbued with Anglo-American aggressiveness."[27] What started out as a "semi-gringo" town and a cultural backwash became practically overnight a booming Yankee commercial center and the best-known place in the entire West.

From the vantage point of the Californios, the most elemental change lay in the chopping up of the ranchos into farms and towns, a process long under way but now dramatically speeded up. Although the economic boom converged on the city of Los Angeles, the chief activity concerned the rancho-blanketed suburbs. In 1887 Los Angeles real estate men and buyers daily engaged in thirty to seventy transactions and exchanged as much as $100,000. The evolution of the ranchos involved a variety of legal and business transformations, all of them well tested in California in previous years. Among the most common were forfeiture of loans, conveyance of mortgages to new

27. Op. cit., p. 226.

owners, tax delinquency, family litigation, legitimate sales, division of undivided interest by court order, and bankruptcy proceedings or sheriff's sales. No set pattern emerges in these transformations, but the eroded claims of the original claimants washed away steadily and flowed into the hands of the newcomers—financiers, railroad developers, town promoters, cooperative colonizers, and irrigation companies.

Some of the larger southern California ranchos, it is true, seemingly impervious to the usual ravages of death and taxes, acquired a kind of immortality of their own. The Irvine Ranch and Dominguez Estates are two venerable properties whose twentieth-century boundaries correspond closely to those of the original Spanish and Mexican grants. More than 24,000 acres remained with Don Manuel Dominguez at his death in 1882, and his will divided them up among his six daughters in 1885.[28] In turn, Dominguez' grandchildren also kept a good hold on their property and were able to lease and develop the estates without selling outright. These durable properties have, however, changed internally with the times. Recent aerial photographs show the sprawling Dominguez properties dotted with oil fields, airports, factories, freeways, shopping centers, and suburban homes, as the city now totally surrounds the rancho that once was set apart by 20 miles of open range. The Yankee-owned Irvine Ranch was operated as a cattle ranch until a decade ago and is only now slowly being urbanized, through carefully controlled regional planning.

More than a hundred towns and thousands of orchards and farms were platted out in southern California before the boom of the eighties collapsed in 1888. But even those evanescent communities, which disappeared as quickly as they arose, had gone through financial and legal gyrations which permanently disrupted the legal basis of most ranchos, much as the drought of the sixties had disrupted the way of life and the economy of those same estates.

---

28. Robert Cameron Gillingham, *The Rancho San Pedro* (Los Angeles, 1961), p. 271. See also Robert Glass Cleland, *The Irvine Ranch of Orange County, 1810–1950* (San Marino, Calif., 1952), pp. 148–150.

William R. Locklear,
"The Celestials and the Angels:
A Study of the Anti-Chinese Movement
in Los Angeles to 1882"

President Chester A. Arthur signed a bill in 1882 prohibiting further
Chinese immigration to the United States for a period of ten
years, the first of a series of such exclusion acts which remained
in force until 1943. Although the most virulent and unremitting
exhibitions of anti-Chinese sentiment came from citizens of San
Francisco, prejudice against the new immigrants was not confined to
that city. The willingness of Chinese-Americans to work for low
wages, and particularly their use as strikebreakers, created animosity
throughout the country. William R. Locklear, in "The Celestials
and the Angels," examines the growth of anti-Chinese feeling in
Los Angeles. Although the Chinese population of Los Angeles
was not large, the success of the newcomers in the laundry and
vegetable businesses generated a jealous hostility from the whites.
Fanned by inflammatory orators from San Francisco, anti-Chinese
prejudice soon became politically expedient in Los Angeles and led
to the passage of local ordinances aimed at forcing Orientals from
the city. Los Angeles and the rest of California played a role in
making Chinese exclusion a national political issue and bringing
about the passage of the Act of 1882.

The Celestials and the Angels: A Study of the Anti-Chinese Movement in Los Angeles to 1882

William R. Locklear

The anti-Chinese movement in California which led to the Chinese exclusion act of 1882 was essentially a product of agitation in San Francisco and Northern California. It was here that the population of the state, both Chinese and non-Chinese, was concentrated, and it was here that agitation against the Chinese originated and developed.[1] Yet, one event in Southern California history—the massacre of nineteen Chinese at Los Angeles in 1871—brought nation-wide attention to the California movement, and this event has come to represent, or rather to misrepresent, the character of Los Angeles' role in the campaign to restrict Chinese immigration. The facts are, however, that agitation in Los Angeles developed far later than it did in San Francisco, was more difficult to arouse and sustain, and was, on the whole, less passionate and less violent.

California's resentment to the "Celestials"[2] was first manifested among the miners of Northern California when the Chinese became numerically ominous in 1852. As large Chinese populations congregated in northern cities agitation spread among the urban laborers,

Abridged from William R. Locklear, "The Celestials and the Angels: A Study of the Anti-Chinese Movement in Los Angeles to 1882," *Southern California Quarterly*, XLII (1960), pp. 239–256. Reprinted by permission of the author. Some notes have been renumbered; they appear at the end of the article.

who feared the results of competing with them. Over the years, sympathetic and ambitious officeholders produced a mass of state and local legislation designed to stem the tide of immigration and to drive the Chinese away, but the courts declared most of the acts unconstitutional. The pulse of this agitation seems to have quickened during depression years or years in which immigration was particularly high, and it subsided to dormancy only when some relief from either "evil" was obtained.[3]

In justification of the agitation a series of objections to the Chinese was voiced, of which the validity of several is still open to debate. But whether factually true or not the Californians responded to them as if they were, and, thus, they became a semiconscious part of almost every citizen's perspective. The Chinese immigrant was characterized as merely a slave of another color—an intolerable situation after 1865. Moreover, because his needs were few, he could work at a very low rate of pay, thereby underselling white labor, throwing Americans out of jobs and causing their destitute families to turn to crime and prostitution. He was further described as a heathen and inveterate liar who had no respect for American social, religious or political institutions. He lived in "herds" amid squalor, gambled, smoked opium and forced Chinese women into prostitution, thus endangering the health and morality of the community. An ironic complaint was added that he—this "immoral, filthy heathen"—refused to assimilate with the white population![4]

Underlying these objections, many of which were applicable to the white community as well, was a deep-seated racial prejudice among the Caucasians which had previously been vented against the Indian, the Negro and the dark-skinned Frenchman and Latin-American. The refusal of the Chinese to adopt American dress and customs tended to intensify this basic animosity. But the critical element seems to have been the great numbers of Chinese who immigrated. To many Californians there was a very real threat of a Mongolian invasion that would extend the frontiers of the Chinese empire into California. As late as 1882 there was published "A Short and Truthful History of the Taking of California and Oregon by the Chinese, in the year A.D. 1899," written by a "survivor." At one time or another all of these elements found expression in Los Angeles, but usually on a very reduced scale.[5]

Popular sentiment against the Chinese did not appear in Los

Angeles until 1876, the massacre of 1871 notwithstanding. This was almost two full decades after organized labor opposition expressed itself in San Francisco. Of the several factors which account for this delay the lack [of] a sizeable Chinese population is paramount. In 1850 only two Chinese resided among 1,610 Angelenos. Ten years later, while the city's population had risen to 4,385, there were just nine Chinese present. The Chinese community grew considerably during the sixties, totaling 172 in 1870, but this was still only three per cent of the city's population. In contrast, San Francisco housed over 2,700 Chinese in 1860 and more than 12,000 in 1870. Railroad construction around Los Angeles after 1875 drew "carloads" of Chinese into the area and set the stage for local agitation.[6]

A second factor in Los Angeles' delayed reaction derives from the local economy. Southern California was "cow country" in the fifties and sixties. Most of the town's business enterprise was devoted only to meeting the more immediate of local needs and was conducted by self-employed craftsmen. It was only after severe droughts decimated the herds in the sixties that agriculture and horticulture became serious endeavors. When they took hold in the seventies and gave Los Angeles new life, the population then increased rapidly and introduced a laboring force that could identify itself with state-wide labor opposition to the Chinese.[7]

The lack of economic opportunity partially explains the slow growth of a Chinese community as well. More significant, however, was the surplus of opportunity which existed, in spite of racial antagonism, in and around San Francisco, the port-of-entry for Chinese immigrants. Then, too, the early reputation of Los Angeles did little to attract visitors. A primitive and undeveloped town, it had a "larger percentage of bad characters than any other city" in the country. . . .

If there was ever any direct competition between Chinese labor and white labor in early Los Angeles it must have been brief and of no serious proportion. By the seventies the Chinese were concentrated in a few occupational fields which, for all intents and purposes, had become their particular fortes. As domestic help they were well regarded and came to replace the Indians and Negroes who had formerly monopolized such endeavors. In 1872 eleven Chinese laundries employed nearly half of the city's "Celestial" population while only two "white" laundries were operating. During the seventies

Chinese gardeners undertook to supply Los Angeles homes with vegetables, and they came to dominate that field, too. Though individual Chinese appeared in other occupations their total number was never significant.[8]

During the sixties the clannish "Celestials" congregated in one area—along a short street which in the Mexican period had been known as *Calle de los Negros*, but since then called "Nigger Alley" by the race-conscious whites. Long before the arrival of the Chinese this vicinity had deteriorated into a slum and was the established center of gambling, drinking and prostitution in Los Angeles. The selection of this site seems to have been voluntary on the part of the Chinese rather than as a result of any restrictions against their lodging in other parts of town. It is likely that low rents were a major consideration in the selection. Negro Alley (as the name appeared most often in print) was about forty feet wide and 500 feet long and was bordered on either side by veranda-fronted adobes. Most of the Chinese living and business activities were stuffed into its narrow, multi-roomed apartments. (In the main only washhouses were located in other parts of town.) This became the nucleus of a gradually expanding Chinatown, and it was here that the Chinese set up their opium dens and houses of prostitution.[9]

With the introduction of the first Chinese woman in 1859 Angelenos became acutely aware of one facet of the objections to Chinese immigration. Within six weeks of her arrival this first "Celestial" lady tried to commit suicide. And though the chivalry of the *Star's* editor allowed, "Family squabbles seem to have driven her to the rash undertaking," it is more likely that her after-hours assignment was the motivation. In mid-1861 over a dozen other females arrived, and the Chinese community was immediately taken to task for its "unblushing conduct." Strangely enough, the Chinese merchants, who were also the owners of the prostitutes, enjoyed favorable reputations among the citizens of Los Angeles.[10]

There was, to be sure, a local awareness of the agitation being conducted in the north during this period, and in time the insulation of distance and difficult communication gave way before the mounting cries of the anti-Chinese. With the gradual influx of disappointed gold-seekers and "busted" businessmen from up-state, first-hand Chinese prejudices were introduced, for it was common practice among the northerners to attribute all their misfortunes to the "yellow-skinned" scapegoat. And though it took considerable time for these seeds to blossom, they had been planted in a fertile soil where racial animosity was currently being directed toward the Indian, Negro and a sizeable Mexican population.

As early as 1857 the topic discussed at a meeting of the local Mechanics' Institute was: "Is the importation of Chinamen into this State advantageous to the people thereof in its present and future results?" At that time there were only three Chinese living in the city. The word "importation" is indicative of the attitude most often expressed in Los Angeles throughout the next decade. There seems to have been real moral indignation which grew out of the belief that Chinese laborers were actually slaves. An 1867 editorial in the *Semi-Weekly News* analyzed Chinese "coolieism" and concluded that it possessed "more than all the evils of African slavery, without any one of its redeeming virtues."[11]

In the late sixties there is occasional evidence of changing attitudes. When Benjamin D. Wilson was campaigning for state senator in 1869 he was "slanderously" accused of employing Chinese while posing as a friend of labor, and in 1870 real concern arose over the possibility of Chinese being given the right of naturalization. Two new laundries began business in 1870, basing their advertising appeal on not employing Chinese. And in April 1871 a warning was posted in the Mexican section of town that no Chinese should try to settle there. However, these were isolated cases and did not reflect wholesale public resentment to the Chinese. There had been no local reaction to the signing of the Burlingame Treaty in 1868 in which the United States and China recognized "the inalienable right of man to change his home ... and the mutual advantage of the free migration and emigration of their citizens ... for purposes of curiosity, of trade or as permanent residents." Nor did Los Angeles send any representatives to the anti-Chinese convention held in San Francisco during August, 1870.[12]

Even from the vantage point of history, nothing occurred in the months immediately preceding the 1871 massacre that would have permitted its prediction. Nonetheless, on the evening of October 24 a mob of 500 "Angels," enraged over the killing of a white by some "Celestials," stormed through Negro Alley leaving eighteen dead Chinese in its wake—fifteen of them suspended from make-shift gallows. A nineteenth victim died from bullet wounds three days later. In addition to the slaughter the Chinese quarters were looted of over $30,000 in money and personal property.[13]

One cannot contest that this was a very real expression of anti-Chinese sentiment among a portion of the population. The mob did not seek out the guilty parties, but gave way to blind racism in taking revenge against the entire Chinese community. However, no evidence exists to suggest that this attitude was representative of Los Angeles as a whole. There is no way of knowing how many people swelled the ranks of the mob merely out of curiosity or from a compelling sense of horror. A heroic few actively opposed the onslaught, and through their efforts reduced the number of victims by perhaps as many as ten. Others tried less successfully to temper the crowd with words. Elsewhere in town whites were hiding Chinese in their homes in case the mob should enlarge its hunting ground. The following day, the newspapers agreed in blaming the "scum and dregs of the city" for the outrage, and though this smacks of civic white-wash, judging from Los Angeles' reputation, the figure of 500 may not have been large enough to embrace even the "bad" element in town. Moreover, the extensive pillage that took place and the fact that the Chinese settlement was located in the center of the local slum lessens much of the skepticism such a statement arouses. On October 26 a City Council member stated that some of the police, apparently seeking to share in hidden Chinese savings, offered bribes to incite the mob.[14]

Within the context of this study a most important point regarding the massacre of 1871 is that it was not a part of any anti-Chinese movement. It was not an attempt to drive the Chinese from town nor to discourage others from coming. At this time there was no anti-Chinese movement afoot in the city. The Chinese population was still quite small and was engaged in occupations which did not directly compete with any significant number of whites. And though 1869–71 were depression years economic pressures were easing by mid-1871, and just two weeks before the massacre the Star observed, "There are fewer idlers and men out of employment in Los Angeles than in any other city of its size on the Pacific Coast." The murdering and looting of October 24 seems to have been more the dying breath of a period of general lawlessness than an expression of any city-wide sentiment against the Chinese.[15]

Except for a single, insignificant meeting in 1873 the anti-Chinese movement did not gain expression in Los Angeles until 1876. Anti-coolie clubs in northern California revived agitation in 1873 when a new influx of immigrants intensified an already unfavorable employment situation, and Los Angeles responded in June with its own anti-Chinese meeting. But no enthusiasm could be generated among the Angelenos, and the agitation died out immediately. Actually Los Angeles took a critical view of the northern agitation. Of the anti-Chinese legislation being considered in San Francisco the *Star* editorialized, "To cut off the queues ('pigtails') of those who are here, and to awe away from us those who are in our midst by refusing to let them remove the bones of their dead to the sacred soil of their fathers, is a recourse unworthy of intelligent men." It also pointed out that "this kind of persecution will weaken the cause of the anti-Chinese, and make friends for the Mongolians," and suggested that the energy of the agitators be directed toward obtaining Congressional action.[16]

State-wide agitation reached new heights in 1876. Recent immigration had been greater than any time since 1852, while economic conditions had deteriorated measurably. By this time every political party in the state and nation included anti-Chinese planks in their platforms, and sufficient pressure was finally brought to bear in Congress that a Joint Special Committee was sent to San Francisco in late 1876 to investigate Chinese immigration.[17]

Even Los Angeles entered into the agitation and organized an Anti-Coolie Club in May. The club was favorably endorsed and initially grew rapidly. But though the meetings it sponsored during the summer were well attended, club membership never exceeded 300. In its platform the club sought abrogation of the Burlingame Treaty and Congressional action to restrict Chinese immigration. It denounced the use of illegal or violent measures and circulated anti-Chinese petitions which were forwarded to representatives in Congress with 2,500 signatures. The only concrete achievement of the club, however, was inducing the City Council to award no public works contracts to persons who employed Chinese. The insignificance of Los Angeles in the over-all movement is effectively implied in the *Report* of the Joint Special Committee—of over 1,200 pages of testimony recorded, only two referred to the local situation.[18]

Despite the meager immediate results of this agitation in Los Angeles, the short-lived Anti-Coolie Club left a legacy of some consequence. Local laborers now identified themselves closely with state-wide labor opposition to the Chinese. Furthermore, membership in the club had transcended class lines by enlisting some of the "wealthiest and most prominent men" of the community, and some of these influential sympathizers were later to lead the workingmen in their political attempts at correcting various social and economic evils.

Local agitation in 1876 and subsequent years resulted from several factors. Construction of the Southern Pacific and other railroads brought large numbers of Chinese into the area after 1875, and the unemployed of Los Angeles saw in them the cause of all their misfortunes. In anticipation of the rail connection with San Francisco local business men overextended themselves. This was forcibly brought home when, instead of ushering in an era of prosperity, completion of the railroad in 1876 introduced an after effect to the Panic of 1873. Coupled with a serious drought in 1876–77 this brought on a depression which lasted to the end of the decade.[19]

For these ills the Chinese, the railroads and "big business" were variously blamed, but the larger part of the Los Angeles populace remained aloof from anti-Chinese activities. A visitor to the city in 1876 noted that while anti-Chinese sentiment was "highly developed" there was still a great demand for Oriental labor and domestic help. In this regard, annual attempts by workingmen after 1876 to organize boycotts against Chinese and Chinese-employing businesses, though heavily pledged to, failed miserably.[20] . . .

The Chinese had dominated the laundry business since the sixties, and in 1879 Chinese laundries probably outnumbered the non-Chinese by nearly ten to one, while employing close to 300 of their countrymen. As for the vegetable peddlers, 200 Chinese truckmen employed at least fifty wagons in carrying out their door-to-door trade. In 1876 Chinese vegetable peddlers had outnumbered non-Chinese forty-seven to two. To maintain their monopoly they gathered in Negro Alley each morning at dawn and exchanged particular items of produce to insure that each peddler had a full selection to offer his patrons. It was reported in 1879 that nine out of ten families relied upon the Chinese for their vegetable supplies.[21]

Under the tax ordinance proposed in January, 1879, "regular" laundries (as differentiated from "poor women who do washing") were to be taxed $25.00 per month, instead of $5.00 as formerly. The vegetable peddlers, who had been paying $3.00 per month per wagon since 1877, were now to pay $20.00 each month. For vegetable peddlers who walked, a monthly tax of $10.00 was to be levied. And so as not to miss the rest of the Chinese community, a tax of $5.00 per month was proposed for "all aliens ineligible to the privilege of becoming citizens of the United States, who were employed in any capacity in the city of Los Angeles."[22]

The simple economics of this tactic and the public conscience of the council proved to be stumbling blocks, however. In order to meet municipal expenses and to liquidate a part of the large city debt it would be necessary to recoup the revenue losses that would result from a Chinese exodus. To accomplish this no tax reduction was given to other businesses (one of the other Workingmen's [Party] campaign promises); it was, in fact, increased five-fold on some, and for the first time in Los Angeles a tax-was to be made on professional pursuits.[23]

Thus, the ordinance drew criticism from many quarters. And an editorial in the *Herald* suggests that there was not unanimous agreement even over the Chinese provisions:

> ... The question as to whether a man of whatever color, race or previous condition of servitude, can be legislated out of his means of earning a livelihood, is a grave one, and it is by no means concluded when a City Council has announced its sovereign pleasure. The Chinese should go, but the place to secure this going is the National Capital.[24]

Under such an economic threat the myth of "docile John Chinaman" was quickly exploded. The Chinese vegetable peddlers taxed themselves $2.00 each to obtain legal aid in testing the constitutionality of the law. And to enlist public sympathy they gave two-days' notice and then went on strike, intending to remain out three weeks. However, some doubts apparently arose about the wisdom of this tactic, and they returned to their wagons after four days. The laundrymen, on the other hand, chose to adopt a wait-and-see attitude, but rumor soon had it that the "wily Mongolians" were plotting to establish an enormous laundry under one roof, thereby having to pay only one tax.[25]

With the very real possibility of expensive litigation facing the city, the Council reduced the fees to $6.00 and $12.00 per month on laundries and vegetable wagons, respectively, and withdrew the tax on employed persons not eligible for citizenship. Although the laundrymen quietly accepted the new tax, which was merely a 20% increase over the former, the vegetable vendors pushed a test case before the courts and won. A county court justice found the tax "oppressive, partial, unfair and in restraint of trade and therefore void." Encouraged by this success the vendors refused to pay even the revised fee of $5.00 and went on strike again in May. Available sources did not reveal the success or failure of this particular effort, but the vendors were soon back at work. In August they petitioned the Council for a reduction to $2.00 and enlisted enough sympathy among customers that several petitions from local housewives asked that the license tax on vegetable peddlers be completely abolished. These efforts, however, gained no further concessions.[26]

In conjunction with trying to tax the Chinese out of town the Workingmen had simultaneously organized a boycott against Chinese goods and labor. There was even established an "Anti-Chinese Vegetable and Produce Market." Though subscription to the boycott was heavy the pledges were most often observed in their neglect. The only pledge reported honored by the *Star* was the replacement of all Chinese help with whites by the United States Hotel in March.[27]

If there was any one aspect of the Chinese issue upon which public opinion was united it was the blight of Chinatown. Though a number of non-Chinese still lived along Negro Alley, the health menace caused by accumulated filth was attributed solely to the "Celestials." The Chinese themselves owned no real estate in Los Angeles, and their landlords had regularly refused to cooperate with earlier efforts to eliminate the eye-sore. In 1877 a frustrated City Council had to settle for merely changing the official name of Negro Alley by incorporating it into Los Angeles Street. When the Workingmen took office public hopes were high that at last some progress would be made, but the best the Workingmen could do was to prorate among the owners the cost of fumigating the area. Later attempts to improve the situation were equally unsuccessful, until 1888 when Los Angeles Street was physically extended, and the adobe apartments of Negro Alley were demolished.[28]

The Workingmen suffered one defeat after another in their campaign against the Chinese. The state "Lodging House Law of 1876," better remembered as the "Cubic Air" law, required that 500 cubic feet of air exist for each tenant of a building. That no effort was made to apply the law in Los Angeles before 1879 reflects the general lack of active resentment to the Chinese, and the conditions under which it failed in that year certainly suggest a continuation of public apathy. In January of 1879 the City Health Officer caused ten Chinese to be arrested for violation of the law. But the city was unable to get a conviction. With absolute evidence on the side of the prosecution, the jury disagreed nine to three for acquittal. Instead of ordering a retrial the judge dismissed the case, explaining that the city could lose a fortune in pursuing such a hopeless cause. Thereafter the law became a dead-letter in Los Angeles.[29]

Anti-Chinese sentiment in Los Angeles decreased rapidly during late 1879 and 1880. The failures of the Workingmen and their defeat in the next election, the improvement of economic conditions, and the departure of large numbers of Chinese for railroad construction in Arizona, all were factors. At the height of the Workingmen's agitation in 1879 the Chinese population may have exceeded 1,000, but the 1880 census recorded only 605 Orientals among more than 11,000 inhabitants. And by the end of the year that figure had been "substantially reduced." The temporary blossoming of agitation in early 1879 can best be attributed to the political advantage labor interests held during the year, although the size of the Chinese community should not be disregarded. That the campaign lasted as long as it did illustrates the determination of the Workingmen, rather than prolonged public endorsement.[30]

In November, 1880, a new treaty was negotiated with China in which the United States was permitted to "regulate, limit or suspend" the immigration of Chinese laborers. This was a major step toward achievement of the anti-Chinese movement's goal, but Los Angeles gave it no particular attention. Jobs were plentiful enough and sentiment against the Chinese was so reduced by July, 1881, that the Los Angeles Woolen Mills began replacing white laborers who refused to work a 15-hour day with Chinese, and no issue was made of the action.[31]

In the early months of 1882, when statewide agitation over the impending passage of a Chinese restriction bill was high, the *Los Angeles Times* put forth a distasteful and unsuccessful campaign to arouse the citizenry. A series of articles attributed the majority of major crimes in California to the Chinese, representing American hoodlums as "tame and insignificant" in comparison. Other articles purported that a "prominent physician" held Chinese wash-houses responsible for the appearance of cases of mysterious "syphilitic sores" among "moral persons." The *Times* supported these accusations with the "well known fact that so impure has become the Chinese nation as a whole that the custom of handshaking is unknown among them."[32]

Seated amid the snowballing excitement in Northern California, the governor set aside March 4, 1882, as a legal holiday for the purpose of each locality helping to demonstrate state-wide opposition to further immigration. The Los Angeles rally was well attended. The city band played, a cannon was fired which "smashed every window in the neighborhood," and a resolution was drawn up and sent on to Washington to encourage Congress. This jubilant holiday may have occasioned the half-hearted attempt in April to exclude the Chinese from the city, relying upon the 1879 state constitution and subsequent laws for the authority to do so. However, the matter was immediately dropped when the city attorney pointed out the obvious conflict of such an ordinance with the federal constitution.[33]

In 1882 local newspapers showed mixed reaction to President Arthur's veto of a twenty year restriction bill. The *Evening Express* called it an abuse of the veto power while the *Times* agreed with the president that such a long period of restriction amounted to exclusion and thereby constituted a spiritual breach of the new treaty with China. In other parts of the state the President was being hanged in effigy. Some localities organized anti-Chinese leagues with the express purpose of expelling the Chinese forcibly. However, no such reaction found expression among Angelenos. On May 6, 1882, President Arthur signed a bill which provided for suspension of the immigration of Chinese laborers for ten years. While most of California celebrated, Los Angeles accepted the news without any demonstration. The rabidly anti-Chinese *Times* extended a soft note of thanks to Pacific Coast congressmen without further comment. At the next meeting of the City Council the achievement was not even mentioned.[34]

Anti-Chinese agitation in Los Angeles did not die with the passage of this act in 1882. In a very real sense it had died in 1879 with the demise of the Workingmen. The indifference exhibited by Angelenos when restriction finally was achieved was representative of the local attitude throughout most of the pre-1882 campaign. The slaughter that occurred in 1871 is misleading when regarded as an episode of the anti-Chinese movement. The only relation that might be drawn is that the massacre tended to retard such a movement in Los Angeles and perhaps exerted a sobering influence on the character of the local campaign. Over most of the period covered here there were too few Chinese in the city to warrant concerted agitation. Nor was the laboring element of Los Angeles either large enough or well enough organized in these years to arouse and sustain popular sympathy for their cause, especially among a population that obviously found Chinese services and prices irresistible.

An enlarged laboring class resurrected anti-Chinese agitation from its grave in 1885-1886, but with results similar to those of 1879. The futility of the anti-Chinese movement in Los Angeles is well illustrated by the "death-bed" appeal of the 1886 campaign—that the City Council should at least compel Chinese launderers to write their tickets in English![35]

Notes

1. The standard works on the anti-Chinese movement are Mary Roberts Coolidge, *Chinese Immigration*, New York, 1909, and Elmer C. Sandmeyer, *The Anti-Chinese Movement in California*, Urbana, Ill., 1939. The former is the more exhaustive study, but the less objective.

2. This was one of several popular terms of reference to the Chinese and appears to have been second only to "John Chinaman" in usage. In California it was frequently used to ridicule the "obviously non-celestial" Chinese immigrant. The term probably derived from "Celestial Empire," an Occidental name for China.

3. Coolidge, *op. cit.*, 30-31. John Walton Caughey, *California*, Englewood Cliffs, N. J., 1957, 383. Sandmeyer, *op. cit.*, chap. 3, gives concise coverage of the early legislation. Lucile Eaves, *A History of California Labor Legislation*, Berkeley, 1910, 134–140. Grace Heilman Stimson, *Rise of the Labor Movement in Los Angeles*, Berkeley, 1955, 10.

4. Sandmeyer, *op. cit.*, chap. 2. Ira M. Condit, *The Chinaman as We See Him and Fifty Years of Work for Him*, New York, 1900, 21–22.

5. Caughey, *loc. cit.* Condit, *op. cit.*, 22. Sandmeyer, *op. cit.*, 109–110, 120.

6. Stimson, *op. cit.*, 10–11. Ira B. Cross, *A History of the Labor Movement in California*, Berkeley, 1935, 78. *Seventh Census of the United States, 1850*, 969. Maurice H. and Marco R. Newmark, *Census of the City and County of Los Angeles, California, for the Year 1850*, Los Angeles, 1929, 30–31, 67, 115, 117. *Eighth Census of the United States, 1860*, I, 29. *Ninth Census of the United States, 1870*, I, 90; the actual population of the city being 5,728. Sandmeyer, *op. cit.*, 17.

7. Stimson, *op. cit.*, 3. Caughey, *op. cit.*, 394.

8. Harris Newmark, *Sixty Years in Southern California*, Boston, 1930, 123. *Star*, March 22, 1872. All newspapers cited are of Los Angeles; City of Los Angeles, *Register of Licenses*, 1872; contains records of 1872–1873 and 1875–1877.

9. Marco R. Newmark, "Calle de los Negros and the Chinese Massacre of 1871," *Historical Society of Southern California Quarterly*, XXVI, Nos. 2 and 3 (June, September, 1944), 98. Harris Newmark, *op. cit.*, 30–31. Edwin R. Bingham, *The Saga of the Los Angeles Chinese*. (Unpublished M. A. thesis, Occidental College, Los Angeles, 1942), 23. *Evening Express*, March 4, 1880.

10. *Star*, October 15, November 26, 1859; April 27, June 8, August 17, 1861; August 27, September 6, November 1, 1870; June 2, 1875.

11. *Star*, January 24, March 21, 1857. *Semi-Weekly News*, June 21, 1867.

12. *Star*, September 4, 1869; July 9, 16, 21, 24, August 16, 1870; April 27, 1871. Sandmeyer, *op. cit.*, 78. Stimson, *op. cit.*, 10.

13. *Star*, October 25, 26, 27, 1871. Chester P. Dorland, "Chinese Massacre at Los Angeles in 1871." *Historical Society of Southern California, Annual*, Vol. III (1894), 22–26. Remi A. Nadeau, *City-Makers*, Garden City, N. Y., 1948, 63–70. Hubert Howe Bancroft, "California Inter Pocula," *The Works of Hubert Howe Bancroft*, XXXV, San Francisco, 1888, 563–568. Paul M. De Falla, "Lantern in the Western Sky," *Historical Society of Southern California Quarterly*, XLII, No. 1 (March, 1960), 57–88, No. 2 (June, 1960), 161–185. For a much-questioned account see Horace Bell, *On the Old West Coast*, New York, 1930, 166–177.

14. Harris Newmark, *op. cit.*, 434. Dorland, *op. cit.*, 25–26. *Star*, October 25, 1871. City of Los Angeles, *Records of the Common Council*, VII, 387.

15. Cross, *op. cit.*, 63–64, *Star*, October 9, 1871. Stimson, *loc. cit.* A story has been perpetuated that a "heavy indemnity" was paid to China by the United States government as a result of the Los Angeles riot. Available sources reveal no such payment. It is possible that payments in 1887 and 1889 for Chinese property losses in Wyoming and Washington riots have led to this misconception. Compare Marco R. Newmark, "Calle de Los Negros and Chinese Massacre of 1871," *loc. cit.* and Marco R. Newmark in *Jottings in Southern California History*, Los Angeles, 1955, 41.

16. Stimson, *op. cit.*, 10–11. Cross, *op. cit.*, 84. *Star*, May 30, June 5, 27, 1873. *Evening Express*, May 28, June 2, 1873.

17. Sandmeyer, *op. cit.*, 57–58, 81–82. Cross, *op. cit.*, 85. Stimson, *op. cit.*, 11. U. S. Congress, *Report of the Joint Special Committee to Investigate Chinese Immigration*, 44th Congress, 2nd Session, Report No. 689, Washington, 1877, 1.

18. *Evening Express*, May 6, 10, 11, 17, 26, June 30, August 23, 1876. *Star*, May 9, 18, 25, August 24, 1876. Stimson, *op. cit.*, 11–12. U. S. Congress, *op. cit.*, 1140–1141.

19. Harris Newmark, *op. cit.*, 504. Stimson, *op. cit.*, 7, 9–12.

20. Ludwig Louis Salvator, *Los Angeles in the Sunny Seventies* [trans. by Marguerite Eyer Wilbur], Los Angeles, 1929, 41, 43.

21. The number of Chinese laundries in 1879 is estimated at 30, based upon a general trend found in compiling occupation totals from the *Register of*

Licenses, 1872 (see note 8); the figures are: 1875, 17; 1876, 24; 1877, 25. The *Star*, January 29, 1879, estimated that each Chinese laundry employed an average of 10 workers. *Tenth Census of the United States, 1880,* XIX, 781. *Star*, January 14, 1879. *Herald*, February 29, 1879.

22. *Star*, December 15, 1878. *Herald*, January 28, 29, 1879.

23. *Herald*, January 28, 29, 30, 1879. Stimson, *op. cit.*, 25.

24. *Herald*, January 29, 1879.

25. *Herald*, January 29, February 2, 1879. *Star*, February 2, 3, 6, 1879.

26. *Records of the Los Angeles Common Council*, XII, 759–767, XIII, 318, 434, 766. *Star*, February 6, 7, 10, 14, 21, May 14, 1879. *Herald*, January 29, February 2, 7, 9, 14, May 2, 4, August 8, September 26, 27, 1879. *Evening Express*, May 2, August 4, 1879. Stimson, *loc. cit.*

27. *Star*, January 14, 29, February 13, March 11, 27, 1879. *Herald*, February 19, 1879.

28. City of Los Angeles, *Deeds From the City of Los Angeles*, III. City of Los Angeles, *Assessment Roll*, 1862, 1867–1873, 1876, 1879, 1881. Marco R. Newmark, "Ordinances and Regulation of Los Angeles, 1832–1888," *Historical Society of Southern California Quarterly*, XXX, No. 2 (June, 1948), 105. *Star*, March 24, 1879; June 17, 1879. *Herald*, January 12, June 6, 13, 1879. William M. Caswell, compiler, *Revised Charter and Compiled Ordinances and Resolutions of the City of Los Angeles*, Los Angeles, 1878, 452. *Records of the Los Angeles Common Council*, XIII, 207.

29. Cross, *op. cit.*, 82. Sandmeyer, *op. cit.*, 63. *Herald*, January 31, February 4, 5, 1879.

30. *Star*, January 12, 1879. The speaker at a Workingmen's rally referred to the "herd of 1500" Chinese in Los Angeles. Carey McWilliams, *Southern California County*, New York, 1946, 84–85, shows a 1879 figure of 236 for Los Angeles, but he does not indicate his source. His 1880 figure is 1170, considerably higher than the census figure and the mayor's calculation at the end of the year. *Herald*, December 13, 1879. *Evening Express*, March 4, June 19, December 23, 1880. *Tenth Census of the United States, 1880*, I, 416. The total population reported for Los Angeles was 11,183.

31. Eaves, *op. cit.*, 172–173. Sandmeyer, *op. cit.*, 91–92. *Evening Express*, December 28, 31, 1880. *Herald*, May 15, July 27, August 19, 1881.

32. *Times*, January 26, 27, 28, 31, February 1, April 7, 8, 1882.

33. *Times*, March 5, April 9, May 2, 1882. *Records of the Los Angeles Common Council*, XV, 342, 343.

34. *Times*, April 5, 19, May 9, 1882. *Evening Express*, May 10, 1882. *Records of the Los Angeles Common Council*, XV, 381–392.

35. Stimson, *op. cit.*, 66; the 1885–1886 anti-Chinese campaign in Los Angeles is given excellent coverage in chap. 5, "Union Against the Chinese."

Part VI
Time of Transition,
1900-1940

Time of Transition, 1900–1940

Many United States citizens entered the twentieth century bent on reforming the political and economic structure of the nation. Partial success at reform by Progressives at home and abroad preceded a period of reaction and retrenchment in the twenties. The depression which followed spawned the New Deal and its wide-ranging efforts at social and economic planning. But these reform impulses offered little to the nation's burgeoning nonwhite population. In fact, white reformers frequently attacked minorities as obstructions to the national progress.

Only during the New Deal did a shift begin in the basic attitude of whites toward nonwhites. Even then, gains for these minorities failed to keep pace with the improved status of the remainder of the population. The experience of the various nonwhites was broadly similar in that all remained second-class citizens, but the circumstances of each group varied according to its economic and organizational resources, and, for Orientals and Chicanos, according to the nation's foreign policy.

Blacks, for example, confronted a rash of lynchings, segregation laws, and political restrictions by organizing associations such as the NAACP, Marcus Garvey's Back-to-Africa movement, and A. Philip Randolph's union, the Brotherhood of Sleeping Car Porters and

Maids. They also fought back, as exemplified by riots in St. Louis (1917) and Longview, Texas (1919). In search of better opportunities, other black Americans migrated from country to city and from the South to the North and West. Many blacks also switched their political allegiance from the Republican to the Democratic party, especially during the administrations of Franklin D. Roosevelt.

Dependent upon an often heedless national government, American Indians had few possible means of ameliorating their plight. Unarmed, stateless, poorly clothed, ill-fed, and decimated in population, they were vulnerable to the machinations of whites. The Indians were restricted to reservations or encouraged to take up farming on small, impoverished tracts of land as whites enforced acculturation on the red man. Government funds and supplies were siphoned off by unscrupulous Indian agents and other whites. Education provided by the boarding school plan separated youths from their families and sent them east in an effort to sunder them from parental authority as well as the body of Indian tradition. One response of the Indians was to withdraw, as evidenced by the Native American Church, a blend of Christianity and native religions emphasizing peyote-induced visions. Eventually, white policy began to change; in 1924 all Indians were granted citizenship, and in 1934 the Indian Reorganization Act enabled tribes once more to acquire land and allowed self-government on the reservations.

The Chinese fell victim to United States exclusionary tactics and their own pattern of immigration. Because of the series of exclusion acts in force from 1882 to 1943, few Chinese were able to come to the United States. Those who had immigrated were generally men who had the goal of working in order to send the proceeds back to the families they left behind or to return to their homeland themselves. Their return to China and the lack of females inhibited natural population increases, which, together with the exclusion policy, caused their population in California to decline from approximately 73,000 in 1890 to 36,000 in 1930.

Japanese, who increasingly immigrated to the United States, as demonstrated by their growth in the population of California from 10,000 in 1900 to 97,000 in 1930, soon encountered the tactics that were employed against the Chinese. The San Francisco School Board precipitated an international incident in 1906 when it segregated Japanese pupils. Shortly afterward, Theodore Roosevelt negotiated the infamous Gentlemen's Agreement in which Japan promised to limit immigration to the United States. By 1924 anti-Japanese forces dominated the political scene, and Congress closed off further immigration.

More Mexican nationals also entered the United States, partly as a result of political disturbances in Mexico and partly to take advantage of economic opportunities in the United States. But conditions were barely tolerable for the Mexican-American, whether he lived in ramshackle rural housing and toiled as a farmhand or inhabited a southwestern city barrio and worked as an industrial laborer. Enmity between Anglos and Mexicans, encouraged by United States military invasions of Mexico during Woodrow Wilson's administration, separated the latter from the white culture and legal system. In some areas, most notably south Texas during and after World War I, Anglos murdered Mexicans with impunity.

In some respects, the years between 1900 and 1940 modified the dismal conditions in which nonwhites lived. Overt discrimination decreased, employment opportunities improved, and the national government responded more vigorously to minority problems. But these gains were limited; significant improvements awaited the mid-century mark and a new spirit of militancy by nonwhites.

Randolph C. Downes,
"A Crusade for Indian Reform, 1922–1934"

For American Indians survival required contending with a federal government which vacillated in its policies according to the pressure by whites for Indian lands and which developed specious rationalizations to support the displacement of the tribes. For example, land speculators and their governmental allies proposed that Indians develop small farms to foster acculturation. The farm allotments were to come from the reservations, but any excess Indian land could be sold. Under this scheme approximately ninety million acres of the best remaining Indian land came into the possession of whites. Randolph C. Downes, in "A Crusade for Indian Reform, 1922–1934," details the efforts of reformers and administrators, culminating in the Indian Reorganization Act of 1934, to eradicate the more reprehensible aspects of the allotment system.

A Crusade for Indian Reform, 1922–1934

Randolph C. Downes

The 8th of February, 1887 "may be called the Indian emancipation day."[1] Thus spoke the reform-minded, government-sponsored Board of Indian Commissioners in 1887 in reporting to the Secretary of the Interior on the passage of the Dawes Act for the allotment of tribal land in individual farms to the American Indians. Forty-seven years later, on June 18, 1934, President Franklin D. Roosevelt signed the Wheeler-Howard Act which had for its aim the restoration and revival of Indian tribal life, and the stoppage of all further individual allotting of land. Said John Collier concerning this event: "Whether that date shall be known hereafter as the Independence Day of Indian history will be determined by the Indians themselves. . . . The Allotment law—the agony and ruin of the Indians—has been repealed."[2] Thus spoke the reform-minded, government-sponsored Commissioner of Indian Affairs as he set about the job of inaugurating a typically

Abridged from Randolph C. Downes, "A Crusade for Indian Reform, 1922–1934," *Mississippi Valley Historical Review*, XXXII (December 1945), pp. 331–334, 336–337, 339–345, 349–354. Reprinted by permission of the Organization of American Historians. Some footnotes have been renumbered.

1. "Annual Report of the Board of Indian Commissioners, 1887," in *Report of the Secretary of the Interior . . . 1887* (Washington, 1887), 6.

2. *Indians at Work* (Office of Indian Affairs, Washington, D.C.), I, July 1, 1934, p. 1.

twentieth-century collectivistic reform to replace a typically nine-teenth-century individualistic one. . . .

"The allotment act," said Commissioner Collier in submitting his draft[3] of the reform bill to the Indian Affairs committees of Senator Burton K. Wheeler and Representative Edgar Howard, "contemplates total landlessness for the Indians of the third generation of each allotted tribe."[4] He pointed out that since 1887 the total Indian land holdings had decreased from 138,000,000 acres to 48,000,000 acres, 20,000,000 of which were arid or semi-arid. Three kinds of sales had accounted for this diminution: sales of "surplus" lands left over on a reservation after the members of the tribe had received their allotments; sales by Indians after they had received full title to their allotments; and sales of allotments divided into small pieces by parents who never increased the size of their holdings, but who either divided the land in their wills evenly among their children or who died intestate. The continuation of these sales, especially of the third type, for two more generations "mathematically insures and practically requires that the remaining Indian allotted lands shall pass to whites." This means that there was a gradually accelerating fragmentation of the Indian lands especially by division among the heirs of the original allottees and this fragmentation was reducing the size of the holdings to unworkable dimensions. The process usually took the form of a lease or sale of the small parcels of land to neighboring white farmers so that Indian lands were becoming "mere islands within a sea of white-owned property." "The Indians," concluded Collier, "are practically compelled to become absentee landlords with petty and fast-dwindling estates, living upon the always diminishing pittances of lease money."[5] . . .

3. A dispatch to the New York Times of February 14, 1934, p. 8, stated: "The bill was drafted in the Office of Indian Affairs with the help of Nathan R. Margold, Solicitor of the Interior Department." See also New York Herald Tribune, Feb. 14, 1934, p. 4.

4. "Readjustment of Indian Affairs," Hearings on H. R. 7902, House Committee on Indian Affairs, 73 Cong., 2 Sess., Part 1, p. 17.

5. For more detailed treatment of the allotment system see ibid., 15–21; D. S. Otis, "History of the Allotment Policy," ibid., Part 9, pp. 428–89; Lewis Meriam, et al., The Problem of Indian Administration (Baltimore, 1928), 469–72; John Collier, "A Lift for the Forgotten Red Man, Too," New York Times Magazine, May 6, 1934, pp. 10–11; and Felix S. Cohen, Handbook of Federal Indian Law (Washington, 1942), 206–236.

Before the administrators of Indian affairs could take hold of the job of reform, the problem had to go through the muckraking stage. Conditions had to be played up, even exaggerated, by those who could focus public attention on the problem through the publicity of episodes seemingly illustrative of particularly outrageous treatment of the Indians. And it would have been unusual if the scandal-ridden years of the early 1920's had not provided grist for reformers of Indian affairs. It is not surprising then that in 1922–1924 the fight against the so-called Bursum Pueblo Land bill provided an appropriate episode, and that the principal villain should be the ill-starred Secretary of Interior Albert B. Fall of Teapot Dome fame. It was this affair which gave birth to the dynamic, crusading American Indian Defense Association,[6] and it was this association, through its indefatigable executive secretary, John Collier, which sparked the reform movement that reached its climax in the adoption of the Wheeler-Howard Act....

...The summer of 1923 saw the issuance by the newly-formed American Indian Defense Association of a statement of general principles drawn up by Dr. [Herbert J.] Spinden [of the Peabody Museum at Harvard] in collaboration with the Indian Welfare Committee of the General Federation of Women's Clubs. The program emphasized the need of developing Indian "'group loyalties and communal responsibilities,'" including tribal landholding, self-government, and religious freedom, the creation of an organization to promote the sale of genuine products of Indian arts and craftsmanship, and a complete reorganization of the education, health, and irrigation services.[7] Not to be outdone, the 42-year-old Indian Rights Association revamped its services with the aid of a grant from John D. Rockefeller, Jr., and in February, 1924 began to issue a monthly bulletin known as *Indian Truth*.[8] The two associations collaborated in an exposé of the exploitation of Oklahoma's Indians, but eventually found themselves at var-

---

6. John Collier, "No Trespassing," *Sunset*, L (May, 1923), 60.

7. *The Survey*, L (Aug. 1, 1923), 501. In 1925 the Indian Defense Associations of California began the publication in San Francisco of a periodical called *American Indian Life*. In 1927 the publication was announced as being "issued on behalf of the American Defense Association." See *American Indian Life*, Bulletin 1, June, 1925; and Bulletin 8, May, 1927.

8. *Forty-Second Annual Report of the Board of Directors of the Indian Rights Association* (Philadelphia, 1924), 5.

iance because of the more radical aims and less quietistic policies of the Indian Defense Association of which the militant Collier was executive secretary.[9] . . .

An orgy of muckraking ensued. Alleged government maladministration in tribe after tribe was set before the public. Loudest and longest in the attack, though not first, was *Sunset*, "the West's Great National Magazine," which, from November, 1922 until June, 1924, had only six issues without at least one leading article denouncing the Indian Bureau.[10] Lead-off man was novelist Stewart Edward White, whose article "Our Treatment of the Indians," called the story of American Indian affairs American history's blackest page. White's article was accompanied by one written by Indian storyteller James Willard Schultz, entitled "America's Red Armenians," which accused the Indian Bureau of blocking private relief to the starving Blackfeet of Montana. . . .

The climax came early in 1924 with the publication by the Indian Rights Association of a pamphlet entitled "Oklahoma's Poor Rich Indians," and subtitled "An Orgy of Graft and Exploitation of the Five Civilized Tribes—Legalized Robbery." It was written by Gertrude Bonnin, Research Agent of the Indian Welfare Committee of the General Federation of Women's Clubs, Charles H. Fabens of the American Indian Defense Association, and Matthew K. Sniffen of the Indian Rights Association. It asserted that, as the result of the transfer in 1908 to the county probate courts in Oklahoma of all jurisdiction over the estates of Indian minors and incompetents, the Indians were being "shamelessly and openly robbed in a scientific and ruthless manner." It was claimed that in many counties the Indians were virtually at the mercy of groups or rings of judges, guardians, attorneys, bankers, merchants, and undertakers, all of whom regarded the Indian estates as "legitimate game."[11]

These charges made the Oklahoma tribes the leading Indian sensation in the press for the next two years. In the spring of 1924 the House of Representatives ordered an investigation by its Committee on Indian Affairs which in turn sent a subcommittee to Oklahoma to

9. *Indian Truth*, I (Feb., 1924), 1; (May, 1924), 2–3; (Aug.–Sept., 1924), 3.
10. *Sunset*, XLIX (Nov., 1922) to LII (June, 1924).
11. Gertrude Bonnin, Charles H. Fabens, and Matthew K. Sniffen, *Oklahoma's Poor Rich Indians* (Philadelphia, 1924), 11–17.

conduct hearings. On February 19, 1925 the subcommittee reported,[12] declaring that "the wholesale charges made against the judges, attorneys, business and professional men of Oklahoma are not sustained by any evidence," but that in the oil producing districts inhabited by the Osages there were some "reprehensible and indefensible practices carried on ... by unconscionable attorneys and persons who make it a profession to obtain appointments as guardians." The result was the passage of the act of February 27, 1925, greatly increasing the guardianship powers of the Indian Bureau over wealthy Osages.[13]

The Pueblo Lands Board Act of 1924 and the Osage Guardianship Act of 1925 were signs of a new day. It was not long before administrators began to see that, in order to avoid the embarrassment of these pin-prick reforms, a general review of the entire Indian service would be a good thing. The occasion for this was the accession in 1923 of Hubert Work as Secretary of Interior in the place of Fall. With the air full of slurs on the quality of the Indian Service, Work sought to clarify the situation by inviting one hundred leaders in the field of Indian welfare to constitute a National Advisory Committee on Indian Affairs. A heterogeneous collection of seventy-five advisers thereupon assembled in Washington on December 11 and 12, 1923, and, after two days of futile wrangling and parliamentary ineptitude, passed a series of innocuous resolutions in which, save for a health proposal, "not one fundamental proposition ... was put across," to use John Collier's words.[14]

Secretary Work was no radical reformer, but he could see, as Collier saw, the amateur quality of the report of the Advisory Com-

---

12. "Indian Affairs in Oklahoma," *House Report 1527*, 68 Cong., 2 Sess., 7, 8. See pamphlet of Indian Rights Association by M. K. Sniffen, " 'Out of Thine Own Mouth'—An Analysis of the House Subcommittee Report Denying and Confirming the Looting of Oklahoma's 'Poor Rich Indians' " (Philadelphia, March 10, 1925), 1–5.

13. *House Report 1527*, 68 Cong., 2 Sess., 10; *Statutes at Large*, XLIII, 1008.

14. John Collier, "The Red Slaves of Oklahoma," *Sunset*, LII (March, 1924), 100; O. G. V. [illard], "For the Indian's Sake," *Nation*, CXVII (Dec. 26, 1923), 734–5; Elizabeth Shepley Sergeant, "The Red Man's Burden," *New Republic*, XXXVII (Jan. 16, 1924), 199–201. For a summary of the resolutions passed, see letter by Arthur C. Parker, the committee's chairman, in *New York Times*, Jan. 20, 1924, Section 8, p. 8.

mittee. Therefore, on June 23, 1925, ignoring temporarily Collier's proposal to engage the fact-finding services of the institute for Government Research, he called upon the 55-year-old advisory Board of Indian Commissioners to investigate and make recommendations. "These reiterated charges and counter-charges," said Work, "give rise to a desire on my part to have a competent body of observers such as is to be found in the membership of your board, and unconnected with the Department of the Interior, formulate their views after proper inquiry."[15] The Board's unpublished report of January 26, 1926 was a whitewash. It said that all charges against Commissioner Burke were "puerile," and that those against Superintendent Wallen of the Five Civilized Tribes in Oklahoma were "politics." It recommended that the office of Superintendent of the Five Civilized Tribes be put under the Civil Service and that all Indians having annual incomes of over $5,000 be segregated for special aid in the administration of their estates.[16]

Just what Secretary Work thought of the Board's report he kept to himself. But it evidently soon became clear to him that the business of constructive Indian reform required something more than the attention of unendowed part-time committees. By 1926 he had come around to Collier's view that expert, unbiased, and full-time counsel should be consulted. The Board of Indian Commissioners was also of the same opinion in its annual report of June 30, 1926. It admitted the great complexity of the Oklahoma problem, its own inability to cope with it, and the need for outside, unbiased investigation. "We believe," said the Board, "there are organizations, amply financed and manned, which would undertake this task without expense to the Government.... [A] report from a non-Government,

15. New York *Times*, July 24, 1925, p. 12.

16. *Ibid.*, Jan. 29, 1926, p. 10. The report is referred to in *Annual Report of the Board of Indian Commissioners to the Secretary of the Interior, ... June 30, 1926* (Washington, 1926), 1, 17. The Board of Indian Commissioners had been created by Congress in 1869 to consist of nine presidentially-appointed philanthropists to serve as unpaid advisers to the Indian Bureau. Long before 1934, indeed long before 1887, "the Board had demonstrated its inability to effect vital improvements" and had thus turned the reform movement over to outside agencies. Loring Benson Priest, *Uncle Sam's Stepchildren: The Reformation of United States Indian Policy, 1865–1887* (New Brunswick, N.J., 1942), 42–53.

disinterested organization, with a field force of experts, would carry great weight not only with Congress but also with the general public."[17]

Even before the official submission of this report Work had made up his mind, and, on June 12, 1926, had requested W. F. Willoughby, director of the Institute for Government Research, to make a survey of the economic and social conditions of the American Indians. Members of the staff of the Institute headed by Lewis Meriam, aided by nine specially selected experts, at once applied themselves to the job, and, after seven months intensive field work, prepared the monumental report which Willoughby submitted to Work on February 21, 1928.[18]

The Meriam Report was a masterpiece of reform propaganda in the best sense of the word. Its high-minded scientific accuracy was never seriously questioned. Its non-controversial tone commanded the respect of both supporters and critics of the Indian Bureau. Although highly critical of American Indian policy, it avoided personalities. Indeed, it won friends from the very Bureau which it criticized. "The object of the survey," said Willoughby in his letter of transmittal, "has not been to take sides for or against the Indian Office, but to endeavor through constructive criticism to aid insofar as possible in pointing the way toward marked improvement in this important activity of the national government. That was our understanding of your request."[19] Obviously Indian reform was now lifted from the field of controversy and placed in the realm of practical businesslike possibility.

A second piece of scientific research into the Indian service was the Preston-Engle Irrigation Report. This was the result of Secretary Work's request of March, 1927, that a survey be made of Indian irrigation projects with a view to the improvement of Indian farming conditions....

But these investigations had very little effect on the Indian Service during the years of Secretary Work's incumbency. The Commissioner

17. *Annual Report of the Board of Indian Commissioners,* 1926, p. 13.

18. Meriam, vii–x.

19. *Idem.* The Report was widely applauded by the press throughout the country. See New York *Times,* May 23, 1928.

of Indian Affairs from 1921 to 1929 was Charles H. Burke, formerly Congressman from South Dakota, and author of the so-called Burke Act of 1906 speeding up the individual distribution of Indian land under the allotment system. Burke was an avowed rugged individualist. In 1923 he was quoted as saying: " 'I believe in making the Indian take his chance, just the same as white folks do.... Don't fool yourself. The Indian makes good when he has the chance.' "[20] This attitude led the New York Times to say editorially that prior to 1929 the administration of the Bureau of Indian Affairs "never quite overcame the frontiersman's attitude" toward the Indians.[21] This last of the "frontier" Commissioners was quite contemptuous of reformers of the Collier type. Speaking of the Pueblo agitation he said: "It is like going to a lot of children and telling them they ought to start a row for more than they are getting.... Propagandists are touring part of the country with a company of dancing and singing Pueblos in full Indian regalia in order to awaken people to the 'crime' in New Mexico. There is no crime in New Mexico."[22] ...

The pre-New Deal phase of the Indian reform movement really got under way in 1929 when President Hoover appointed Ray Lyman Wilbur, educator, social worker, and president of Leland Stanford University, to be Secretary of the Interior. That Wilbur's appointment presaged progressive measures in the Indian Bureau was seen in the replacement of Burke and Meritt, the last of the "frontier" administrators, by two Quaker humanitarians, Charles J. Rhoads, wealthy Philadelphia banker, and president of the Indian Rights Association, and J. Henry Scattergood, treasurer of Haverford and Bryn Mawr Colleges, Pennsylvania Working Home for the Blind, and Christiansburg Industrial Institute.[23] Reformers rejoiced. John Collier declared the appointment "well nigh incredibly fortunate,"[24] and Ickes predicted: "Mr. Rhoads will write a new and fairer chapter in the terrible story of our treatment of the Indian.... He gives the im-

20. Herbert Corey, "He Carries the White Man's Burden," Colliers (May 12, 1923), p. 13.
21. New York Times, April 16, 1929, p. 28.
22. Ibid., March 16, 1924, section 9, p. 3.
23. Indian Truth, VI (May, 1929), 1–2.
24. American Indian Life, Bulletin 14, May, 1929, p. 6.

pression of sympathy and understanding, of justice and fair dealing."[25] . . .

No aspect of the Indian reform problem illustrates the difficulty of preparing the red men for individualized farming better than that of Indian irrigation. Unaided by systematic education, the Indians were less able to compete with whites on irrigable land than on fertile land. As the Meriam Survey pointed out: "To win success from a small area of high cost irrigated land requires far better farming than is necessary on a similar area of low cost land watered by natural rainfall." The Preston-Engle report declared: "The development of an irrigated farm . . . [requires] far more capital, ingenuity, and perseverance than most Indians possess. . . . If such a small proportion of our own race can make a success of irrigated farming . . . how can it be expected that every Indian can succeed as an irrigation farmer?" And yet in arid country the allotment system of the Dawes Act had been carried out without regard to segregation and future irrigation projects so that, as the Preston-Engle report stated, there resulted "a condition that brought both Indian and white lands under the same irrigation system," and the Indian Service was frequently put "in the position of operating and maintaining irrigation systems more for white people than for the use of the few Indians under the system." The inevitable result had been that the "vast majority" had either leased or sold their lands and the net result was paradoxically enough "to encourage indolence and improvidence." It was estimated that as soon as "irrigated Indians" received unrestricted titles to their lands "70 to 90 per cent . . . immediately sell their land."[26]

The proposed remedies were in effect a form of default. Implying that it was too late or too difficult for the Indian Bureau to assume its neglected duty of irrigation education, Preston and Engle recommended that the larger projects be turned over to the Bureau of Reclamation, that the remaining personnel in the Indian irrigation service be drastically improved in quality, and that some of the projects be abandoned.[27] About all that Rhoads seems to have been willing to

25. Ickes, quoted in Cong. Record, 71 Cong., 2 Sess., 2498.

26. Meriam, Problem of Indian Administration, 508; Preston-Engle Report, 2235, 2236, 2280.

27. Ibid., 2217, 2222, 2255, 2258–9, 2504, 2528.

do in this respect was to reorganize the irrigation service,[28] and for his failure to follow Preston and Engle in the other recommendations he was severely criticized by Senators William H. King of Utah and Lynn Frazier of North Dakota.[29] Perhaps the most outstanding reform was the cancellation of several million dollars of so-called "reimbursable debts," charged against Indians for various projects deemed no longer useful to the red men.[30] . . .

How much farther along the road to reform Rhoads would have gone if he had not been replaced by Collier in 1933 is, of course, impossible to say. It is true that Collier accelerated reform to a degree to which Rhoads was incapable. But the Collier administration was an acceleration, and not a break. . . .

. . . From 1933 on, as Collier groomed himself to strike down what Rhoads feared to attack, the Rhoads achievements in education, health, and other lines were carried on and supplemented. The transfer of Indian children from boarding schools to day schools near their homes was speeded up as boarding school enrollment dropped from 22,000 in 1933 to 17,500 in 1934, and plans were made for a decrease to 13,000 in 1935.[31] In the meantime the remaining boarding schools were being transformed into institutions for the care of special classes of children: orphans, those with poor home environments, those without local school facilities, and high school pupils needing vocational training not offered locally.[32] A new spirit came into the Indian Service as Collier issued an order based on the most progressive educational and psychological foundations: " 'No interference with Indian religious life or expression will hereafter be tolerated. The cultural history of Indians is in all respects to be considered equal to that of

28. *Annual Report of the Commissioner of Indian Affairs*, 1931, p. 22.

29. *Cong. Record*, 71 Cong., 3 Sess., 1375–6; "Survey of Conditions Among the Indians of the United States," *Senate Report 25 on Irrigation and Reclamation on Indian Lands*, part 4, 72 Cong., 2 Sess. (1932), 8–9.

30. *Statutes at Large*, XLVI, 1519; *ibid.*, XLVII, 564–5; *Annual Report of the Commissioners of Indian Affairs*, 1930, p. 32; *ibid.*, 1932, p. 19; *ibid.*, 1933, p. 103; *Annual Report of the Directors of the Indian Rights Association, 1932* (Philadelphia, 1933), 10; "Some Reimbursable Wrongs Corrected," *American Indian Life*, Bulletin 18, July, 1931, p. 22; "Pima Relief," *Indian Truth*, VIII (March, 1931), 1–2.

31. *Annual Report of the Secretary of the Interior . . . 1934*, pp. 84–5.

32. "Civilizing the Indian," *Nation*, CXXXVIII (Jan. 10, 1934), 33–4.

any non-Indian group. And it is desirable that Indians be bilingual. . . . The Indian arts are to be prized, nourished, and honored.' "[33] . . .

. . . The time of timorous testing was over, and Commissioner Collier was determined to give the new Indian policy a charter basis. Accordingly the Bureau drafted its own bill with great care and, in February, 1934, submitted it to the tender mercies of Senate and House consideration. Then, while the Congressional committees held their hearings,[34] the fighting Collier took to the hustings. Backed by the specific and outspoken endorsement of President Roosevelt,[35] Collier took the bill to the country at large and to the Indians in particular. The press and radio were enlisted to create public sentiment in its favor.[36] Under the auspices of Bureau employees, great Indian congresses were held throughout the West so as to give as many Indians as possible the chance to hear, discuss, and criticize the bill. Characteristically enough most Indians were more or less suspicious and preferred to return to their people and discuss the proposal at their leisure.[37] However, by May 9 fifty-eight tribes comprising a population of 146,194 Indians had voted in favor of the bill and thirteen tribes made up of 15,213 Indians had voted against it.[38]

Although assailed as communistic, pagan, and Bureau-bought, the measure became law with little difficulty. The title itself is an adequate summary: "An Act to conserve and develop Indian lands and resources; to extend to Indians the right to form business and other

33. *Annual Report of the Secretary of the Interior . . . 1934*, p. 90.

34. "Readjustment of Indian Affairs," *Hearings on H. R. 7902*, House Committee on Indian Affairs, Parts 1–9, 73 Cong., 2 Sess. (1934); "To Grant to Indians Living under Federal Tutelage the Freedom to Organize for Purposes of Local Self-Government and Economic Enterprise . . . ," *Hearings on S. 2755 and S. 3645*, Senate Committee on Indian Affairs, 73 Cong., 2 Sess. (April 26, 28, 30, May 3, 4, 17, 1934).

35. *Hearings on H. R. 7902*, 233–4.

36. *Cong. Record*, 73 Cong., 2 Sess., 9265.

37. Congresses were held at Rapid City, South Dakota, March 2–5, 1934; at Santo Domingo Pueblo, New Mexico, March 15, 1934; at Phoenix, Arizona, March 15–16, 1934; at Riverside, California, March 17–18, 1934; and at Muskogee, Oklahoma, March 22, 1934. See Cohen, 84; Minutes of the Plains Congress (Rapid City Indian School, 1934); and Proceedings of the Conference for the Indians of Southern California held at Riverside, Calif., March 17 and 18, 1934, to discuss the Wheeler-Howard Indian Bill (mimeographed, n. p., n. d.).

38. *Hearings on H. R. 7902*, 399.

organizations; to establish a credit system for Indians; to grant certain rights of home rule to Indians; to provide for vocational education for Indians; and for other purposes."[39] Thus allotment in severalty was explicitly forbidden and any surplus lands still remaining were to be restored to tribal ownership. Sales of lands to, and inheritance by, non-Indians were most drastically restricted. The Secretary of the Interior was enabled to acquire land for incorporation into tribal estates and the expenditure of not over $2,000,000 a year for this purpose was authorized. The sum of $250,000 a year might be spent to defray the expenses of organizing Indian chartered corporations. A revolving fund of $10,000,000 was authorized to make loans to such corporations "for the purpose of promoting the economic development" of the tribes. Another sum of $250,000 a year was to be spent for tuition loans to Indians attending "recognized vocational and trade schools." Exemption of Indians from civil service rules was granted to promote an increase in the number of tribesmen in the staff of the Indian Service. Tribal constitutions were authorized to be created and ratified by the Indians themselves to give them extensive rights of political home rule. The act itself was not to apply to any tribe which should vote not to accept it.

And so we return to where we began. If the rugged individualism of the Dawes Act of 1887 and its subsequent administration were completely at variance with the sociological requirements of cultural amalgamation, the needed scientific adjustments were proposed, promoted, and in some measure adopted in the years before the enactment of the Wheeler-Howard Act of 1934. Indeed, in view of this pre-invasion of twentieth-century reform ideals into the anachronistic preserves of a nineteenth-century Indian administration, modernists might be pardoned their flight of fancy in suggesting that, had the Wheeler-Howard Act been passed in 1887, the American Indians might by 1934 have been ready for the Dawes Act.

39. *Statutes at Large*, XLVIII, 984. Two major parts of the bill as originally introduced were omitted, viz., the creation of a Court of Indian Claims and the application of the law to the Oklahoma Indians.

Elliott M. Rudwick,
"DuBois versus Garvey: Race Propagandists at War"

The early twentieth century gave birth to a series of virulent anti-black practices, including lynching, beating, segregation by law as well as in fact, denial of civil rights, and exclusion from politics. In response, black leaders emerged who voiced opposition to the racist behavior of the white majority and introduced programs for improving the lot of their race. Elliott M. Rudwick contrasts the methods of two prominent black leaders in "DuBois versus Garvey: Race Propagandists at War." Although both men were concerned with alleviating the condition of blacks in the United States, they differed in approach, technique, and personality. Marcus Garvey was outspoken, flamboyant, and emotional; he appealed to the masses of black people. William E. B. DuBois was soft-spoken, reasonable, and moderate; he spoke primarily to the well-educated members of the black race. Both leaders, however, emphasized black pride, confrontation with the white community, black nationalism, and the need for action to eradicate the ills of society.

DuBois versus Garvey:
Race Propagandists at War

Elliott M. Rudwick

After World War I, large numbers of Negroes were stirred by race pride and demanded a "spiritual emancipation." They were encouraged to seek improvement of their own living conditions and work for the betterment of the natives on the African continent. During this post-war decade two prominent leaders, W. E. B. DuBois and Marcus Garvey, clashed in their separate plans to establish an African state and an international organization of Negroes. Both men were propagandists. DuBois was editor of the *Crisis*, the official magazine of the N.A.A.C.P. and Garvey owned the *Negro World*. (The Jamaican regularly wrote articles for his newspaper and the editorial writers he hired adopted his tone.) The present article is based primarily on a study of these two publications and seeks to examine the DuBois-Garvey debate which—especially from Garveyite quarters —was abusive and acrimonious.

In 1917, DuBois favored the formation of a "great free central African state" (the amalgamation of German East Africa and the Belgian Congo); later, he declared that the state should be enlarged to include Uganda, French Equatorial Africa, German Southwest

Elliott M. Rudwick, "DuBois versus Garvey: Race Propagandists at War," *Journal of Negro Education*, XXVIII (1959), pp. 421–429. Reprinted by permission of the author and the publisher.

Africa, and the Portuguese territories of Angola and Mozambique.[1] In his conception, a "Brain Trust" of Negro administrators were to be responsible for the establishment of an "industrial democracy," i.e., a socialized system of production and distribution.[2] In 1919, through the help of Blaise Diagne, a Negro Senegalese representative in the French Chamber of Deputies, DuBois received permission from Prime Minister Clemenceau to organize the First Pan-African Congress in Paris. The delegates (from the United States, West Indies, Europe, and Africa) asked the League of Nations to guarantee political, social, and economic rights to the African natives and set up a legal code for the "international protection" of these people. The League was requested to consider the Africans in "international labor legislation" and to provide for native representation within the organization.

According to the Pan-African Congress, "Negroes of the world demand" that the natives should hold title to all African land which they could "profitably" cultivate. The conclave petitioned for effective controls upon the white capitalists in order to prevent further economic exploitation. The conferees also maintained that the Africans should receive assurances that elementary, vocational, and college education would be available to them.[3] To create international racial unity, DuBois proposed to found the *Black Review* (with English, French, and perhaps Spanish and Portuguese editions). He hoped that American Negroes would learn to speak French and Spanish and he was certain that Negro literature and art would thereby gain momentum in all nations. He suggested that U.S. Negroes should travel to Europe on "*personal rencontres* for information and propaganda."[4] The League paid little attention to DuBois's Pan-African Congress, nor did any other group consider the conclave as "representative of the Negro race." The convention had no real grass roots organizational support; only on paper was the N.A.A.C.P. headquarters concerned and the N.A.A.C.P. branches simply ignored the Pan-African Congress. However, DuBois seemed undaunted and con-

1. *Crisis* XV (1917–1918), p. 114.
2. *Crisis* XVII (1918–1919), pp. 119–120.
3. *Crisis* XVII (1918–1919), pp. 271–274.
4. *Crisis* XVII (1918–1919), pp. 269–270.

tinued to grind out propaganda which was moderate in tone and intellectual in approach.

Unlike DuBois, Marcus Garvey was able to gain mass support and his propaganda had a tremendous emotional appeal. He established the Universal Negro Improvement Association in New York (with branches in many U.S. cities and several foreign countries). The aim of the organization was the liberation of Africa. By 1919, he set up the Black Star Line and the Negro Factories Corporation. In August, 1920, Garvey called a month-long convention of the U.N.I.A. in New York City. In the name of "400,000,000 Negros of the World," he declared that Africa must be free. He did not bother to display the restraint which characterized Pan-African leaders and many of his remarks were inflammatory. He warned that his race was prepared to shed its blood to remove the whites from the natives' rightful land in Africa.[5] His convention delegates and members paraded through Harlem. Tens of thousands of Negroes were excited by the massed units of the African Legion in blue and red uniforms and the white-attired contingents of the Black Cross Nurses. Garvey's followers sang the new U.N.I.A. anthem, "Ethiopa, Thou Land of Our Fathers" and they proudly waved the Association's flag (black for Negro skin, green for Negro hopes, and red for Negro blood). Never again was the race to have a leader who could produce such a wonderful show.

DuBois publicly ignored Garvey until December of 1920 and this tardiness of editorial recognition was probably due to the Crisis editor's ambivalence toward him. DuBois was profoundly impressed by "this extraordinary leader of men," and he acknowledged that Garvey was "essentially an honest and sincere man with a tremendous vision, great dynamic force, stubborn determination and unselfish desire to serve." However, the Crisis editor also considered him to be[6]

dictatorial, domineering, inordinately vain and very suspicious....
The great difficulty with him is that he has absolutely no business sense, no flair for real organization and his general objects are so shot through with bombast and exaggeration that it is difficult to pin them down for careful examination.

5. New York Times, August 3, 1920. See also Negro World, September 11, 1920.
6. Crisis XXI (1920–1921), pp. 58–60.

The following month, after DuBois had requested (and failed to receive) a financial statement from the Jamaican on the Negro Improvement Association and the Black Star Line, the *Crisis* editor wrote:[7]

> When it comes to Mr. Garvey's industrial and commercial enterprises there is more ground for doubt and misgiving than in the matter of his character.

Originally, DuBois believed that his own hopes for Africa's reclamation and an international black economy could be achieved through Garvey's mass appeal. He concluded that the failure of the Garvey Movement, which had generated so much "spiritual" potential, might seriously damage racial self-confidence. He was impressed by the "bold effort and some success" of the Jamaican, who, after all, had sent ships ("owned by black men") to sea. However, the editor of the *Crisis* announced that Garvey was expending funds for current expenses instead of using the money for capital improvements. (The flamboyant Garvey seemed more interested in public relations than in buying ships.)

Nevertheless, the *Crisis* editor saw a bright future if Garvey was willing to eschew certain tactics which had been employed in the past:

1. Garvey "introduced" the Jamaican black-mulatto schism to the U. S., where DuBois claimed it had no relevance and only bred disunity. (One of DuBois's own errors was that he minimized this conflict.)
2. Garvey alienated the British by his tactlessness, and the help of Great Britain was required in his international trade plans.
3. He did not seem interested in establishing a friendly relationship with the N.A.A.C.P. and went out of his way to antagonize its officials.
4. His relations with the Liberian Government were less than satisfactory, even though he hoped to establish headquarters there.
5. With inadequate material resources, he still made bellicose statements about conquering Africa.

7. *Crisis* XXI (1920–1921), pp. 112–115.

DuBois's comments showed remarkable temperateness in view of the fact that the Garvey Movement had been attacking him for more than a year. Just before the Pan-African Congress in 1919, Garvey alleged that DuBois talked so mildly and equivocally to French reporters about American race relations, that the Jamaican's "High Commissioner" abroad found his own work sabotaged.[8] DuBois denied the accusation. The Negro World instructed its readers that the Crisis was basically reactionary and was published from an "aristocratic Fifth Avenue" office.[9] After a Crisis editorial on Woodrow Wilson's faithlessness, and following a DuBois comment on the post-war imperialist resurgence in England, the Negro World reminded the N.A.A.C.P. propagandist that Garvey had foreseen these developments as early as 1918, when the editor was counseling cooperation with the United States Government. DuBois was pictured as a fallen old warrior whose contributions to the race were at an end. With relish the Negro World also took up the cry of A. Philip Randolph's Messenger that DuBois was "controlled" by white capitalists on the N.A.A.C.P. board.[10] When the Crisis editor was awarded the Spingarn Medal in 1920 for "founding" the First Pan-African Congress, Garvey's paper charged that the entire affair was "a discreditable fraud."[11] (The N.A.A.C.P. citation ignored a 1900 Pan-African conclave. By juggling words, DuBois had "founded" the first Congress because he argued that the 1900 organization was called the Pan-African "Conference.")[12] As far as Garvey was concerned, the 1919 Pan-African Congress had accomplished little and he asserted that William Monroe Trotter's National Equal Rights League had contributed more to the race when it presented its petition to the Peace Conference in Paris:[13]

But perhaps Mr. Villard [one-time N.A.A.C.P. board chairman] and the other gentlemen of the Committee on award regard Mr.

8. Crisis XXI (1920–1921), pp. 112–115.
9. Negro World, May 24, 1919.
10. Negro World, March 13, April 3, 1920.
11. Negro World, June 19, 1920.
12. Crisis XXI (1920–1921), p. 198.
13. Negro World, June 12, 1920.

Trotter as too radical, perhaps they do not regard him from a white man's point of view as safe and sane a leader as Dr. DuBois.

At the 1920 U.N.I.A. convention, Garvey called the *Crisis* editor "the associate of an alien race," and his remark received "the most enthusiastic applause" of the session. The *Negro World's* editorial reaction to DuBois's lengthy critique was typical: "subtle, shrewd, untruthful in its professed sincerity, cunning and adroit in its attempt to blow hot and cold at the same time." The N.A.A.C.P. propagandist was accused of petty jealousy and of being quite possibly "more of a white man than a Negro and [he] seems to be only a professional Negro at that." Garvey mounted the platform to chide DuBois for ignoring the masses and believing in a "bastard aristocracy." In contrast, the Jamaican recalled how he "always walked among [his own] ordinary humble people . . . (cheers)." Garvey proved his ability to write demagogic propaganda:[14]

> Where did he [DuBois] get his aristocracy from? He picked it up on the streets of Great Barrington, Mass. He just got it into his head that he should be an aristocrat and ever since that time he has been keeping his very beard as an aristocrat; he has been trying to be everything else but a Negro. Sometimes we hear he is a Frenchman and another time he is Dutch and when it is convenient he is a Negro (Derisive cheers and laughter). Now I have no Dutch. I have no French, I have no Anglo-Saxon in me, but I am but a Negro now and always (thunderous applause). I have no Frenchmen to imitate, I have no Anglo-Saxon to imitate; I have but the ancient glories of Ethiopia to imitate. (Great applause.) The men who built the Pyramids looked like me, and I think the best thing I can do is to keep looking like them. Anyone you hear always talking about the kind of blood he has in him other than the blood you can see, he is dissatisfied with something, and I feel sure that many of the Negroes of the United States of America know that if there is a man who is most dissatisfied with himself, it is Dr. DuBois.

In order to demonstrate that displeasure with DuBois was mounting in various quarters of the race, the *Negro World* reprinted several

14. *Negro World*, January 8, 1921.

comments and editorials from other Negro papers. The Richmond *Planet* believed that DuBois was much out of his element for having the audacity to reproach Garvey, the "man of action." The Oakland *Sunshine* expressed similar sentiments: "DuBois is talking big things and Garvey is doing big things. We rather admire the man that does rather than talks." According to this newspaper, the N.A.A.C.P. propagandist was hurting the Association by his anti-Garvey campaign. The *Sunshine's* editor contended that the Garvey organization was larger and more powerful than the N.A.A.C.P. and was dedicated to DuBois's principles of improving the status of Negroes in the United States. The *National Review* took DuBois to task for editorializing on Pan-African movements and omitting the U.N.I.A. For this incompleteness, DuBois was dubbed, "king of journalistic jugglers."[15]

The *Negro World* was resentful because of the *Crisis's* tone of superiority and public omniscience. DuBois was castigated for thinking that Negroes who wanted to start race enterprises were obliged to appear before his inquisition.[16] A Garveyite published a pamphlet in 1921 entitled, "The Mistakes of Dr. W. E. B. DuBois," which was designed to show its victim's feet of clay:[17]

Garvey's old, unseaworthy wooden ships are still plowing through the turbulent waters of old Father Neptune's salty domains. Unlike the wreck of the Niagara Movement, they are not lying high and dry upon the weather-beaten shores of Disaster.

Such remarks brought forth DuBoisian retaliation, and he blasted the Garveyites as "scoundrels and bubble-blowers" who were causing havoc within the race. He denounced them for damning all whites and exploiting the Negro masses. (He claimed that the white supremacists were retreating and that the N.A.A.C.P. would liberate the Negroes in another quarter of a century.[18] In the past, DuBois had also condemned whites in wholesale fashion, but in fighting Garvey, he undoubtedly tried to appear more optimistic about interracial relations than he actually was.)

15. Reprinted in *Negro World*, January 29, March 5, and May 21, 1921.
16. *Negro World*, May 14, 1921.
17. Wheeler Sheppard, *Mistakes of Dr. W. E. B. DuBois*, pamphlet, New York, 1921.
18. *Crisis* XXII (1921), p. 8.

During the early months of 1921, DuBois was preparing for the Second Pan-African Congress which he announced for the fall. He promised to invite not only the Negro Governments, but "all Negro organizations interested in the peoples of African descent." He also mentioned that colonial powers would be encouraged to send delegates to the conclave which was to be held in Europe again.[19] Realizing that his organization would be confused with and compared with the Garveyites, he stressed that the Second Pan-African Congress was not convening to prepare a "scheme of migration." Shortly before the Congress, the *Negro World* reminded DuBois that only about one-fourth of the delegates to his first Congress were from Africa, and since the ratio had been so small, the term "Pan-African" was unrealistic. The N.A.A.C.P. propagandist had only recently printed a letter from the Liberian President, and the note was intended to rebuke the Garveyites. (The Liberian chief of state warned that his country would not allow itself to serve as a base of operations from which the Garvey Movement could harass other governments in Africa.)[20]

DuBois found it necessary to make a public statement after it became known that Garvey had not been invited to the coming conclave, and the *Crisis* editor announced that the U.N.I.A. leader was ignored because his movement was "dangerous" and "impracticable."[21] The *Negro World* told its readers that such studied neglect was all that could be expected of DuBois, who directed his Pan-African Congress like "an exclusive college function."[22] The newspaper followed up this criticism with another entitled, "Is Dr. DuBois Misled or Is He Misleading?" In this piece, DuBois was advised to join forces against the "white beasts."[23] (Garvey predicted a race war, and he asserted that DuBois and the old-time leaders were not really preparing for it.) The *Crisis* editor was invited to attend the second convention of the U.N.I.A.[24]

Strategically, Garvey decided to call his own international con-

19. *Crisis* XXI (1920–1921), p. 101. *Crisis* XXII (1921), p. 5.
20. *Crisis* XXII (1921), p. 53.
21. New York *Age* note reprinted in *Negro World*, July 2, 1921.
22. *Negro World*, July 2, 1921.
23. *Negro World*, July 23, 1921.
24. *Negro World*, July 23, July 30, 1921.

clave in New York a few weeks before the Pan-African Congress. Unanimously, the U.N.I.A. delegates condemned DuBois's movement (and they dispatched their caustic comments to European newspapers). Garvey considered it an absurdity for the Pan-African Congress leaders to ask white representatives of the imperialists to attend their meetings:"[25]

> Just imagine that! It reminds me of the conference of rats endeavoring to legislate against the cats and the secretary of the rats convention invites the cat to preside over the convention.

The Jamaican tried to create the impression that DuBois represented "the antithesis" of the U.N.I.A.—on the alleged grounds that the *Crisis* editor's policy was racial amalgamation. Contending that the whites would always hold firmly to their racism, Garvey suggested that the Negro develop[26]

> a distinct racial type of civilization of his own and . . . work out his salvation in his motherland, all to be accomplished under the stimulus and influence of the slogan, 'Africa for the Africans, at home and abroad!'

His speech was delivered at a special meeting "called unexpectedly" after press dispatches of the Second Pan-African Congress (condemning the U.N.I.A.) arrived from Europe.

The Second Pan-African Congress met in London, Brussels, and Paris, in late August and early September of 1921. As in 1919, the conclave promulgated its belief in the physical, social, and political equality of all races. The Negroes were to be guaranteed "the ancient common ownership of the land and its natural fruits and defence against the unrestrained greed of invested capital." The League of Nations was asked to set up one agency to study Negro problems and another to insure that native labor was not exploited. England, Belgium, and France were accused of taking advantage of the natives. However, within the Pan-African movement itself there was a rupture between the American-British delegation who favored a critical ap-

25. *Negro World*, August 6, 1921.
26. *Negro World*, September 17, 1921.

proach to colonialism and the French-Belgian delegates, who desired an accommodation to the status quo.[27]

In Belgium, the Pan-African leaders were regarded as Garvey's henchmen, and white European newspapers continually asked if DuBois expected to eject the whites from Africa.[28] Repeatedly, the Pan-African Congress spokesmen asserted that they eschewed "any policy of war, conquest, or race hatred."[29] However, the moderate propaganda approach received the sympathy of some newspapers. The Paris *Humanite* stated:[30]

> The black and mulatto intelligentsia which the Congress revealed or permitted us to know better, showed by its very existence that the black race is not naturally or essentially an inferior race, and that it is not destined to remain so forever.

After the Second Pan-African Congress, Marcus Garvey challenged DuBois's group "to fight to a finish" (applause).[31] He laughed at those who argued that they owed their primary allegiance to the nations in which they lived. When one Pan-African leader said that he would "lose everything" if he returned permanently to Africa, Garvey jibed that "everything" meant Parisian white women. Garvey charged that the American whites were encouraging European immigration in order to replace the Negro "and cause him to die by starvation."[32] The Jamaican argued that it was only a matter of time before the whites would exile Negroes from all countries. However, he declared that some members of the race would remain in the United States for another hundred years; he announced that they would occupy a higher status because their welfare would be guaranteed by the prestige of the African Republic.

Although he excoriated N.A.A.C.P. leaders, Garvey denied that

---

27. *Crisis* XXIII (1921–1922), pp. 5–8. See also, Jesse Fauset, "Impressions of the Second Pan-African Congress," *Crisis* XXIII (1921–1922), p. 13.

28. *Negro World*, October 8, 1921.

29. W. E. B. DuBois, "A Second Journey to Pan-Africa," *New Republic* XXIX (1921–1922), p. 41.

30. Jesse Fauset, *op. cit.*, pp. 12–18.

31. *Negro World*, September 17, 1921.

32. *Ibid.*

he hoped for the demise of the organization. He announced that he would not "originate an attack" on the Association, but that he was prepared to defend the race against "our bitterest enemies [who] are not so much those from without as within; men who will continue to find faults where there are no faults." He asked the N.A.A.C.P. to send its representatives to the third convention of the U.N.I.A. and to permit "the real leadership" to assume command of the race.[33] The Jamaican wanted his followers to believe that DuBois lived in fear of being dropped by the Association—"the National Association for the Advancement of (Certain) Colored People."[34]

During all of this time, DuBois was still requesting the U.N.I.A. to issue a financial statement of its activities, and the Negro World's reply was that this interloper had no right "to say what people should do with their money and what other organizations should do." The Garveyites declared that their leader supplied jobs to twelve hundred Negroes, when one included such enterprises as the U.N.I.A., the Negro World, the Negro Times, a printing plant, the Negro Factories Corporation, a hotel, restaurant, steam laundry, and a doll factory.[35]

In sharp contrast to the Garveyite hysterics, DuBois's comments about the Jamaican's program were usually calmly delivered and based on objective data. Since he viewed the Black Star Line as crucial in a consideration of the leader's fame and influence, DuBois examined the development of this business venture. He proceeded to recount the history of Garvey's mismanagement of the enterprise. DuBois described the unseaworthy Yarmouth's voyage to the West Indies. The ship carried a cargo of whiskey, much of which was stolen; the American Government fined the vessel's owners. Since the ship was old, much money was spent on repair bills, and the Yarmouth was finally sold in order to pay off the creditors. Another vessel, the Antonio Maceo, was also lost to the Black Star Line after it was beached in Cuba because it required extensive repairs. A third ship, the Shadyside, suffered the same ignominious fate, after it served a short propaganda stint as an excursion boat up the Hudson. In

33. Negro World, October 29, 1921. Negro World, February 4, 1922.
34. Negro World, September 9, 1922. Negro World, November 4, 1922.
35. Negro World, July 8, 1922. Negro World, January 6, 1923.

early 1921, the Jamaican said he purchased the Phyllis Wheatley in order to handle the African trade, and later he stated that some of his associates had absconded with funds which had been designated as a deposit for the ship. Since Garvey had announced sailings and sold passage on the Phyllis Wheatley, he was indicted for fraud. In 1922, after the Black Star Line collapsed, DuBois wrote feelingly, "Here then is the collapse of the only thing in the Garvey Movement which was original or promising."[36]

The *Crisis* editor also attempted to learn how many members of the U.N.I.A. there actually were. Garvey claimed four million by August of 1920[37] and for 1921 he listed two figures. (During the early part of the year he stated that there were still four million members, but two years later, he recalled that there were six million members in 1921.)[38] The year after Garvey's indictment, DuBois estimated the membership in the U.N.I.A. for the period of September, 1920 to July, 1921. (He divided the annual dues into the total sum which was collected.) The *Crisis* editor calculated that there were fewer than ten thousand "paid up members," between ten and twenty thousand "active members," and very much less than a hundred thousand "nominal members."[39]

DuBois reached a white public when he analyzed the Garvey Movement in *Century* magazine, and while he made no attempt to mask his disapproval of the organization, he did try to account for it. He viewed Garvey as a disoriented victim of the color line:[40]

All his life whites have laughed and sneered at him, and torn his soul. All his life he has hated the half-whites, who rejecting their darker blood, have gloried in their pale shame.

DuBois referred to the Jamaican as a "little, fat, black man; ugly, but with intelligent eyes and a big head." Garvey made the most

36. *Crisis* XXIV (1922), pp. 210–214.

37. Marcus Garvey, "The Negro's Greatest Enemy," *Current History* XVIII (1923), p. 955.

38. Speech of Marcus Garvey to the Beulah Baptist Church of Cincinnati, Ohio. Typescript, February 19, 1921. (Located at Hampton Institute Library.) See also Garvey, "The Negro's Greatest Enemy," *Current History* XVIII (1923), p. 956.

39. *Crisis* XXV (1922–1923), p. 120.

40. W. E. B. DuBois, "Back to Africa," *Century* CV (1922–1923), p. 544.

of this description, replying that his physiognomy was "typical of the African":[41]

Anything that is black, to him [DuBois] is ugly, is hideous, is monstrous, and this is why in 1917 he had but the lightest of colored people in his office, when one could hardly tell whether it was a white show or a colored vaudeville he was running at Fifth Avenue [the offices of the N.A.A.C.P.].

The *Crisis* editor was labeled as an apostle of "social equality," which in Garvey's thinking represented the kind of person who demanded to squire a white woman to a dance at the Waldorf-Astoria Hotel.[42] The Jamaican said that the U.N.I.A. was the only agency which was able to protect the darker-skinned Negro masses against the DuBois-led "caste aristocracy" of light mulattoes, many of whom were "intellectuals."[43] Paradoxically, Garvey denied that he was prejudiced against mulattoes, and he argued that all men had equal opportunity in the U.N.I.A.

In 1923, Garvey was convicted of mail fraud. After the trial, DuBois reprinted an editorial from a West Indies newspaper, wherein the U.N.I.A. leader was termed a "transparent charlatan."[44] Frustratedly, DuBois declared once again that his own attempt to settle the race problem on an international scale (through "cooperation" with the whites) was "harmed by the tragedy and comedy of Marcus Garvey."[45] The Jamaican refused to accept his defeat. In his prison cell, he continued to write diatribes, and DuBois angrily denounced him as "the most dangerous enemy of the Negro race in America and in the world. He is either a lunatic or a traitor."[46]

Since DuBois had been his chief critic, Garvey charged that the *Crisis* editor was responsible for his indictment and conviction. He blamed the N.A.A.C.P. propagandist for all of his difficulties and he asserted that the editor's malevolence had prevented the Black Star Line from sending "dozens" of ships to sea. During the summer

41. *Negro World*, February 10, 1923. *Negro World*, February 17, 1923.
42. *Negro World*, March 3, 1923.
43. *Negro World*, March 1, 1924.
44. *Crisis* XXVI (1923), p. 230. See also, *Crisis* XXVIII (1924), pp. 8–9.
45. *Crisis* XXVII (1923–1924), p. 9.
46. *Crisis* XXVIII (1924), pp. 8–9.

of 1924, the U.N.I.A. exiled DuBois from the Negro race.[47] However, such sentiments were only the last breaths of the movement. The Liberian Government announced that no members of the Garvey organization were welcome in the country. In January, 1925, President King remarked that his administration would not support any organization which dedicated itself to stirring up racial animosity. DuBois, who had recently been in Liberia as American Envoy Extraordinary and Minister Plenipotentiary, was identified by Garvey as the leader in the Liberian plot to destroy him.[48]

During the same years in which the Garvey Movement attracted thousands of average Negroes, DuBois's Pan-African Congress barely managed to survive. However, in 1923 and 1927, he was finally able to persuade the National Association of Colored Women to sponsor his conclaves.[49] These Congresses attracted few people and DuBois's large hopes to arouse the Negro were unrealized. In his leadership of the movement DuBois did not seem to understand that a truly effective propagandist related his work to a functioning organization. Since he did not build a real machine and did not have N.A.A.C.P. aid, his movement faded away.

This article has examined the intra-racial battles between DuBois and Garvey. During the 1920's, in the pages of the *Crisis* and the *Negro World*, they employed the same propaganda style and approach in their attacks on each other as they used in their organizational pronouncements on Africa. Garvey's expressions were explosive, irrational, and flamboyant. Their emotional appeal attracted large numbers of frustrated, uneducated blacks. DuBois's remarks were usually moderate, thoughtful, and analytical and were directed to a minority within the minority.

47. *Negro World*, April 10, 1924, New York *Times*, August 29, 1924.
48. Edmund D. Cronon, *Black Moses* (Madison, 1955), pp. 129–131.
49. *Crisis* XXVII (1923–1924), p. 122, 170. *Crisis* XXXIV (1927), p. 264.

Manuel P. Servín,
"The Pre-World War II Mexican-American:
An Interpretation"

Mexican nationals migrated to the United States in increasing
numbers during the early twentieth century, a movement which
added approximately one million legal and illegal immigrants to
the population by 1930. Most of the new immigrants settled in the
Southwest, which was enjoying an economic boom in industries
such as oil, cotton, and railroads, but Mexican-Americans were
seldom participants in the rising prosperity. They provided manual
labor for the growing area, filling the need for unskilled workers
created by whites who moved up the economic ladder. In addition,
as whites left tenant farming for the cities and towns, many
Mexican immigrants, working as migratory laborers paid by the
piece rather than by the hour or day, were relegated to the fields
of the Southwest. Manuel P. Servín, in "The Pre-World War II
Mexican-American: An Interpretation," depicts the life styles of
these immigrants, destroying in the process numerous white myths
regarding them.

The Pre-World War II Mexican-American: An Interpretation

Manuel P. Servín

The Mexican-American resident in the United States constitutes this nation's most unique, if not mystifying, minority group. Descendant of the aboriginal American inhabitants and of the first European settlers in the New World, the Mexican-American, despite the fact that he preponderantly lived and still lives in areas that were wrested from him, has until the recent war years been considered not an American but a foreigner. This fact has been so evident that even European immigrants, whose accents patently reveal their very recent arrival in the United States, did not hesitate to regard the Mexican-American not as an American but as a Mexican, whom they considered less American than themselves.

That such an attitude should prevail is clearly understandable to those possessing an historical insight into early North American-Mexican relations. Incredible as it may seem, the Mexican became a minority group—a despised minority—not when he immigrated to the North American Republic, but rather when the North American migrated to Mexican Texas and California, finding on the whole a

Abridged from Manuel P. Servín, "The Pre-World War II Mexican-American: An Interpretation," *California Historical Society Quarterly*, XLV (1966), pp. 325–338. Reprinted by permission of the author and the California Historical Society. Notes have been renumbered and appear at the end of the article.

poor class of Hispanic settler. Consequently, despite his residence on his own national soil, it was the Mexican who became the backward, somewhat unassimilable foreigner.

This attitude toward the Mexican, particularly in Texas, was further intensified by the wars affecting the North Americans and Mexicans. With the few exceptions of the *ricos* (the few wealthy ones) who passed themselves off as Spaniards, the Mexican truly became a minority group in the worst sense of the word. Generally despised in Texas, dispossessed of his lands in California, and denying his racial heritage in New Mexico, he lacked an acknowledged Mexican aristocracy—social, economic, and clerical—which would visibly prove to him that he was capable of achieving success and status....

The decades that followed the 1880's North Americanization of the Southwest and preceded the early twentieth-century wave of Mexican immigration are in an historical sense extremely quiet concerning North American and Mexican-American relations. Perhaps it would not be too rash to surmise that the Mexican-American of this period generally resigned himself to a fate that previous historical events had cast upon him. He was, at least in the eyes of the North American, an inferior being, a half-breed, if not a coyote; he was unassimilable, especially if he was dark skinned; he was treacherous; he was cowardly; he was lazy; and thus he was not an American but a Mexican whose lot was to exist in poverty, subservience, and isolation.

That such was the fate of the Mexican after the 1880's is attested to by the treatment of the Mexican immigrant who arrived in the United States in the early twentieth century after the fall of Don Porfirio Díaz.

Unfortunately for this new Mexican immigrant, he was neither prepared for the treatment that he would receive nor would he be able to understand the reasons for it. Because of the great changes, relative progress, and social and political stability imposed upon Mexico by the benevolent dictator Porfirio Díaz, the twentieth-century Mexican immigrant was a different person from his early predecessor in the Borderlands. He was far from lawless—Díaz's *rurales* had created respect for law and order. He was not the idle, lazy Greaser so eloquently characterized by early American writers— he had been oppressed in peonage for much too lengthy a period. Generally speaking, he was a moral and religious man—he had emigrated generally from the highly religious areas of Mexico. Finally, he was meek and submissive—Díaz's policy of *pan ó palo* had been effective.

It was this humble and meek person who began arriving in 1901 in great numbers to reside permanently in the United States. His increasing immigration, as determined by the United States Census of 1930, reflected the chaotic condition of Revolutionary Mexico and the need of North American cheap labor. Thus in 1901-1910 over 93,000 Mexicans legally entered the United States and remained at least until 1930; in 1911–1914 approximately 77,000; in the War years of 1915–1919 about 137,000; in 1920–1924 over 135,000, and in 1925–1930 just under 109,000.[1] By 1930 there were about 617,000 legal Mexican immigrants residing in the United States, constituting almost one-half of the legal Mexican population in the nation.[2] Actually, however, it is quite safe to state that if the illegal entrants —the predecessors of the wetbacks and fence-climbers—were taken into account, the majority of the Mexicans then residing in the United States were foreign born.[3] And, perhaps even more significant than the rate of foreign born Mexicans are the sound indications that they were not predominantly a rural group, as is often asserted, but were perhaps in the majority emigrants from urban areas.

This wave of legal and illegal Mexican immigration, plus the birth rate of the early Spanish Borderlands' Mexican, swelled the total legal Mexican population in the United States in 1930 at least to just under one and one-half million.[4] Although Mexicans migrated in some numbers to such states as Michigan, Illinois, Kansas, and Indiana, it was in the Southwest, the former Mexican territory, that the overwhelming majority—some one and one-quarter million—settled.[5] By 1930, Texas, long reputed among Mexicans as the most racially bigoted state, had the largest Mexican population, some 683,000. California had approximately 368,000; New Mexico, possibly 200,000 (although only 59,000 of these descendants from the early colonizers confessed to being Mexican to the census taker); Arizona, just over 114,000; and Colorado, about 57,000.[6] . . .

The panoramic picture presented of the early twentieth-century Mexican, who was born before 1926 and who did not enjoy the social and economic opportunities resulting from World War II, is interesting. . . . Arriving in poverty, unable to speak English, and inheriting the anti-Mexican prejudice engendered decades before, the Mexican was definitely at a disadvantage and greatly in need of help. Unfortunately, such help was not given, particularly by the groups from which the Mexican expected aid. The Spanish-speaking aristocracy —old Mexicans who disguised their heritage under such euphemisms as Californios, Spanish-Americans, and Hispanos—generally not only ignored but apparently despised the immigrant.[7] The Roman Catholic Church, aside from building churches and stationing refugee Mexican priests in Spanish-speaking parishes, did little to aid materially or socially.[8] Paradoxically, it was certain Protestant churches, especially the Methodist, that appeared to be most cognizant of the plight of the immigrant.[9] It is, therefore, not strange that bitterness toward the Spanish-speaking aristocracy and some antipathy toward the Church should have developed—a bitterness characterizing the aristocracy in a most unprintable manner and an antipathy resulting in the conversion of many Mexicans to Protestantism.

Unaided by their own groups and unable to obtain work in their previous occupations, the Mexicans were forced to take the lowest paying jobs as well as the most difficult work. In the agricultural areas of Texas, Colorado, and California they became the neglected, underpaid, exploited migratory farm workers. In the north central areas of the nation they performed various forms of low-paid unskilled labor. In Chicago and the Calumet area, for example, they worked in the railroad sections and in the meat packing plants. In Minnesota they worked in the sugar beet industry. And, in the area of Bethlehem, Pennsylvania, they became unskilled steel workers. Thus, the Mexicans were consciously relegated to the lowest working positions.[10] Perhaps the classical example of this policy was best expressed to Dr. [Paul S.] Taylor by an executive in the Chicago and the Calumet area who bluntly stated the hiring policy found in the area:

> We use no Mexicans. We have more refined work and have not had to resort to the greasers. They use them for rough work and around blast furnaces.[11]

But regardless of the demeaning work which they were assigned, the Mexicans, despite conflicting testimony, appear to have been good but not excellent workers. Preferred in California and Texas as farm laborers, the Mexicans did not merit this preference and achievement because they were built closer to the ground and possessed a physical advantage. The preference was simply economic: they were unorganized, apparently docile, and did not demand decent wages and living conditions.[12] In the industrial areas their record, as in the farming areas, was also respectable. They compared both favorably and unfavorably with the Slovaks, Wends, Negroes, and Irish.[13] Perhaps the most favorable report on the Mexicans' work occurred in Bethlehem when Dr. Taylor interviewed a number of executives, one of whom stated that he

> rated the Mexicans as equals or possibly the superior of the two important groups of Europeans available for the same work: 'The Mexicans are a good class of men as a whole; the majority are good steady workers. As a class their intelligence is above the Slavish [Slovaks] and Wendish. They are a bright, keen race, and good workers.' And in response to my observation [Dr. Taylor's] that in other localities some persons regard Mexicans as possessing low intelligence, he added, 'If some people think the Mexicans are dumb, they should see some of our Irish. . . .'[14]

Notwithstanding the Mexican's at least average work record, he, along with the Negro, was the lowest paid of the workers, both on the farms and in the plants. Unlike the Japanese who was disliked by his fellow workers because of his industriousness and efficiency, the Mexican was unacceptable to his co-workers for a number of reasons. The reasons generally cited were that he lowered wages and weakened union organization.[15] But the racial difference, the dark skin, unhygienic appearance, and quaint dress habits appear to be, at least to me, the more basic reasons. Following almost an identical pattern of the well-known segregation that existed in Arizona, California, and Texas, the Mexican had difficulty renting in better neighborhoods. . . .

The low wages received by the Mexicans, regardless of area, plus their own cultural and racial drawbacks, of course, had a very essential influence upon their living conditions. While Texas has always possessed among both Mexicans and dogmatic liberals the worst reputation for oppressing Mexicans and for retaining them in the lowest substandard living conditions, it is my judgment—as a person who has traveled in Texas, attended school in New Mexico, journeyed extensively through Arizona, and was reared in California—that the living conditions, with some very few exceptions in New Mexico, were equally as poor in utopian California as in Texas, Arizona, and other areas.[16]

Southern California, whose record for indiscriminate, hypocritical discrimination is difficult to excel, possessed perhaps the Southwest's most blatant opposing living conditions between the White North American and the Indian-Spanish Mexican. Few Mexican *barrios* could compete in poverty with that of Maravilla Park in Los Angeles County where two and sometimes three shacks built of scrap lumber, old boxes, and other salvage were erected in one small lot; where there were forty houses to a city block; where the average family income in 1928 was $795; where almost all workers were unskilled laborers; and where out of 317 houses only ten had cesspools connected with flush toilets.[17]

But in reality Maravilla Park was not an exception in California. Similar living conditions could be found in El Centro, San Fernando, and the outskirts of Montebello, Whittier, and El Monte—and, incidentally, in various cities of the San Joaquin Valley, even today.[18]

Actually, such poverty was not unknown to the Mexican in his home country, and would not be a great source of unhappiness. What did strike the Mexican was the irrational prejudice and disdain that he encountered. In many areas he could not eat in the same restaurant with the North American, nor could he swim in the same pools. In other areas he could not attend the same theatres, or if allowed to do so, he would have to sit in a segregated section; but this segregation, similar to his living among his own people, did not seem to bother him—perhaps he inwardly considered himself equal or even superior to the Americans in some areas.[19]

Yet despite all the disheartening and degrading conditions that he encountered, the Pre-World War II Mexican not only maintained a good record but made certain remarkable achievements.

Although he inherited the poor reputation for crime from the very early Mexican settlers, his crime record, basing it on random examples, was not outstandingly bad.[20] In the Chicago and the Calumet area, a two-year survey—1928–1929—revealed that 1.4 percent of all persons arrested were of Mexican nativity, while the Mexican population constituted only .57 percent of the total population.[21] In Los Angeles City the 1927–1928 percentage of Mexican arrests, revealing narcotics (probably marihuana), drunkenness, and vagrancy as the rising element, amounted to 17.5, while the Mexican population of the city was slightly over 10 percent.[22] In rural Imperial Valley, an important farming area, where the Mexican in 1925 was supposed to be responsible for 75 percent of all crimes, it was authoritatively found that he was responsible for only one-fourth of all crime, while he constituted approximately one-third of the population.[23] Thus, seeing that the rural crime rate was less in proportion to that of the urban, one might conjecture (perhaps somewhat dangerously) that since the Mexican population in the United States was almost equally divided between rural and urban, its crime rate was in proportion to, or even lower than, its total population.

A similar picture is found in California regarding juvenile delinquency—a reflection of family life. In Los Angeles County as of March of 1928, 19 percent of the Mexican boys and 28 percent of the Mexican girls were on probation—figures which were far above the estimated 11 percent total Mexican population.[24] Yet in Imperial Valley the picture was reversed. The percentage of Mexican children involved in juvenile court was proportionately much less than the total Mexican population, and incidentally less than that of old North American stock.[25]

Besides possessing a rather good work record and not a bad adult and juvenile crime rate, the Mexican also possessed fairly good records in marital relations and relief. Insofar as married life was concerned, there is little doubt that his divorce rate was less than either that of the Negroes or Whites.[26] His public relief record, based upon statistics of California—the nation's most magnanimous or perhaps most foolish state—was not quite as good, but it was apparently below his proportional maximum. Despite unfavorable relief records in Los Angeles, Orange, and Riverside counties, and despite the low and seasonal wages he was paid, it is evident from Governor C. C. Young's Report that the Mexican in California was not only not a burden on the state but that he received only a slight amount above his just proportion of relief funds.[27] That such a case seems to have been true throughout the nation appears most plausible from the Report of the Governor's Interracial Commission in Minnesota and from the Mexicans' practice of organizing societies such as the Cruz Azul for helping each other financially and otherwise.[28]

Undoubtedly the Mexican's area of least success and greatest failure was in obtaining an education. Coming from a culture failing to prize mass education, finding it necessary to put even his elementary-age children to work, and perhaps feeling frustrated that an education would not help him overcome the prejudices and disdainful treatment he received throughout the Southwest, the Mexican failed drastically to take advantage of the educational opportunities opened to him. Of all the groups listed in the Census of 1930, he had the lowest percentage of school attendance—a factor of course that in the long run militated and still militates against him and his future advancement.[29]

Yet despite the Pre-War Mexican's lack of educational interest, language barrier, and racial and cultural prejudice, he made some formidable breakthroughs in addition to gradually changing his portrait in the areas of work, crime, family life, and relief. Unlike some other persecuted minorities, he established a very good, cultural Spanish press, as exemplified by the Los Angeles La Opinión. He broke into the motion pictures and produced respectable and respected stars such as Ramón Novarro, Dolores del Río, and Gilbert Roland. In the East he gave such distinguished professional men as conquistador-descended Harold Medina, the jurist; Alonso E. Escalante, American Maryknoll missionary bishop for Mexico; and American-trained dancer-choreographer, José Limón. In crime, he at least showed some ability to think "big" as exemplified in the case of the fugitive Los Angeles police lieutenant, Peter Del Gado. In music he developed popular crooners such as Andy Russell and more serious singers as José Mojica and Tito Guízar. And, in higher education, in addition to the colonial-descended and highly distinguished Espinoza family, he came forth with such academic limelights as Carlos Eduardo Castañeda and George Isidore Sánchez, both from the University of Texas.[30]

Breakthroughs into North American life were not, however, the only achievement that the Pre-World War II Mexican attained. He also made some contributions to United States culture—and I do not mean just the adding of tacos, tamales, and margaritas to the North American diet. He contributed, as Henry Lopez's recent interview with Katherine Anne Porter in Harper's Magazine indicates, an incentive for enriching American letters.[31]

The period of [the] Pre-World War II Mexican in the United States came to an end with opening of hostilities late in 1941 and early in 1942....

Notes

1. U. S. Bureau of Census, *Fifteenth Census of the United States, 1930: Population* (Washington, 1933), II, 498.

2. *Ibid.*, II, 25, 27, 405.

3. *Ibid.* For an estimate of illegal immigration see Emory S. Bogardus, *The Mexican in the United States* (Los Angeles, 1934), p. 15; also see Leo Grebler, *Mexican Immigration to the United States: The Record and Its Implications* (Los Angeles, 1965), pp. 7–11, 17–29.

4. *Ibid.*, II, 27; Enrique Santibañez, *Ensayo acerca de la inmigración Mexicana en los Estados Unidos* (San Antonio, 1930), pp. 47–48.

5. *Fifteenth Census of the United States, 1930: Population*, II, 35.

6. *Ibid.*

7. Interview with José Bravo, Los Angeles, September 11, 1965; interview with Dionisio Rodríguez, Los Angeles, September 11, 1965.

8. The Rev. Francis J. Weber, "His Excellency of Los Angeles: The Life and Times of the Most Reverend John J. Cantwell," MS, pp. 96–103, Archives of the Archdiocese of Los Angeles, Los Angeles, California; *Notes: Outline of Protestant Proselytism in the United States* (Los Angeles, 1945), pp. 1–8, 54–55, 66–82; *Notes: The Mexican Problem and its Latin American Background* (Los Angeles, 1942), *passim*, Kathryn Cramp et al., "A Study of the Mexican Population of Imperial Valley, California," MS, p. 23, Bancroft Library, Berkeley.

An example of the Catholic Church's neglect of the Mexican is graphically illustrated by the late date (1944) that the Bishop's Committee for the Spanish Speaking was formed. See Rosemary E. Smith, "The Work of Bishops' Committee for the Spanish Speaking on Behalf of the Migrant Worker" (master's thesis, The Catholic University of America, 1958), p. 4.

9. In order to obtain a true insight of the zeal and efforts of the Methodists in working with Mexicans of the period it is only necessary to read the *Minutes of the Southern California Conference of the Methodist Episcopal Church, 1879–1939*, Conference Headquarters, Los Angeles. For a very limited view into Methodist Church activities see Edward Drewry Jervey, *The History of Methodism in Southern California and Arizona* (Los Angeles, 1960), pp. 90–100. Also see *Notes: The Mexican Problem and its Latin American Background*, *passim*.

10. For the work the Mexican performed see Paul S. Taylor, *Mexican Labor in the United States*, published in the University of California Publications in Economics. Dr. Taylor's different studies utilized in this essay and cited individually are: *Mexican Labor in the United States: Imperial Valley* (Berkeley, 1928); *Mexican Labor in the United States: Valley of the South Platte, Colorado* (Berkeley, 1929); *Mexican Labor in the United States: Dimmit County, Winter Garden, South Texas* (Berkeley, 1930); *Mexican Labor in the United States: Bethlehem, Pennsylvania* (Berkeley, 1931); *Mexican Labor in the United States: Chicago and the Calumet Region* (Berkeley, 1932). Also see Kathryn Cramp et al., "A Study of the Mexican Population in Imperial Valley, California," MS, 1926, Bancroft Library; Santibañez, *Ensayo acerca de la inmigración Mexicana en los Estados Unidos*, especially p. 53; The Governor's Interracial Commission, *The Mexican in Minnesota* (Minneapolis, 1953); and Carey McWilliams, *North from Mexico* (Philadelphia, 1949).

11. Taylor, *Mexican Labor in the United States: Chicago and the Calumet Region*, p. 80.

12. For a summary of Mexicans' [efforts] to unionize agriculturally in the early 1900's see Federal Writers' Project, "Organization Efforts of Mexican Agricultural Workers," (Oakland, 1939), MS, Bancroft Library. For other areas see Cramp et al., "A Study of Mexican Population in Imperial Valley, California," pp. 1–2, 6–11; George L. Cady, *Report of Commission on International and Interracial Factors in the Problem of the Mexicans in the United States* (1926), pp. 11, 21; State of California, *Mexicans in California: Report of Governor C. C. Young's Mexican Fact-Finding Committee* (San Francisco, 1930), pp. 159–171, especially 171, and also pp. 123–150, 176–179.

13. Taylor, *Mexican Labor in the United States: Chicago and the Calumet Region*, pp. 81–87; Taylor, *Mexican Labor in the United States: Bethlehem*, pp. 13–14.

14. Taylor, *Mexican Labor in the United States: Bethlehem*, p. 13.

15. For examples of lowering wages see Taylor, *Mexican Labor in United States: Chicago and the Calumet Region*, pp. 77–80.

16. The information compiled by George L. Cady, *Report of Commission on International and Interracial Factors in the Problem of the Mexicans in the United States*, as well as Paul Taylor's studies on Mexican Labor in California, Texas, Colorado, Chicago and the Calumet, appear to bear out this writer's evaluation.

17. *Mexicans in California: Report of Governor C. C. Young's Mexican Fact-Finding Committee*, pp. 177–178. For an all enclosing view of the poverty of Mexican communities in Chicago, Colorado, Texas, New Mexico, Arizona, and California see W. Rex Crawford, "The Latin American in Wartime United States," *The Annals of the American Academy of Political and Social Science*, 223 (September, 1942), 127.

18. *Mexicans in California: Report of Governor C. C. Young's Mexican Fact-Finding Committee*, pp. 178–179.

19. A fine example of almost complete segregation is contained in Cramp et al., "A Study of the Mexican Population in Imperial Valley, California." A partial list of segregated living and school districts in California is found in *Mexicans in California*, pp. 176–177. Also see Bogardus, *The Mexican in the United States*, pp. 28–29, for an area in which the Mexican did not consider himself inferior to the North American.

20. George L. Cady in his *Report of Commission on International and Interracial Factors in the Problem of Mexicans in the United States* gives a fine example of this pre-World War II exaggeration, p. 10. A somewhat different interpretation, indicating "an unusually high rate of crime and delinquency," is found in Bogardus, *The Mexicans in the United States*, pp. 52–58.

21. Taylor, *Mexican Labor in the United States: Chicago and the Calumet Region*, p. 144.

22. *Mexicans in California*, pp. 175–176 and 203.

23. Cramp et al., "A Study of the Mexican Population in Imperial Valley, California," p. 11, also see p. 12.

24. Mexicans in California, p. 204.

25. Cramp et al., "A Study of the Mexican Population in Imperial Valley, California, pp. 10 and 25.

26. Fifteenth Census of the United States, 1930: Population, II, 842.

27. Mexicans in California, pp. 190–191, 195–196.

28. The Mexicans in Minnesota, pp. 44–45; Taylor, Mexican Labor in the United States, Bethlehem, p. 17; Taylor, Mexican Labor in the United States: Chicago and the Calumet Region, pp. 124, 128–129, 132–133; Cramp et al., "A Study of the Mexican Population in Imperial Valley, California," pp. 13–14; interview with José M. Bravo, Los Angeles, September 11, 1965.

29. Fifteenth Census of the United States, 1930: Population, II, 1094–1095; Pauline R. Kibbe, Latin American in Texas (Albuquerque, 1946), p. 92, presents a fine example of the frustration encountered by enthusiastic Mexican students.

30. For biographical data on Ramón Novarro, Dolores del Río, and Gilbert Roland see Langford Reed and Hetty Spiers, eds., Who's Who in Filmland (3rd ed.; London, 1931), pp. 84, 227, 259.
Judge Harold Medina's Mexican ancestry is discussed in Time Magazine, LIV (October 24, 1949), 23. Bishop Alonso E. Escalante's biographical data are found in the Dictionary of the American Hierarchy, 1789–1964, p. 84. Biographical data on José Limón are published in the Celebrity Register (New York, 1963), p. 375.
For Peter Del Gado's part in the Shaw administration in Los Angeles see Time Magazine XXXII (December 5, 1938), 14; interview with Mr. Richard Rodríguez, Los Angeles, September 29, 1965.
For the Mexican singers of the period only Tito Guízar is listed in Otto Mayer-Serra, Música y Músicos de Latinoamerica (Mexico, 1947), I, 459. For José Mojica, who entered the Franciscan Order, see The Tidings (Los Angeles), January 14, 1966. Andy Russell's biographical data are found in J. T. Mize (ed.), The International Who Is Who in Music (Chicago, 1951), pp. 359–360.
Professors Carlos Eduardo Castañeda and George I. Sánchez are listed in Jacques Cattell, Directory of American Scholars: A Biographical Dictionary (3rd ed.; New York, 1957), pp. 122, 653.

31. Katherine Anne Porter, "A Country and Some People I Love: An Interview by Hank López," Harper's Magazine 231 (September, 1965), 58–68.

Masakazu Iwata,
"The Japanese Immigrants in California Agriculture"

Japanese immigrants to the United States arrived in the twentieth century with expectations and backgrounds similar to those of the Chinese who, beginning with the Exclusion Act of 1882, had been barred from entering the United States. The Chinese had worked in the gold mines, on the railroads, in agriculture, and in their own small businesses. Most of the Japanese, on the other hand, engaged in farming. As Masakazu Iwata indicates in "The Japanese Immigrants in California Agriculture," they were generally quite successful and became landowners. Japanese efficiency and flair for reclaiming previously undesirable land fanned the wrath of white Californians, who in most other instances, had emphasized the need for immigrant settlers in the state but now enacted legislation curtailing alien land ownership.

The Japanese Immigrants in California Agriculture

Masakazu Iwata

The noteworthy contributions made by the Japanese immigrants to California's agricultural development before World War II are undeniable. Indeed, a study of their history reveals that the realization of the agricultural potentialities of the State has been due in no small measure to their endeavors. The Japanese, as in the case of most European immigrants to this country, were induced to leave their homeland because of unfavorable economic conditions. Arriving in ever increasing numbers after the turn of the twentieth century, the Issei[1] settled in the Pacific Coast states where most of them worked as ordinary laborers in various industries. Spurred on by the desire for wealth which would enable them to return to and retire in Japan, the Japanese worked diligently under the most trying circumstances. Their vaulting ambitions soon enabled them to make successfully the

Abridged from Masakazu Iwata, "The Japanese Immigrants in California Agriculture," *Agricultural History*, XXXVI (1962), pp. 25–37. Reprinted by permission of the author and the Agricultural History Society. Some footnotes have been renumbered.

1. *Issei* literally means "first generation." The children of the first generation Japanese in the United States are called *Nisei*, or "second generation." The bulk of the Japanese-American students in high schools and colleges today are *Sansei*, or third generation Japanese.

transition from laborers to tenant farmers. As farm operators, the *Issei* continued a life of struggle not only against the elements but also against adverse social, economic, and political pressures. But despite such discriminatory legislation as the anti-alien land laws, the Japanese, many of whom sought protection in organization, made notable advances in agriculture. Hence by 1941, they, along with the *Nisei* who in the meantime had joined their parents in farming, were producing between thirty and thirty-five percent by value of all commercial truck crops grown in California as well as occupying a dominant position in the distribution system of fruits and vegetables, both wholesale and retail. Many of the immigrant farmers were also engaged in the production of fruits and nuts and in the raising of flowers and poultry. Although the significance of the *Issei* in agriculture was virtually terminated as a result of the Second World War,[2] it would be remiss if history should fail to recognize the vital part they have played in the growth of California agriculture.

In general, the history of Japanese immigration to the United States varies very little from that of other new immigrant groups who came to this country. The Japanese, like the Europeans, were motivated by a desire to better their economic situation. They were likewise compelled to engage in the more menial tasks in their initial efforts to earn a livelihood, and in time were to arouse hostility among groups within the economy. Finally, as in the case of other immigrants, the Japanese were to gain for themselves a foothold in limited fields of endeavor, predominantly agriculture.[3]

Japanese immigration to the United States prior to the turn of the twentieth century was insignificant. Before 1900 arrivals from Japan comprised less than one percent of the total annual volume of im-

2. At the beginning of World War II the average age of the *Issei* was already in the sixties. Consequently, after the evacuation interlude, only a small minority among them had the necessary energy, inclination, and capital to re-establish themselves in farming. The *Issei* are a fast disappearing generation. For statistics regarding their average age, see United States Bureau of the Census, *United States Census of Population: 1950*, Vol. IV, *Special Reports*, Part 3, Chapter 13, Nonwhite Population by Race (Washington: Government Printing Office, 1953), p. 86.

3. See United States Congress, *National Defense Migration*, Fourth Interim Report of the Select Committee Investigating National Defense Migration (House Report No. 2124), 77th Congress, 2nd Section, May, 1942 (Washington: Government Printing Office, 1942), p. 59. Hereafter cited as U. S. Congress, *National Defense Migration*.

migration to this country.[4] The earliest Japanese entrants were shipwrecked seamen, the most famous of them being apprentice sailor Hikozo Hamada who in the 1850's was adopted and educated by the collector of customs in San Francisco.[5] In 1870 only fifty-five Japanese lived in the United States, but by 1890 two thousand more had reached the country.[6] An increasing number of Japanese aliens were admitted after 1900; during this one year alone more than 12,000 new arrivals were counted. The peak was reached in 1907 when more than 30,000 migrants reached the "land of promise." Thereafter the annual influx steadily declined as the result of the Gentlemen's Agreement of 1908 which curtailed the migration of Japanese nationals to the United States and Hawaii. By the eve of World War I, however, the migration figures had once more begun an upward trend with 10,168 Japanese admitted in 1918, a reflection of America's willingness to receive aliens to compensate for the dearth of laborers in the national emergency. Finally, after the passage of the Oriental Exclusion Act of 1924 the flow of immigrants became a mere trickle. In 1928, for example, only 522 Japanese were admitted to the United States.[7]

Figures indicate that among the Japanese entering the various Paci-

4. In 1899 the immigrant aliens admitted from Japan numbered 3,395 out of a total of 311,715 immigrant aliens who entered the United States. See United States Department of Labor, Bureau of Immigration, *Annual Report of the Commissioner General of Immigration: 1928–1929* (Washington: Government Printing Office, 1929), p. 194.

5. Yamato Ichihashi, *Japanese in the United States* (Stanford: Stanford University Press, 1932), pp. 19–21. It is said that members of the Japanese race came to California as early as 1610. Three years later a group of Japanese Catholics on its way to Rome landed here. See Tomatsu Murayama, "Tokyo Topics: First Japanese Landed in California Near Mendocino," *Pacific Citizen*, December 17, 1954, Sec. B, p. 9; James Murdoch, *A History of Japan* (London: Kegan Paul, Trench, Trubner and Co., Ltd., 1925), II, p. 595 ff. A San Francisco newspaper gives an account of "a party of refined Japanese gentlemen, one of whom had been the Governor of Jedo [sic]," who in 1868 were compelled to flee Japan and come to the United States because of their liberal ideas. These Japanese, who spoke English and French, leased a farm in Alameda County and hired a few intelligent white men to instruct them in farm methods. Their venture subsequently produced handsome profits. Editorial in the San Francisco *Chronicle*, June 17, 1869.

6. United States Bureau of the Census, *Fifteenth Census of the U. S.: 1930. Population*, Vol. II. General Report (Washington: Government Printing Office, 1933), p. 32.

7. United States Department of Labor, *Annual Report of the Commissioner General of Immigration: 1928–1929*, pp. 194–196.

fic Coast ports a large percentage of them drifted to and eventually settled in California. Hence the proportion of all Japanese in continental United States settled in California increased from 42 percent in 1900 to 57 percent in 1910 and 65 percent in 1920. The Chinese in contrast were in the beginning exclusively in California and later dispersed to other parts of the United States.[8] Obviously the Japanese were drawn to California by its climate and increasing agricultural and business opportunities.

The Japanese were motivated to come to America primarily by economic factors. To many of them emigration was a means by which they could escape the hardships of life in an impoverished homeland where, especially after the Russo-Japanese War of 1904–05, living conditions progressively worsened. Japan's population density had increased from 1,335 per square ri[9] in 1872 to 1,885 in 1903 which meant that with each successive year a country with limited resources and land area had to satisfy the needs of more and more people.[10] Intense competition among the working classes forced millions of them to live under great economic pressure. The workers, together

8. Varden Fuller, *The Supply of Agricultural Labor as a Factor in the Evolution of Farm Organization in California*, United States Congress, Senate, Committee on Education and Labor, *Violation of Free Speech and Rights of Labor*, Hearings before Subcommittee, 76th Congress, 3rd Session, on S. Res. 266, January 13, 1940, Pt. 54, *Agricultural Labor in California* (Washington: Government Printing Office, 1940), p. 19828. In 1900 out of the total of 24,326 Japanese residents in the country over 10,000 of them lived in California while by 1940 these figures had risen to 126,947 and 93,717, respectively. The following is a breakdown of figures of the California Japanese population into native and foreign-born elements covering the period 1900–1940:

Year	Foreign Born	Native Born	Total
1900	10,008	143	10,151
1910	38,184	3,172	41,356
1920	51,138	20,814	71,952
1930	48,477	48,979	97,456
1940	33,569	60,148	93,717

See United States Bureau of the Census, *Fifteenth Census of the United States: 1930. Population*, Vol. 11, p. 32; United States Bureau of the Census, *Sixteenth Census of the United States: 1940. Population*, Vol. 11, Characteristics of the Population, Pt. 1, U. S. Summary (Washington: Government Printing Office, 1943), pp. 21, 518.

9. A square ri equals 5.9552 square miles.

10. Yosaburo Yoshida, "Sources and Causes of Japanese Emigration," *The Annals of the American Academy of Political and Social Science*, Vol. XXXIV (September, 1909), p. 158.

with the farmers upon whom fell a disproportionate share of the tax load, eagerly came to the United States, hoping to make a quick fortune while at the same time avoiding military conscription. A smaller group of immigrants came specifically to attend American schools.[11] Once in America the immigrants themselves advertised the benefits of life in the new land and thereby induced other Japanese to venture across the Pacific. Like their European counterparts, the Japanese in America delineated in their letters to friends and relatives an often exaggerated picture of American opulence and opportunities. Such correspondence, as well as magazine and newspaper articles dealing with success stories among the Japanese residing in the United States, encouraged migration as did emigration societies which advertised for emigrants through newspapers and traveling solicitors.[12]

The early Japanese immigrants were mostly unmarried males, the majority of whom were under thirty-five years of age,[13] who began their careers in this country as common laborers. Most of them worked as railroad, cannery, and logging camp laborers while a smaller number were employed in the mining, meat-packing, and salt industries. Their willingness to accept even lower wages than laborers of other races enabled the Japanese to secure employment readily.[14] In a number of instances they were used as strike breakers in the mines of Colorado and Utah.[15] The Japanese, in contrast to the Chinese, were unable to enter manufacturing establishments in the cities, such as the cigar, shoe, and clothing factories, partly as a result of the earlier agitation against the Chinese who were employed in these industries and because there was an adequate supply of European immigrant labor for these jobs.[16]

Unable to enter the ranks of the more desirable occupations and unwilling to remain as laborers in non-agricultural employment, the

11. *Ibid.*, pp. 159–160.

12. *Ibid.*, pp. 163–164. See also Yamato Ichihashi, *op. cit.*, pp. 87–88; United States Immigration Commission, *Reports of the Immigration Commission* (Washington: Government Printing Office, 1911) I, p. 662. Hereafter cited as U. S. Immigration Commission, *Reports*.

13. U. S. Immigration Commission, *Reports*, XXIII, p. 8.

14. *Ibid.*, p. 58. For a comparison of the pay received by the Japanese and other races in the railroad, lumber, fishing, mining industries, see *ibid.*, pp. 37–41, 47, 48–49, 53, 56.

15. U. S. Immigration Commission *Reports*, I, p. 664.

16. U. S. Immigration Commission, *Reports*, XXIII, p. 33.

Japanese even prior to 1910 showed a strong inclination to leave their original work for employment in agriculture. This movement into farm work was motivated by a desire for higher earnings in an occupation that had always been looked upon with respect in Japan and for which the Japanese were better fitted through experience.[17] ...

The predominance of Japanese immigrant labor in California agriculture by 1910 was due to several factors. During the nineties when there was a general abundance of agricultural laborers[18] the newly arrived Japanese resorted to wage-cutting to gain a foothold in the various farming districts.[19] After 1902 a labor vacuum drew heavily on the large number of incoming migrants from Japan.[20] Other characteristics of Japanese labor favored their employment in the intensive type of agriculture of the State. The localities in which intensive farming was carried on usually specialized extensively in one or only a few crops, a situation which required large forces of laborers for short seasons only. The Japanese, present in large numbers after 1900, had few family ties and property and were therefore less reluctant than the white men to engage in seasonal agricultural work which required migrating from one district to another.[21] The organization of *Issei* laborers in gangs under Japanese bosses, which was as much

17. *Ibid.*, p. 59. In the Japanese social structure under Tokugawa feudalism (1600–1867) the farmer ranked above the merchant and below the warrior class.

18. Although Chinese exclusion had cut off the source of Chinese labor by the nineties, the stagnation in non-agricultural industries beginning in 1889 and extending throughout the 1890's caused the release of a large number of white workers who drifted into farm work. Fuller, *op. cit.*, p. 19830.

19. *Ibid.* In one community where the Chinese were paid five dollars per week, the Japanese first worked for thirty-five cents per day in the early nineties. In another district the wages of the Japanese varied from sixty to ninety cents as against one dollar per day, including board, for white laborers. U. S. Immigration Commission, *Reports*, XXIII, p. 63. Although they at first worked for lower rates than either Chinese or whites, the Japanese received a progressively increasing amount of wages. By 1910 both Chinese and Japanese rates were approximately equal to those of the whites. Fuller, *op. cit.*, p. 19834.

20. The progressively decreasing number of Chinese farm laborers and the outflow of many white workers who, with the return of prosperity in the nonagricultural industries after 1900, created by 1902 a farm labor vacuum into which the Japanese stepped. Fuller argues that the Japanese, coming at a crucial period in California's labor history, enabled the perpetuation of the State's farm organizational pattern established during the period of Chinese labor dominance. Hence had the Japanese not come when they did the California farmers might have had to change their employment policy, i.e., giving laborers drawn from other ethnic groups better housing, etc. Fuller, *op. cit.*, pp. 19830.

21. U. S. Immigration Commission, *Reports*, XXIV, p. 15.

a boon to the laborer as it was to the employer, served also to secure the position of the Japanese as farm workers.[22] The Japanese labor agents located in various farming communities conducted boarding houses and stores where their men lived on a cooperative plan. The bosses not only obtained work for their gangs and carried on all the necessary wage negotiations with the employers but collected the wages for men and paid them their individual earnings. Under these conditions the employers could keep their bookkeeping at a minimum, having to pay only the labor agent the contracted sum, and be assured of a supply of reliable labor. Hence California ranchers made little effort to secure white laborers for whose services the employers had to negotiate individually, whose wages had to be paid to each personally, and whose reliability was doubtful because only those of an irregular, nomadic class were attracted to farm work.[23]

The Japanese contract labor system which prevailed in California, furthermore, helped to create conditions favorable for the transition of the Japanese from wage-earners to tenants or farm owners. In many instances California farmers resorted to leasing their holdings to the Japanese as a means of securing the nucleus of a labor supply and of transferring to the tenants the task of obtaining the other laborers needed. The Japanese, moreover, venturesome and ambitious to become independent producers, were sought as tenants by landowners because of their willingness to pay higher share or cash rents, to make improvements upon lands and to tolerate conditions not acceptable to white tenants in matters of housing.[24] Furthermore, their operations brought high yields and proportionately high profits to the landowners who rented on a share basis. Again the fact that the Japanese required little or no capital to begin with encouraged them to undertake independent farming. Competing packers and commission merchants financed the Japanese growers after taking liens upon the crops while storekeepers and landlords themselves made generous cash advances. Lastly, their willingness to form partnerships and pool their

22. Labor gangs were not peculiar to the Japanese. The Chinese were earlier organized in the same manner. For a discussion of the various tactics employed by Japanese labor contractors in obtaining work and bargaining for wages for their men, see Lloyd Fisher, *The Harvest Labor Market in California* (Cambridge: Harvard University Press, 1953), pp. 24–31.

23. U. S. Immigration Commission, *Reports*, XXIV, pp. 16–17.

24. U. S. Immigration Commission, *Reports*, XXIII, pp. 81–82.

money in leasing land was of considerable advantage to the *Issei*, a form of cooperation which the other races seldom undertook to better their economic position in agriculture.[25]

Thus by shrewd bargaining, industry, and the ability to tap credit sources the Japanese were able to climb the agricultural ladder from farm laborer to share tenantry, to cash tenantry, and finally for some to farm owner. While in 1900 there were only thirty-nine Japanese farmers in the United States (thirty-seven of whom were operating in California) with an aggregate holding of 4,698 acres, by 1910 there were 1,816 *Issei* farm operators in California alone.[26] In 1904 the Japanese in the State owned 2,442 acres, leased 35,258 acres for cash and 19,572 acres for a share of the crops. By 1909 the corresponding figures had risen to 16,449, 80,232 and 59,001 acres.[27] By 1920 the Japanese had been written off as an appreciable source of farm labor....

For the Japanese farmers the struggle was not only against the elements but also against discrimination. Having inherited the prejudices which the Chinese had earlier aroused, the *Issei* were made the focus of attack from various political and economic groups. Systematic opposition began with the formation in May, 1905, of the Asiatic Exclusion League which had the avowed purpose of halting Japanese immigration and preventing by legislation the sale of land to Japanese aliens.[28] In 1909 no fewer than seventeen different bills relative to the

25. *Ibid.*, pp. 81–84; U. S. Immigration Commission, *Reports*, XXIV, pp. 635–639.

26. United States Census Office, *Twelfth Census of the United States: 1900. Agriculture*, Vol. V (Washington: United States Census Office, 1902), p. xciv; United States Bureau of the Census, *Thirteenth Census of the United States: 1910. Agriculture*, Vol. V (Washington: Government Printing Office, 1913), p. 176; U. S. Immigration Commission, *Reports*, XXIII, p. 79.

27. *Ibid.*

28. *Ibid.*, p. 169. Among organizations which supported the exclusion movement in California were the American Federation of Labor, American Legion, National Grange, and the Native Sons of the Golden West. For views expressed by representatives of the Asiatic Exclusion League on behalf of Japanese exclusion, see United States Congress, Senate, Committee on Immigration, *Japanese Immigration Legislation*. Hearings before the Committee on Immigration, 68th Congress, 1st Session, on S. 2576, March 11, 12, 13, and 15, 1924 (Washington: Government Printing Office, 1924), pp. 3, 21–38, 38–51, 103–143, 146 ff. Fuller maintains that "general anti-Japanese feeling in the rural districts dates from the years subsequent to 1910 and not before as some writers have supposed." Fuller, *op. cit.*, p. 19837.

Japanese were introduced in the California legislature including an alien land bill and a school segregation measure, neither of which passed.[29] In the campaign of 1910 in California, the platforms of the Republican, Democratic, and Socialist parties contained exclusion planks.[30] In 1913 an anti-alien land bill finally became law. It provided in essence that the Japanese might lease agricultural lands for a maximum of three years, that lands already owned or acquired in the future in satisfaction of existing liens, might be retained but could not be bequeathed to heirs under a citizenship disability though proceeds from the sale of the land would be turned over to such heirs.[31] This was a severe blow, but the Japanese circumvented the ownership provisions of the law by purchasing agricultural land in the names of their minor children born in the United States or by paying American citizens to buy land and hold it for them or their children.[32]

During World War I, economic antagonism against the Japanese ceased as industrial expansion stepped up labor demand. With farm laborers and operators alike leaving the rural areas for factory employment, the Japanese were eagerly sought as tenants. Hence well over 70,000 Japanese aliens entered the country between 1913 and 1920, among whom the farmers and farm laborers formed the largest group. This influx was a reflection of the relaxation in the enforcement of the Gentlemen's Agreement.[33] From 1916 through 1918 nearly 10,000 immigrants of these two categories were admitted.[34] . . .

After the first World War, agitation against the Japanese farmers was revived. Agitators found no difficulty in winning adherents for the anti-alien movement among the stream of returning doughboys

29. U. S. Immigration Commission, *Reports*, XXIII, pp. 171–172.

30. *Ibid.*, p. 173.

31. U. S. Congress, *National Defense Migration*, pp. 77–78. For the full text of the land law of 1913, see Eliot Grinnell Mears, *Resident Orientals on the American Pacific Coast* (Chicago: University of Chicago Press, 1928), pp. 473–475.

32. *Ibid.*, p. 253; U. S. Congress, *National Defense Migration*, p. 78.

33. Specifically the provisions of the governmental agreement stated that Japan of her own accord would refrain from issuing passports to Japanese laborers desiring to enter territories contiguous to continental United States and would recognize the right of the United States to refuse the admission to continental United States of Japanese of the laboring class whose passports did not include continental United States. Albert H. Elliot and Guy C. Calden, *The Law Affecting Japanese Residing in the State of California* (San Francisco, 1929), p. 68.

34. U. S. Congress, *National Defense Migration*, pp. 78–79.

and workers released from war industries, many of whom now felt their own economic insecurity in contrast to the established position of the Japanese. The movement was abetted by Japan's aggressions in Siberia, Manchuria, and Korea, and by the awarding of Shantung to Japan in 1919. American nativists made the best of the situation in California at the expense of the Japanese farmers.

The proponents of Japanese exclusion used a plethora of arguments after 1919, among which the economic was not the least of those stressed. The white farmers were told, for example, that the ever-increasing number of Japanese family farms where the father, mother, and children worked in the field would present unfair competition. V. S. McClatchy, a virulent representative of the Japanese Exclusion League of California, filed a skeleton brief with the Secretary of State of the United States in which he said:[35]

The Japanese possess superior advantages in economic competition, partly because of racial characteristics, thrift, industry, low standards of living, willingness to work long hours without expensive pleasures, the women working as men, etc. Combine with these characteristics extraordinary cooperation and solidarity, and the assistance of the Japanese Government, through associations acting for it or in its behalf, and the Japanese, concentrating in communities or industries, are easily able to supplant the whites.

The Japanese were also accused of having "secured the control of one-eighth of all the irrigated lands of California, which are the State's richest," and that they were organizing a market trust.[36]

The champions of the Japanese argued that the Japanese had taken up much of the worst lands in California and made them fertile, thus helping to reduce the cost of food for the city consumers.[37] Evidence

35. V. S. McClatchy, *Japanese Immigration and Colonization*, Skeleton brief with the Secretary of State, 67th Congress, 1st Session, Senate Document No. 55 (Washington: Government Printing Office, 1920), p. 14.

36. *Ibid.*, pp. 14–15. Besides the economic agreements, the exclusionists charged that the Japanese were unassimilable, that they owed primary allegiance to the Japanese emperor, and that the birth rate of the Japanese residents would enable them in time to outnumber the whites.

37. The American Committee of Justice, *Arguments Against the California Alien Land Law* (Oakland, 1920), p. 11. See also U. S. Congress, *National Defense Migration*, p. 84.

indicates that the Japanese did indeed develop undesirable lands. The refractory hog wallow lands in western San Joaquin Valley were actually shunned by the white man, but the Japanese succeeded in conquering them. Subsequently, vineyards and orchards were to cover such lands from Seville to Lemon Cove. It was the Japanese who pioneered the rice industry and produced the first commercial crop of rice on hard pan and goose lands "that were not worth paying taxes on."[38] These are not isolated examples; they were the general condition throughout the State in areas where the Japanese farmed. Through intensive cultivation and the application of scientific techniques, the Japanese had succeeded by 1920 in producing on improved lands crops valued at $67,000,000.[39]

Despite the presentation of evidence favoring the presence of Japanese farmers in California agriculture, the opposition forces persuaded the State legislature in 1920 to pass an amendment to the land law of 1913. The amended law deprived the Japanese of the right to lease agricultural land and to act as guardian for a native-born minor if his estate consisted of property which the Japanese could not hold under law.[40]

Whether as a result of the land law[41] or not, Japanese agricultural development in California was checked during the third decade of the twentieth century. In 1921, for example, the Japanese produced 12.3 percent of the total farm products raised in the State, whereas in 1925 the percentage had dropped to 9.3.[42] A corresponding decrease is to be noted in the census figures enumerating the number of Japanese farms and acreage under cultivation for the years, 1920 and 1930:[43]

38. J. P. Irish, "Orientals in California," Overland, Vol. 75, April, 1920, p. 333.

39. The American Committee of Justice, op. cit., p. 10.

40. For a synopsis of the alien land law of 1920 as amended in 1923 and 1927, see Elliot and Calden, op. cit., p. 25 ff.

41. The effectiveness of the alien land laws has been questioned. One source even goes so far as to say that they actually increased Japanese ownership because landowners who might otherwise have rented to Japanese tenants, after 1920 sold outright to their American-born minor children. U. S. Congress, National Defense Migration, p. 86.

42. Ibid., p. 87.

43. United States Bureau of the Census, Sixteenth Census of the United States: 1940. Agriculture, Vol. 1 (Washington: Government Printing Office, 1942), p. 684.

	1920	1930
Number of Japanese farms	5,152	3,956
Acreage	361,276	191,427

The decline in the number of Japanese engaging in agriculture in the 1920's is said to have been reinforced by the disinclination of the Nisei to remain on the farms,[44] but this was an insignificant factor. After all, the great majority of the Nisei during this decade were not even in their teens and hence would have had little bearing on the decline of Japanese agriculture.[45] The agricultural depression of that decade may have been a weighty factor in forcing some of the Issei to leave farming, but the legal barriers, the land law and the Oriental exclusion act of 1924,[46] did much to discourage the Japanese from entering farming or expanding their operations.

By the eve of the Second World War, however, the number of Japanese farmers in California nearly equaled that of the 1920 figure although the acreage farmed was much lower. Hence in 1940 there were 5,135 farms operated by this race with a total acreage of 220,094.[47] During the previous decade the maturing Nisei had become a factor in agriculture, and their participation in this occupation undoubtedly accounted for the small increase in the number of farmers classified in census figures as "Japanese"; yet, even at this late date the management and operation of Japanese farms were still in the hands of the Issei male.[48]

With respect to land tenure among the Japanese immigrant farmers only a small percentage of them actually owned their farms. In California only twenty-five percent were owners or part owners, less than

44. U. S. Congress, National Defense Migration, p. 87.

45. For a table showing the age by sex of the Japanese population in California, see United States Bureau of the Census, Sixteenth Census of the United States: 1940. Population, Characteristics of the Nonwhite Population by Race (Washington: Government Printing Office, 1943), p. 98.

46. For an explanation of the Immigration Law of 1924, see Elliot and Calden, op. cit., p. 13 ff.

47. United States Bureau of the Census, Sixteenth Census of the United States: 1940. Agriculture, Vol. III, General Report (Washington: Government Printing Office, 1943), p. 224.

48. Leonard Bloom and Ruth Riemer, Removal and Return (University of California Publications in Culture and Society, Vol. IV, Berkeley and Los Angeles: University of California Press, 1949), p. 76.

five percent managers, while the majority of them, seventy percent, rented their farms. In Los Angeles County, where almost thirty percent of all Japanese farms were located, approximately ninety percent of the operators were tenants. In contrast, in the counties of Fresno, Merced, Placer, and Sacramento only fifty percent of the Japanese growers were in this category.[49] Apparently there were more tenant farmers in truck and field-crop-producing areas of the State than in those regions where considerable fruit and other perennial crops were cultivated.

Various theses have been presented to account for the low rate of decline of tenancy among the Japanese farm operators. In 1910, eighty-five percent of them were classified as tenants and thirty years later, in 1940, seventy percent of them were still in the same category. True the laborious method by which they worked up the agricultural ladder had not enabled many of them to accumulate the money necessary to purchase and equip a farm. But the reasons are more fundamental. Students of the problem have stated that although doubt was expressed as to the effectiveness of the alien land laws, the forces which effected these measures deterred many eligible Japanese from acquiring tenure status, particularly farm ownership, in regions where local sentiment was not favorable to the Oriental. Because of this uneasiness, say the experts, many may have preferred tenure of land which would enable them to move on short notice, and a type of farming, i.e., truck farming, which required a minimum of capital investment for permanent structures and perennial crops. The restrictive measures, to the extent that they discouraged farm ownership, probably contributed to establishing an unstable tenure pattern among the Issei agriculturalists with associated undesirable features inherent in short-term leasing, insecurity of land occupancy, and high tenant mobility.[50]

The Japanese, whether farm owner or tenant, usually farmed on a small scale. In 1940 their farms averaged a little over forty acres[51]

49. U. S. Congress, National Defense Migration, p. 117.

50. Adon Poli and Warren M. Engstrand, "Japanese Agriculture on the Pacific Coast," Journal of Land and Public Utilities Economics, Vol. XXI (November, 1945), pp. 354–355.

51. U. S. Bureau of the Census, Sixteenth Census of the United States: 1940. Agriculture, Vol. III, General Report, p. 224.

as compared with the national average of two hundred acres.[52] The *Issei* generally preferred to cultivate small acreages intensively, as did their counterparts in Japan, in order to grow crops with high returns per acre. Consequently only a very insignificant number of the race were engaged in livestock farming which requires extensive acreages of forage crops.[53] ...

The noteworthy aspect of pre-World War II Japanese farming was the ability of the farmers of this ethnic group, each growing on a small scale, to compete successfully with large vegetable grower-shippers. The Japanese were not out-competed because they possessed aptitude for the type of agriculture in which most of them were engaged. They possessed special skill in soil preparation, crop and seed selection, planting, cultivation, irrigation, and spraying. They were also able managers. "Japanese capacity for labor in the fields, growing, cultivating, and marketing truck crops is secondary to their managing ability," said one observer who was acquainted with their ways.[54] Another reason for their success in agricultural competition was their willingness to organize cooperative farm organizations.

A cohesive group, the Japanese immigrants very early in their careers as independent farmers cooperated to meet common problems. The early Japanese farm organizations, local in character, aided their members in finding ranches, served to limit the competition for land by fixing a maximum rental that a Japanese should pay, assisted in marketing the crops and obtaining supplies, interested themselves where disputes arose between a landlord and tenant, and disseminated scientific knowledge of agriculture and horticulture through publications of their own. Many of these local associations served as mutual benefit societies as well.[55]

In southern California, Japanese farmers' associations (*nogyo kumiai*) were more extensive in their operations than elsewhere in the State. Such organizations were connected with marketing associations in Los Angeles for channeling crops from farm to market.

52. *Ibid.*, p. 81.
53. Küchi Kanzaki, *California and the Japanese* (San Francisco, 1921), p. 97.
54. U. S. Congress, *National Defense Migration*, p. 118.
55. U. S. Immigration Commission, *Reports*, XXIII, pp. 85–86; U. S. Immigration Commission, *Reports*, XXIV, pp. 341–343, 396–397.

The two types of associations were also joined in a service federation which for a fee provided its members with daily newspaper and radio broadcasts of produce prices.[56] ...

In the course of their rise to a distinctive position in California agriculture, the Japanese immigrant farmers were condemned by their critics for various uncommendable practices. In their desire to become independent farmers, it was asserted, the *Issei* paid comparatively high rent for land which led to an increase in the rental value of land and to a certain extent caused the displacement of farmers of other ethnic groups.[57] Another charge made against the Japanese was that the value of land diminished in areas where they settled which forced the white population to move away. This was undoubtedly true, especially with respect to residential property, but evidence to the contrary is also available. Hence in a certain section of Fresno County a Japanese was the first to settle and begin farming. Within four years two of his countrymen and four white families moved into the area. While the first settler paid thirty-five dollars an acre for the hay land, the later purchasers were compelled to pay sixty dollars for the same type of land.[58]

Early in their careers the Japanese were also criticized for over-specialization and over-production of crops such as berries and asparagus, a consequence of their eagerness to acquire quick profits. The practice is said to have resulted in the lowering of market prices of such crops which forced non-Japanese farmers to withdraw from producing them. But actually the white farmers did not generally grow the type of crops in which the Japanese specialized, and therefore the effect upon the farmer was minimal. Instances, moreover, in which prices were adversely affected because of Japanese competition were comparatively few.[59]

A further practice attributed to the *Issei* growers was "mining" the soil. The allegation was not entirely without foundation because, as already indicated, the Japanese were predominantly tenants, not owners, a situation which inevitably affected their attitude regarding land improvement. But at the same time it is important to note that

56. Poli and Engstrand, *op. cit.*, p. 358.
57. U. S. Immigration Commission, *Reports*, XXIV, p. 309.
58. *Ibid.*, p. 643.
59. *Ibid.*, pp. 307–308.

a soil scientist of the United States Department of Agriculture minimized the seriousness of the charge by stating: "I am inclined to believe the thorough and excellent cultivation given land under Japanese farming, which favors aeration and biologic processes promoting soil fertility, may in a large measure offset deterioration through removal of plantfood materials."[60]

Finally, during the early years as farmers the Japanese were taken to task for failing to honor contract agreements.[61] No adequate explanation has been given for this, but the fact that East and West differ in the stress each places upon the inviolability of contract may be a partial reason. No sweeping generalization should be made about the Oriental, however, because the Chinese farmers were not generally accused of breaches of contract.

Various other pertinent data are available which help to form a clearer picture of the Japanese immigrant farmers in California. The standard of living of the average *Issei* farmers prior to 1941 was definitely below that of other ethnic groups engaged in the same occupation.[62] They did not, generally speaking, improve property or build a better class of homes. Most of them were merely rough, unplastered frame structures of three or four rooms.[63] An acute observer has described Japanese farm life in the following words:[64]

In California I met for the first time large groups of Japanese, industrious farmers, fruit growers, and poultry raisers, in the Sacramento and San Joaquin Valleys, from El Centro to Colusa, in and around Los Angeles and Fresno and Sacramento. It was comparatively easy to distinguish between the Japanese ranches and

60. Mears, *op. cit.*, pp. 245–246.

61. U. S. Immigration Commission, *Reports*, XXIII, pp. 87–88.

62. A comparison of the data for the Japanese and Italian truck gardeners around Sacramento prior to 1910 reveals that the Japanese farm homes were generally rated from bad to fair in repair while those of the Italians were rated fair to good. In Los Angeles County the Japanese homes were in fairly good repair. The Scandinavian farmers in Santa Clara County and the Germans in Anaheim had homes kept in good condition. Cf. Tables 119, 209, 255, and 289 in U. S. Immigration Commission, *Reports*, XXIV, pp. 838–840, 864–865, 884–889.

63. *Ibid.*, p. 399.

64. Konrad Bercovici, "The Japanese in the United States," *The Century*, CX (September, 1925), p. 608.

the white man's farm ... Either because of the insecurity with which the Japanese has regarded his holdings in this country, the farm home of a Japanese, even of a wealthy farmer, is far below that of a home of a white man owning a similar piece of ground or of similar wealth.[65] The neatness of the field ... is in direct contrast with the flimsy, improvised condition of the living quarters of the Japanese.

This is a faithful picture of Japanese farm houses in the 1920's and, in general, it had not changed considerably by 1941. The shifting and unsettled nature of the Japanese farmers induced by the land law and the inability of the Issei to become naturalized citizens prevented many from establishing themselves permanently in any community. Under such conditions there was little incentive to build permanent homes. In the settled districts, however, chiefly around Fresno, where there were large Japanese landholdings, the standard of living was surprisingly high.[66] ...

By 1941 the Japanese immigrants in agriculture, the majority of whom had come to America as "birds of passage," intending to make enough money and then to return to Japan, had settled down in various farm communities. They were rearing their native-born children in the American tradition. For most of the Issei there was now no longer any strong desire to leave the country in which they had resided the greater part of their lives. ...

... Very few, however, even among the Japanese themselves, realize the important role the Japanese immigrants collectively played in California agricultural history. Coming in large numbers after the turn of the twentieth century, they filled the farm labor vacuum and thus prevented a ruinous slump in those lines of agriculture for which California is noted, namely, in the growing and harvesting of intensive crops. As independent farm operators, the Japanese with

65. In the 1930's the writer had occasion to visit the home of a Japanese operator of one of the largest growing and shipping concerns in California. The owner of a large packing shed and a grower of crops on thousands of acres of well-tilled land, this operator lived in a humble unpainted frame home surrounded by huge sheds housing hundreds of thousands of dollars worth of trucks, tractors, and other farm equipment. The picture, in view of his wealth, was incongruous to say the least.

66. E. Manchester Boddy, *Japanese in America* (Los Angeles, 1921), p. 107.

their skill and energy helped to reclaim and improve thousands of acres of worthless lands throughout the State, lands which the white man abhorred, and made them fertile and immensely productive. They pioneered the rice industry and planted the first citrus orchards in the hog wallow lands in the San Joaquin Valley. They played a vital part in establishing the present system of marketing fruits and vegetables, especially in Los Angeles County, and dominated in the field of commercial truck crops. From the perspective of history, it is evident that the contributions of the *Issei* to California's economy far outweigh the evils that have been attributed to their agricultural activities. They were undeniably a significant factor in making California one of the greatest farming states in the Union.

Part VII
Struggle for Status, 1940 to the Present

Struggle for Status, 1940 to the Present

At the mid-point of the twentieth century in the United States, nonwhites grappled with material and psychological obstacles. During the years from 1940 to date some progress seemed evident to casual observers, but particularly in relation to the white population, cold statistics showed improvement to be largely illusory. Spurred on by heightened expectations and growing bitterness and abetted by an awakening white conscience, nonwhites embarked on a sustained drive to upgrade their status and achieve coexistence and equality with the white world.

The effort to improve the lives of nonwhites borrowed heavily from the tactics of earlier militants who had appeared intermittently during the previous two hundred years, only to be ruthlessly put down. The new approach emphasized pride in their color, heritage, and culture. Nonwhites rejected those values of the white culture which seemed inappropriate to their experience. But for many the most important consideration continued to be subsistence; rat-infested housing, inadequate food and clothing, and unemployment persisted as daily problems.

Black Americans led the struggle for status, and many of their tactics were adopted or modified by other nonwhite groups. From A. Philip Randolph's threatened march on Washington in 1941 to the Black Panther party program of 1971, black Americans organized and confronted the white establishment. Their techniques included the legal battles of Roy Wilkins, the political activities of Shirley Chisholm and Julian Bond, the nonviolent demonstrations of Martin Luther King, the religious and nationalistic appeals of Elijah Muhammad and Malcolm X, and the black power program of Stokely Carmichael. Some joined forces with white Americans while others aligned themselves with the Third World; some were violent while others insisted on peaceful protest, but all were determined to create an equitable place for the black man in American society.

Other nonwhites developed similar patterns of resistance. The new American Indian created a "red power" movement which exhibited his disenchantment and militancy; the invasions of Alcatraz Island and the other efforts to reacquire land by force, as well as by legal means, epitomized their strategy. The success of the grape strike at Delano, California, initiated by Filipino farm workers and carried through by Cesar Chavez and his Mexican-American followers, illustrates another kind of resistance through labor union organization and methods. While the family structure and living habits of Orientals who have remained within the culture work toward separation from the currents that often agitate American life, young people such as the Maoist-leaning youth guards and the alienated Wah Ching, the Hong Kong born young men of San Francisco's Chinatown, have asserted a militancy not shared by their parents.

The objectives of minorities were not confined to a demand for parity with the white world; nonwhites also called for self-determination within their communities, and particularly for the control of schools and businesses. The movement for community control ironically was fostered by the isolation of nonwhites in ghettos and more recently by the movement of economically secure whites to the suburbs. The growth of ghettos led to an enlarged nonwhite population in the great central cities of the nation and a concomitant increase in the political influence which nonwhites could assert. Thus by midcentury nonwhite mayors and congressmen were placed in office by city electorates.

The discriminatory policies that herded nonwhites into ghettos opened the way to the development of alternative life styles and promoted the pluralism which Americans have simultaneously prized and attempted to prevent by homogenizing their white population.

The structural assimilation of which Milton M. Gordon (Part I, "Assimilation in America: Theory and Reality") speaks did not apply to nonwhites, and the effect was the promotion of separate cultures that often had only a tangential relationship to that of the majority.

Nonwhite demands for correcting the imbalance between their world and that of the whites created a population that was no longer quiescent. Nonwhites gave voice to their frustrations and unhappiness in a manner that shook the foundations of the nation. For not only did they demand equitable treatment by the economic and political system, but some also confronted the social system and rejected it in favor of a culture that derived from their own experience.

Ronald O. Haak,
"Co-opting the Oppressors:
The Case of the Japanese-Americans"

The attack on Pearl Harbor which brought the United States into
the Second World War had disastrous results for those Japanese-
Americans who lived on the west coast. A wave of fear and hatred
produced hysterical rumors of sabotage and Japanese-American-
aided invasions of the coast. A flagrant violation of human rights
occurred as over 117,000 people, two-thirds of them American
citizens, were moved to ten relocation camps in the interior of the
nation solely because of their race. The Japanese submitted peacefully
and, professing their loyalty, aided in running the camps and
laboring in surrounding areas. Ronald O. Haak, in "Co-opting the
Oppressors: The Case of the Japanese-Americans," argues that the
Japanese drew on their cultural heritage in order to endure the
oppression and emerge from the ordeal.

Co-opting the Oppressors: The Case of the Japanese-Americans

Ronald O. Haak

"A Jap's a Jap," stated Brigadier General John L. DeWitt. As commander of the Western Defense Command in 1942, he was testifying before a congressional committee on the vulnerability of the West Coast to invasion from Japan. Indeed, former Supreme Court Chief Justice Earl Warren, then attorney general of California, testified that the American-born Japanese were even more dangerous to the security of the United States than the alien Japanese. There was a pervasive fear that the Japanese-Americans' knowledge of the English language and American customs would make them excellent saboteurs. To Walter Lippmann the very lack of sabotage and espionage on the West Coast was cause for alarm. Innocuous behavior was merely a ploy to disarm American suspicions, he warned. Plans were soon under way for the harsh resettlement of 112,000 persons of Japanese ancestry. In sealed trains they were dispatched to ten relocation camps, where they were allowed to bring only as much baggage as they could carry in their hands.

The authority for this vast roundup of "undesirables" on the charge of potential treason lay in Executive Order 9066, which

Abridged from Ronald O. Haak, "Co-opting the Oppressors: The Case of the Japanese-Americans," *Transaction*, VII (1970), pp. 23–31. Copyright © 1970 by Transaction, Inc., New Brunswick, New Jersey. Permission to reprint.

President Franklin D. Roosevelt signed on 19 February 1942. The order marked off military areas "from which any or all persons [might] be excluded." General DeWitt, who was made responsible for implementing the executive order, had already recommended "evacuation of the Japanese and *other subversive persons* from the Pacific Coast" (my italics) and had specified that "the word 'Japanese' included alien Japanese and American citizens of Japanese ancestry." In later proclamations and directives, General DeWitt referred to the American-born group, euphemistically, as "American-born persons of Japanese lineage" or as "nonalien persons of Japanese ancestry," and in the *Final Report* of the Western Defense Command, "nisei" was defined as "any person of Japanese ancestry not born in Japan," while the meaning of "Japanese ancestry" was clarified to cover "any person who has a Japanese ancestor, regardless of degree."

The stereotyping was racial, rather than political, since none of America's other so-called enemies-in-residence were so categorized. Germans and Italians in the United States faced no such charges and as a group were never subjected to more than a curfew in the very first days of the war. Moreover, the ideology behind the action had a domestic flavor, even a regional one. The Japanese third of Hawaii's population, 3,000 miles closer to the emperor's charisma, were generally allowed to go about their business, as were the Japanese populations in the Middle West and on the East Coast. For 112,000 people on the western seaboard, however, constitutional guarantees were suspended, and the civilian enclave was subjected to treatment usually reserved for prisoners of war.

Despite this alarming start, within little more than a decade the Japanese were welcomed back into the pantheon of good American immigrants. The oppressed minority, against overwhelming odds and with little hope their efforts would do them any good, induced the white majority to erase the stigmata. How did it happen?

Before the war, the Japanese had earned grudging respect. Neatness, diligence, respect for property, low delinquency rates and an aversion to the dole won them favor so long as they were kept out of the larger competition. Their educational record, for example, compared favorably with the white population at large and exceeded that of any identifiable minority. Yet the fact remains that by 1939 in San Francisco and Los Angeles only one in ten nisei (Japanese:

ni = second, *sei* = generation) employed in trade or nondomestic service was actually working for a "Caucasian" firm. Significantly, their strivings did not seem to require reinforcement from the larger society. In the 1930s, when even members of favored minority groups could find no jobs, the nisei went to school and avidly prepared for that one chance in a thousand. But then came Pearl Harbor and the vicious "preventive detention" of the war years.

Yet it was precisely their wartime record of camp cooperation and combat valor that finally broke down the accusations against Japanese-Americans. Political loyalties were shown not to be fused to ancestry; this was fact. But society, in exonerating this minority, went a step further and attributed the group's performance to Americanization, to the fact that it had assimilated "our" standards and way of life. Moreover, the truth of this explanation seems to have been accepted even by the Japanese-American Citizens League (JACL) which has also consistently stressed the theme of Americanization in its representations to Congress and to the nation at large. In a statement before the West Coast hearings of the House of Representatives in 1954, the JACL stated:

> In spite of threats and intimidation by the disgruntled and disillusioned, as the records show, several thousand Japanese-Americans whose loyalty had been questioned by their own government volunteered to fight, and if necessary to die, for our country. This we submit was a demonstration of *real faith in America and the American way* seldom if ever surpassed (my italics).

Today, the JACL version is probably the standard version of what happened. (Indeed, it may be the only one the majority is willing to accept.)

If, as in the film *Rashomon*, we look at events through the memory filters of the participants, the entire perspective shifts. The California nisei with whom I spoke regard the camp period as attesting to their worth as Japanese. Postwar acceptance by the larger society was tremendously important, but the nisei view it as belated recognition of peculiarly Japanese virtues, virtues that this nation had ignored for 70 years. In short, they attribute their admirable performance to ethnic intensification, not ethnic renunciation.

These findings suggest that when groups are forced into confrontation each takes what it needs from that confrontation and does not perceive it in the same way even when both are moving toward a satisfactory rapprochement. Far from representing this as a lapse in communication, I would generalize that a happy outcome requires each faction to salvage its self-esteem under the common umbrella of mutual misunderstanding.

The Japanese-Americans know they were misjudged from the start. That may be why their recollections are more bemused than indignant. Of Japanese farmers suspected of planting their vegetable rows toward neighboring airfields for the benefit of Japanese bombing runs, they can laugh, "That farmer didn't know anything but his vegetables." Again, Caucasians hidden in bushes reported that farmers stared intently at passing aircraft, coordinating traffic volume, flight schedules and regional air strength. The truth, it turned out, was that the farmer welcomed an excuse to straighten his back and relieve the monotony of his day. There is still much enjoyment over the story of the Japanese hotel proprietor who returned from his roof-top laundry lines with basket and flashlight to find his hotel filled with police searching for "the spy on the roof."

A strong, overbearing, gullible figure is always good fun, and Japanese folk plays (kyogen) dramatize the discomfiture of many. It is embarrassing when a powerful authority brings a cannon to bear upon a flea, while splashing around huge sums of money for guards, camp maintenance, bookkeepers, administrators—not a bit of it necessary. It softens the blow to reflect that the qualities carried here from an old and illustrious civilization should escape the notice of a newcomer like the United States.

But more importantly, Japanese see no point in nursing even grave grievances if there is an appropriate apology. In their view, postwar indemnification, though partial, qualifies as a proper apology and relieves them of all onus. Once again, they see themselves as rewarded not for renunciation of Japanese traits, but for the very tenacity with which they clung to them.

Many first-generation immigrants grew up in the rural Japanese village, with its deeply entrenched tradition of subservience and cooperation. Long before Japan dreamed of modernization, her villages consisted of small, family-centered production units disciplined to the exacting, labor-intensive techniques of wet rice cultivation. Communal performance was severely monitored, and ostracism meant substantial psychological and economic dislocation. When Japan lunged toward modernization, the agrarian sector was chosen to bear the full brunt of initial capitalization. From 1868 until the upturn of Japan's economic growth in 1886, taxes on farm production accounted for 78 percent of the total national revenue. During this period of rather pitiless extraction, class divisions did not appear in the villages, and the farmers did not challenge the directives. They performed according to expectations.

The immigrants, who in America turned to truck farming, flower raising and other related pursuits characteristic of Japanese endeavors on the West Coast, came from a milieu where duty and sacrifice were demanded almost as in war. Rural commitments in Japan were not made provisionally, in the context of interest politics or a battle for subsidies. Rice cultivators have for centuries worked prodigiously for their immediate hierarchical superior. Commentators on Japan often use the term "moral style" to get at just this readiness of the Japanese to invest themselves in an enterprise that brings them no commensurate gain, none even in sight. The rewards are present, of course, in the security and interdependence of the group cocoon, and this is especially pronounced in the rural sector. Urban girls recruited to weave kimonos in Japanese cities prior to World War II kept themselves aloof and moved on to better jobs after their training or contract was over. Rural girls recruited for the same jobs invested themselves lavishly in the small companies, even to bearing the boss's children and bringing them up as little apprentices, with marriage foreclosed from the start. This rural predisposition for self-sacrifice without hope of reward molded the character of the immigrants in this story. It helps explain how they and their children could stick to these priorities of cooperation under the most tremendous provocation, a fidelity the adopted country could account for only by the self-flattering notion of "Americanization."

The camps gave many Caucasians their first contact with Japanese outside the movie houses. A nisei recalled the day the sealed trains delivered their human cargo to an Arizona camp. Nisei girls in crisp, fresh blouses set up registration points, and family representatives queued up to offer data for rosters. The arrival scene slowly acquired some signs of voluntary order and purpose. "Are these the Japanese people?" a government bystander asked in wonder. "Yes," replied the nisei, "that's the way the Japanese are."

The nisei share a common fund of knowledge about the fates and reputations of the ten garrison settlements that stretched from eastern California to Arkansas. The Arizona camp was well known for the prodigious resourcefulness of its people. The internees faced a blazing sun and harsh soil, but gradually they learned that castor beans were viable. Humble as it was, this crop was marketable and brought money into the camp. Cereals were garnered from the nearby Navaho, who startled the Japanese with the specter of minority ruin. The new arrivals quickly came to fear reservation poverty and apathy, particularly among the sansei (san = third, sei = generation) who would be growing up in a potentially demoralizing milieu. This furnished an incentive for the Japanese to do more than merely adjust to their desert exile.

To appreciate the initiative of the Japanese internee, place him in the context of the wardship that was his for the asking. The government assumed the task of providing food and shelter, while conduct of internal camp affairs was in the hands of the Japanese membership. Specialists such as cooks, nurses, doctors and police earned salaries of $12 to $19 a month. There were no additional allowances for clothing replacements and toiletries. Food shipped in was charged against daily allocations of 29¢ to 45¢ per person. The Japanese could have lapsed into sullen and passive dependence, for which the Navaho provided a vivid precedent, but these new arrivals fared better.

Incentives need not be lofty to be effective. The Japanese had no voice in menu composition, and they found the pork hocks, ox hearts and mutton (the most vividly remembered foods) too different from their traditional fare to be palatable. Private purchases of preferred foods from the neighboring countryside outran the capacities of $12 to $19 incomes for specialized workers. The others had even less money, as bank assets had been frozen before the evacuation.

From conferences with nearby Indians, the Japanese learned that where sagebrush grew, vegetables would too. Before their tenure was over, the Japanese were raising all manner of vegetables. Chickens provided plenty of eggs for the whole camp, and even cattle were in evidence. Their initiative produced a bounty that extended beyond the camp. From the year-round growing season of Arizona they were able to ship their surplus to camps in the north.

Timber parties left under escort and returned with harvests that appreciably lowered government coal bills. With 120,000 internees, trimming a dime a day per capita meant $12,000 saved daily from the federal outlay. From nisei recollections, many dimes were pared from maintenance costs by Japanese diligence. As camp food production grew to supplement the official menu, the cooks found themselves able to cut their food purchases. At the end of the first year, a delegation approached their captors and volunteered the money left over from the food budget, all carefully saved and meticulously recorded.

Rumors of the Japanese performance seeped into the Arizona governor's mansion. With the establishment of the camps, the governor had guaranteed to his people that not one Japanese would be allowed to remain in the state when the war was over. The irony of the situation was not lost on the internees who met the governor's reserve, some of them recall, not head-on, but with characteristic finesse. Their response was a gift of three yellow and three white camp-grown chrysanthemums coaxed from the desert soil. The flowers, "big as cantaloupes," waved from two-foot stalks and were replete with rapprochement symbolism. "Did such flowers grow inside *that* camp?" the outsiders asked one another as the present made its way to the statehouse. Soon a local fire department visited the camp for a picnic. The police took the next tour, and finally the governor himself put in an appearance. "They all thought we would be living like Indians, but they found out the Japanese were different," one man remembers. The guests found the sandy glare softened by trees, flowers, a pond, walks and improvised landscaping. (Some internees devoted half their precious hand baggage to prize bulbs, cuttings and the like. Thus, camps favored with better soil sported Chinese elm trees and even manicured lawns.) "How do you keep everything so clean?" the Caucasian visitor of the moment might ask. "Who picks up all the paper?" Shrugging diffidently, the nisei would reply matter-of-factly, "Oh, everyone looks after himself."

By the war's end, the governor was won over. He invited six nisei agriculturalists from the camp to inspect a parcel of property under consideration for his own venture into commercial flower raising. Of the 25 acres, the Japanese judged 15 as promising, and they agreed to develop this acreage as employees of the governor-turned-businessman. Two refrigerated trucks were purchased the first year to convey the flowers to California winter markets. Needless to say, the Japanese are now welcome in Arizona, as they are welcome everywhere.

It would be inaccurate to attribute the Japanese cooperative drive to a spirit of docility. When the government accountant accepted the donation of savings from the food budget, the Japanese did not withdraw, content with a down-scaling of funds for the following year. They requested a hike in the very next allocation for clothes and travel fares so they could "help the war effort" by repairing railroad tracks and harvesting in the fields that had lost workers to the army or higher paying war industries. Although they often met hostility, they traveled throughout the country doing farm work.

Such cooperation has all the earmarks of sheer identification with the American war effort. But within the camps, the elected leadership had their hands full "calming down the people" so as to deal prudently with the Caucasian administrators. Regional and generational fissures, temporarily closed during the stress of evacuation, were reopened inside the camps. Rumors of FBI inquiries and arrests aroused suspicions that there were informers among the internees, and cooperation with the administration was branded as collaboration. Every faction found its convenient scapegoat. Suspected informers were ostracized, threatened or even beaten by their fellow evacuees. Revolt against the administration took the form of major strikes or minor work stoppages during the fall of 1942, and in two projects, Poston and Manzanar, revolt assumed the proportions of riots and was met with force by the administration. . . .

Detention, first considered as a transitory phase in the larger scheme of evacuation and resettlement, bogged down and took on the earmarks of a permanent program. The War Relocation Authority (WRA)—rather more human than the other agencies involved—sought to reinstitute the objectives that its name implied. It sought to extract from the War and Justice Departments the necessary authority to move its people out of the camps. When the War Department decided to reopen the army to loyal Japanese-American volunteers, the WRA saw its chance. It decided to capitalize on the War Department's interest in the male nisei by expanding the loyalty inquiry into a general liberalization of the stalled relocation policy. The War Department was to "process" the male citizen, while the WRA would process the rest of the adults.

For all its good intentions, the questionnaire was clumsily conceived and cast the internees into a state of alarm and consternation. The three points that caused the trouble dealt explicitly with the issue of "loyalty": 1) Are you loyal to the United States, abjuring allegiance to the emperor? 2) Do you hope the United States wins the war? 3) Would you serve in the combat forces of the United States, wherever ordered?

Some nisei found these questions irrelevant to their own feelings of "loyalty" toward the United States, for they perceived them as glossing over legitimate reservations based upon prior violation of their own civil rights. A nisei informant who answered yes in good conscience to questions 1 and 2 could recite in detail his civic reasons for giving a negative answer to the third. Yet this qualified his loyalty. Another nisei recalled that his response to question 2 had been: "There is no winner in a war." Administrator response: "We know that." Nisei rejoinder: "Then why ask me?" This is not as slippery as it may appear, for it is good Buddhist doctrine, but it compromised his status as a loyal citizen in the administration's view. Other nisei were uncertain how they could renounce allegiance to the emperor when they were American citizens and had no contact with Japan. Was this a "Do you still beat your wife?" question?

But the camp debates raged longest about question 1 which, as a condition of loyalty, required alien issei who were barred from American citizenship by statute, to forswear allegiance to the country wherein their citizenship was assigned. If they complied and America lost the war, then what would become of them?

Belatedly, the issei were permitted to affirm that they would "abide by the laws of the United States" and "take no action that would in any way interfere with the war effort of the United States." But their American-born off-spring were required to affirm the original "wife-beating" statement, despite their American citizenship. . . .

As a counterweight to this sketch of uniform Japanese cooperation, I should mention here the militant and outraged Japanese who railed at their imprisonment, refused to take an oath of sympathy toward the United States war effort, beat up the emissaries and the president of the JACL and accused advocates of moderation of being collaborators and informers. They sorted themselves out by their defiant performance on questionnaires and were segregated in a special camp at Tule Lake. It was made possible for these American-born Japanese to renounce their citizenship, and some of them did, though it was later ruled that this renunciation was not binding. A high proportion of these militants were kibei [Japanese born in America but educated in Japan].

Though the West Coast Japanese were thrown back as a group upon their own resources for solidarity and self-worth by harsh outside verdicts, the kibei recoil was compounded by their recent education in Japan. Their memories were fresh and vivid, and their militancy tended to be proportionally stronger. Tanaka, one of my informants, had the added misfortune to be drafted into the army before the war, at a time when he still knew no English. . . .

The vast bulk of the population remained stigmatized throughout the war and were treated "like Japanese." Their forced exile and the cause célèbre of their identity predictably intensified their ethnic consciousness. In conversation today they refer to their wartime capacities and performance as distinctively Japanese solutions to a minority, not a political, problem.

Their solution was an ancestral reflex pattern of self-sacrifice and cooperation with no reward in sight. This was not new. A nisei recalls the exhortations she received from her parents even before the war:

We were abused at school, we were told never to fight back. We were told never to bring disgrace upon our family. Instead, we were told to rise by working hard. We had to do better than Caucasians to earn even equal treatment. We saw our parents had sacrificed everything for us children, and we couldn't disgrace them.

Isn't this a strategy to urge on all minorities striving for a breakthrough? Shouldn't they all follow the Japanese example? Initially, it sounds good, but the more the nisei reveal of themselves, the more they reveal an inheritance that is nontransferable. The diligence, the corporate performance, the respect for authority and parental wishes, shame (more than guilt) as a deterrent to nonsanctioned behavior, the importance of keeping up appearances—all these desirable traits have different roots than their American counterparts, which they outwardly so closely resemble. The Japanese did so well in school, for example, because of their on to their parents, their community and the giri to their name. Already in 1858, Japan's literacy rate of 50 percent outdistanced that of Great Britain, the leading industrial power of that day. In Tokyo (then called Edo), which boasted the world's greatest urban population until London pulled ahead in the early nineteenth century, 85 percent of all children spent at least four years in school despite the low per capita incomes. Throughout Japan, reverence for learning was a national characteristic, and the teacher was held in high esteem. The immigrants brought it with them.

What helped them most in the long run was the way they chose to earn recognition by performance, rather than by claiming it on principle. They steered clear of demands for radical revisions in the national power structure, in the distribution of wealth, in the ethnic composition of political and policy-making bodies. They simply worked and endured until their performance overwhelmed, without contentiousness, society's negative definitions of their worth. . . .

The Japanese cooperated with their captors into submission, but the process was slow. After the close of the war, with the release of the internees and the combat record of the 442nd Regimental Combat Team plainly set forth for all to see, the following discriminatory prohibitions still obtained:

The issei were ineligible for citizenship.

All property was subject to escheat under the alien land laws upon failure to adhere to the legal minutiae of scrupulous reporting procedures. Tenants who improved property after years of hard labor were regularly dispossessed upon the termination of their lease.

There was no equality under law for immigration quotas and procedures.

Intermarriage was prohibited.

Claims for indemnification were unresolved.

General acceptance by their neighbors was still retarded by long-standing majority resentments.

After the close of the war, the Japanese in America chipped in $325,000 to lobby for redress in Congress and were successful on all six points.

Was their wartime performance a calculated strategy? Did the Japanese in America create an impressive record between 1942 and 1945 with explicit intent to silence their critics when the day of adjudication dawned? The clamor over the loyalty questionnaire suggests this was far from the case. Nor is it realistic to expect any minority to trample the response pattern that sustains its identity and self-esteem. The Japanese were faithful to theirs throughout. When the close of the camps was imminent, representatives from each of the garrison settlements convened in Salt Lake City to draw up an agenda for repatriation to the larger society. Caucasians were excluded, but all camp representatives agreed that the last contact with the government should be conciliatory. Demands were minimal. Larger questions of equity under law and economic redress were deferred. From the convention emerged 24 articles providing for such matters as housing and care of the sick and aged. "The government man told us we wouldn't have to sleep under bridges, and he was right." In a California camp of thousands of trailers the Japanese set up their last temporary settlement. The government man arrived weekly with subsidy checks to find many already off securing a beachhead, to speed the day when they could send for their families. The trailers became empty one by one, with the sick and the aged the last to go. Relocated, this time without supervision of forced scheduling, the relief checks were no longer needed. "The Japanese don't like relief," my informant noted. He added, after a pause, "This saves the government money."

How was consistently Japanese behavior reconciled with prevailing American expectations? Not by intent. When projected on the ethnic screen, Japanese values and psychological commitments presented a favorable Rorschach. The majority society read its own priorities into the ethnic tenacity of the Japanese and saw no reason to debate the diverse background and motives that inspired them. Indeed, it is far more flattering to concede that the Japanese had been Americans all along than to entertain the suspicion that ethnicity is admirable in its unredeemed state.

Joan Ablon,
*"American Indian Relocation:
Problems of Dependency and Management in the City"*

Nowhere, perhaps, is the clash of cultures in modern America more apparent than in the case of Indians who have migrated from the reservation to the city. As Joan Ablon emphasizes in "American Indian Relocation," traditional Indian values and reservation life have ill-prepared these newcomers for urban survival. American Indians, schooled in dependency as wards of the government and accustomed to communal life by their heritage, find it difficult to make their way in a complex white urban society which places a heavy value on independence and individualism. While some Indians have managed a successful transition to city life, many others return defeated to their reservations or subsist, unemployed and impoverished, in urban slums. If the movement of Indians to cities is not to constitute simply another disastrous "relocation," much more must be done to make it possible for them to adapt to the demands of urban life while retaining their unique cultural heritage.

American Indian Relocation: Problems of Dependency and Management in the City

Joan Ablon

The diverse population groups that are migrating into metropolitan areas are offering formidable challenges to community agencies who must attempt to understand the particular needs of widely varying groups. More than 60,000 American Indians have immigrated to large urban centers in the last decade to seek stable employment and a new life. American Indians present a peculiar new urban group, a tribal people who have left the primary relationships and cultural world of the folk society to enter a complex industrial order whose basic values violate many of the premises of Indian life. It is the fact of the persistence of tribal and folk values that differentiates the rural, unskilled Indians from other such population groups that are moving into urban centers over the country. This paper will attempt to point up some of the factors involved in the relocation experience, and to analyze typical Indian attitudes of dependency and modes of coping with problems in the new urban milieu.

Most Indian reservations are economically underdeveloped areas. The lack of steady employment opportunities and the prevalence of widespread social and domestic problems have motivated many per-

Abridged from Joan Ablon, "American Indian Relocation: Problems of Dependency and Management in the City," *Phylon*, XXIV (1965), pp. 362–371. Reprinted by permission of the publisher.

sons to relocate to urban areas. For some the venture has proven successful but for many others it has been another contemporary trauma to add to the list of those in Indian history.

Many Indians have moved into urban centers on their own resources and initiative through the years. A great many of these decided to remain in areas where they were stationed or had worked during World War II. However, the greatest impetus for Indian relocation has been recent programs sponsored by the Bureau of Indian Affairs. The Employment Assistance Program (formerly called the Voluntary Relocation Program), which began in 1952, provides financial assistance for the Indian individual or family unit for transportation from the point of origin to ten Field Relocation Offices throughout the country, maintenance and living expenses until the first wages are in hand, and services in the areas of orientation, employment, housing, and general counseling. The Adult Vocational Training Program, a potentially more successful program because it has offered wide educational opportunities for young people, was first broadly implemented in 1957. This program brings Indians between the ages of 18 and 35 to schools across the country where they will receive training in specific marketable skills. The pragmatic sink or swim nature of a move to areas distant from family and community differs qualitatively from all other Bureau programs. The character of the program and its demands requiring certain initiative and independence in thought and action from a people long in wardship status has produced complex and varying responses.[1]

While other rural Americans or even European immigrants who move into urban societies are segments of the broader Western European tradition and share in some part its values and accepted moral system, American Indians, though differing from tribe to tribe in some accepted values and patterns, almost all hold to certain common values which differ from or are completely contrary to those of the dominant white society. Most Indians are not aggressive toward others.

1. This discussion is based primarily on a two-year study (1961 to 1963) of the general adjustment complex and the persistence of Indian values and tradition in the course of the relocation process among government-sponsored and self-relocated Indians in the San Francisco Bay Area. The findings are similar to those of other investigators in other areas. There are, unfortunately, few published works on urban Indians. For more detail on Indians in the San Francisco Bay Area see Joan Ablon, "Relocated American Indians in the San Francisco Bay Area: Social Interaction and Indian Identity," *Human Organization*, Vol. 23, No. 4, Winter 1964.

They do not like to compete. In conflict situations they are more likely to withdraw than to speak out. They would rather share their money and goods than to budget and save. A man's prestige was based traditionally on what he had given away and not on what he had accumulated for himself. The functional realistic time dimension is short and the deferring of educational or economic goals is alien.

Relocatees exhibit a wide variety of tribal backgrounds, educational experiences, and histories of contact with whites. Most have attended all-Indian schools and many have had nominal vocational training in school or in the service, but proportionately few make use of this. Almost half of the relocatees who came in the early years of relocation were veterans, and most have had some form of prototypic work experience in which they were forced to deal with whites. Although the chief reason for relocation is the incentive to find steady employment, this goal is usually compounded by a variety of personal and family problems that the relocatees wish to escape.

Most Indians bring few vocational skills with them, and the unskilled job market is small and uncertain. Lay-offs are common and expected. Many Indians who do remain in the city have treasured the security of jobs in "dirty work" that more educated acculturated persons would not endure. Indeed personal attitudes toward work and a craving for security often appear to be more important in the retention of jobs than previous training or sophistication in the complexities of the job and union markets. Indians tend to live in working-class neighborhoods where a variety of other ethnic and minority groups are also represented. Although dispersed among this general population, they do not often associate with their neighbors and most frequently turn to other Indians, usually tribesmen, for their intimate social relocationships, and to pan-Indian social activities.

Most Indians exhibit temerity and ambivalence in dealing with whites. Often they have experienced great discrimination in the areas peripheral to their reservations and many have been ill-used by whites leasing their lands. Thus in the city they are pleased by the relative freedom from the blatant forms of discrimination they have known. Nonetheless, most Indians never feel relaxed among whites,[2] and true egalitarian relationships with whites occur infrequently. A com-

2. For a penetrating and informal discussion of characteristic personality differences between Indians and whites, see Rosalie Wax and Robert K. Thomas, "American Indians and White People," *Phylon*, XXII 1961, Fourth Quarter, 305–317.

mon type of friendship may be noticed in the form of young Indians being adopted in a dependency relationship by older whites who help them with money, services, and emotional support. This dependency relationship is a distinct carryover from the relations with white federal or local officials that they experienced on the reservation.

Certain gross cultural-tribal common personality characteristics are often readily apparent in the responses of relocatees of the same tribe. Certain of these common tribal characteristics may be highly selective for success or failure in the city. For example, some tribes who have experienced great disorganization and heavy alcoholic problems on their reservations have sent many families on relocation, but these families frequently have grave difficulties in simple survival in the urban situation. Uncontrollable drinking problems which prohibit steady employment and compulsive hospitality and sharing patterns which further complicate an already impoverished condition are common. For instance, most Sioux who have remained and are doing well on relocation have generally been sober and not inclined to follow the hospitality and generosity patterns which their tribe traditionally has emphasized to an extreme. In general it may be said that many Indians tend to exhibit severe ambivalent "marginal man" characteristics which often seem to paralyze action and preclude efficient relations with whites.[3]

There is, however, a wide range of personal characteristics unique to individuals of the same and differing tribes. The importance of the personal psychological characteristics of the individual relocatee cannot be overstated in their influence on the future of the relocation experience, and are so varying that they can rarely be figured in as a generalized "given" when planning for the individual or family unit.

It is indeed difficult to speak in generalities about Indians and the

3. The "marginal man" as an individual caught between the values of two cultural worlds, and often finding himself unable to function acceptably in either, has been treated as a sociological phenomenon by a number of scholars. The original classic article by Robert E. Park, "Human Migration and the Marginal Man," *The American Journal of Sociology*, No. 6, May 1928, 881–893, has been reexamined by others such as Milton Goldberg, "A Qualification of the Marginal Man Theory," *American Sociological Review*, VI, No. 1, February 1941, 52–58; Arnold Green, "A Re-Examination of the Marginal Man Concept," *Social Forces*, XXVI, No. 2, Dec. 1947, 167–171, and Steven Polgar, "Biculturation of Mesquakie Teenage Boys," *American Anthropologist*, LXII, No. 2, April 1960, 217–235.

relocation experience. Each family represents a differing cultural and educational situation, further complicated by the nature and amount of experiences with whites the families have had, and the personal psychological characteristics of the individual relocatees. Often crippling personal problems or drastic homesickness are the factors that finally break the relocation, in spite of a happy employment situation. The treatment by the Bureau and the process of relocation as it occurs is highly significant, as are the simple factors of chance and luck which may determine the pickings of the job market and housing just at that particular time that the relocatee arrives.

Most Indians do not like the city, although they appreciate the many conveniences of urban life. They do not like the crowds, the traffic, the many buildings pushed together, the constant restraints, the bills, the lack of privacy. Yet most enjoy the varied amusements a metropolitan area can offer them, as well as the educational experiences of seeing new things. Indians come to the city seeking work, not to become white men, nor to stop being Indians. Most of them sorely miss their families and reservation life. Their feelings about returning are ambivalent, and negative and positive attitudes occur in their every utterance. If comparable job opportunities at home were available, it is probable that more than 75 percent of the Indians who have relocated would choose to return to their reservations as soon as possible.

The decision of returning to the reservation is a complex blend of objective economic and social factors, and of shifting emotions for most relocatees. In some cases, aside from and secondary to employment opportunities, men think of the much longed-for open spaces, woods, fishing and hunting that they enjoyed at home; women think of the household conveniences of running water, lights and heating, to which they have grown accustomed in the city and which are so painfully important with a large family. They also think of the better educational opportunities available for their children in the city. Many persons argue the pros and cons of easier control and discipline of children in the city as opposed to rural areas. Some fear that their children will become delinquents in the city by being caught up in school, neighborhood, or housing project gangs. Most prefer to raise small children in the country, but say that there the adolescents have more opportunity to run wild and that they will not be able to control their wanderings or drinking. A complicating dimension of both alternatives of reservation and city life is the alcohol problem, which may be more threatening at home where drinking relatives surround one, or more dangerous in the city where anxieties caused by new and alien pressures cause one to wish to lose himself. . . .

The immediate decision to return home may be made in a few minutes or hours, precipitated by illness, death, an overwhelming medical bill, a sudden lay-off, or a traffic offense. It takes only a short time to activate the fever for home in the blood, and one may not stop to think clearly, to remember or care that employment opportunities have not improved, nor have reservation shanties been provided with running water or lights or easy heating. The time for second thoughts will come after the glad return.

The Bureau of Indian Affairs estimates that some 35 percent of those persons who have relocated for employment return to their reservations. Other investigations suggest that although this figure has been accurate for the past several years, in the early years of relocation the return rate was about 75 percent. Some returnees eventually apply for a second or even third relocation, but there is careful screening of these cases, and generally only such objective reasons for return as major illness or death are accepted as a justifiable basis for subsequent sponsorship for a repeat location.

Most Indians still retain vestiges of what may be called a former "primitive world view," which recognized an important and precious relation between man, his fellows, nature and the gods. Man was part of an interdependent harmonious whole.[4] He was a cog in the larger order of his community and nature, and he did not have an individual and independent career. His thoughts were pervaded with mysticism. A person molded in this culture is not equipped to readily adjust to an individualistic, anonymous existence and to the nuclear-family, self-sufficiency pattern of the city-dweller. Members of the middle-class urban society have come to see themselves as objects to be shaped to fit into the requirements of complex modern culture, and to be changed to meet goals which hold promises of rewards. For Indians to become efficient managers of their life situation is a complex process which may never occur. This requires an amount of introspection and

4. For excellent expository discussions of this subject see Robert Redfield, "The Primitive World View," in The Primitive World and its Transformations, 1953; and Laura Thompson, "Attitudes and Acculturation," American Anthropologist, No. 2, April–June 1943, 200–215.

self-awareness of being a unique and malleable entity that is not common to the Indian personality or view of life. An Indian already *is* so to speak; he *is* a Navajo, a clan member, a son, a father, etc.—all stations existing only in relation to his tribe, his family, or the universe.

The nature of governmental relations with Indian communities has compounded the potential for dependency of the tribal man whose resources with which he could maintain his own way of life were rapidly and forcibly removed. The many reservations over the country differ in the detail of their history of federal administration; however, governmental policies have been generally ill-planned and inconsistent. A pervading paternalistic orientation and preemption of decision-making has characterized government policies toward Indian communities. The continuing effect of these policies has been extreme economic deprivation and psychological crippling to most of the several hundred Indian tribes. Two of the more obvious manifestations of this crippling have been a deeply entrenched dependency, and widespread and chronic drinking.

Life in the city is a difficult and puzzling experience for most relocatees. Reservation life has little prepared them for the credit temptations and varied monetary pitfalls of urban society. On reservations Indians have a wardship status and have become accustomed throughout their lives to depend on governmental doles in the forms of money, commodities, and free medical services. They frequently paid little or no rent. In the city they suddenly encounter seemingly endless bills. . . .

Complexities in almost every aspect of life and various sorts of red tape are part and parcel of the urban existence. City dwellers are used to dealing with and manipulating both the small daily problems of life and also larger long-range issues. Middle-class persons usually put emphasis on practical problem-solving through work, thrift, and legal means. Lower socio-economic groups likewise put importance on manipulating their environment; however, they often choose methods such as conning or stratagems of chance, rather than stable employment or long-term education.[5] Such ingenious forms of "alley smart-

5. For an analytic discussion of lower-class values see Walter B. Miller, "Lower Class Culture as a Generating Milieu of Gang Delinquency," *Journal of Social Issues*, XIV No. 3, 1958, 5–19.

ness" contrast sharply to the traditional more pedestrian planning and action patterns of Indians, who may have great knowledge about hunting, farming and other areas not applicable to city life. Also it may be observed that many ethnic groups develop communities with indigenous leadership with urban know-how, and these persons serve as clearing-houses of information and skills for less sophisticated persons and new arrivals. Indians have not developed such functional urban structures, primarily because of tribal differences in political procedure and values.

The most important characteristics that appear to be common to almost all the Indians who have remained in the city are a conformity to white standards, at least on the economic level, by a striving for employment stability and security, and an ability to manage for themselves and to control their life situation. In less crucial aspects of their lives they have made various kinds of adjustments. Families who have made successful relocations exhibit great differences in home atmosphere, life ways, values, and activities that they consider pleasurable and worthwhile. The differences in these homes are far greater than would be found in white homes of the same economic brackets....

Those Indians who have been able to take active control of their situation in the city have separated their own identity as a separate and inviolable entity that does not substantially change, while on the other hand they have mastered the techniques of handling and manipulating their environments. There is no doubt but that the roads through which the development of this control come about are many. A first step is a self-awareness of Indian identity, and a certain introspection about the implications of this. Some persons were fairly sophisticated in dealing with whites before coming; others learned through harsh experience. Members of most tribes can be counted among the controllers, full and mixed bloods, relatively highly educated and sophisticated persons to those less educated and sophisticated.

Those who consciously and actively have controlled their urban life, even if torn by great desire to return to the reservation, will not generally do so until they believe they will be able to control their reservation situation once there, by having a secure job, ridding themselves of dependent relatives, etc. It is probable that a sizeable number of those who have developed sufficient mastery to give them a realization of choice and the meaning and possibility of alternatives have also made the decision to return home, preferring not by default of inability, failure and subsequent withdrawal, but through conscious choice to return home.

Many Indians have survived in the city for years, but exist essentially in the same manner as their relatives on the reservations rocking from daily problem to problem with little ability to better their situation.What criteria can be set up then to distinguish survival from success? The Bureau of Indian Affairs has had no program to follow-up relocatees except through chance encounters or by the "grapevine," and has not followed the progress of self-relocatees at all. Therefore, they tend to almost categorically label a unit they hear has remained over a period of years and has not frequently called on them for aid (which is often a hopeless gesture, as the Indians are well aware) as being a successful relocation.

The crucial question that must be faced is how success is to be defined pragmatically as opposed to mere elemental physical survival in the city. I would suggest that the fact of active mastery of one's everyday situation on a daily operational level is the functional definition of success for a family. Are persons who have developed this control the less Indian for it? On the basis of my observations and interviews which almost universally encountered an everpresent psychological and social awareness of Indian identity, I would suggest that these persons are not less Indian, but are Indians of a little different quality—an urban neo-Indian type. This neo-Indian has a more acute awareness of himself, of the general implications of his identity, and how, as an Indian, he must be able to meet the everyday problems of city living with some equanimity and measure of control to shape the mundane features of his new life....

Alphonso Pinkney,
"Black Power"

Beginning with the 1954 Supreme Court decision, Brown v. Board of
Education of Topeka, which declared that segregated schools
were inherently unequal, and the Montgomery bus boycott of 1955
and 1956, blacks with the aid of some whites, embarked on a
new drive to improve their living conditions. However, by the
middle sixties it become apparent to many blacks that the Negro
Revolt, or the Civil Rights Revolution, had not been particularly
successful. Compared to the rest of the population, blacks lost
ground economically; southern whites were especially unwilling to
permit change, and conditions in the North seemed to be
deteriorating. "Black Power" became a popular slogan, emphasizing
black pride, black nationalism, and self-help. The Black Power
movement alienated some white supporters of the Civil Rights
Revolution because its advocates threatened violence as opposed to
the nonviolence of the earlier struggle, attacked racism in the
North as well as the South, and insisted on black direction and
leadership. In the following selection from his book, Black
Americans, Alphonso Pinkney defines Black Power and explains
its rapid acceptance in the black community.

Black Power

Alphonso Pinkney

For all practical purposes the civil rights movement ended in 1965. The following year civil rights organizations appeared to be searching for some cause around which to rally as a means of continuing their protest activities. Although implementation was lagging, they had won important victories: the Civil Rights Act of 1964, the Voting Rights Act of 1965, and, perhaps most important of all, the recognition by Americans that the low status of black people posed a serious social problem in a world where oppressed people were fighting for freedom and self-determination. The question "Where do we go from here?" was being asked by the leaders of the major civil rights organizations. In June 1966 James Meredith was shot as he started his freedom march through Mississippi. Immediately thereafter the leaders of several civil rights organizations gathered in Memphis, Tennessee, and made plans to turn the aborted march into a major civil rights campaign. During this march Stokely Carmichael, the chairman of SNCC, introduced a new and controversial slogan into the nomenclature of the movement to achieve greater civil rights for Negroes. The concept of Black Power was first used in this context when the march-

"Black Power," pp. 196–203. Alphonso Pinkney, *Black Americans*, copyright © 1969. Reprinted by permission of Prentice-Hall, Inc., Englewood Cliffs, New Jersey. Footnotes have been renumbered.

ers reached Greenwood, Mississippi.[1] Field workers from SNCC had worked in this community, and, at a mass rally, when Carmichael proclaimed, "What we need is black power," he was cheered by the crowd of poor Mississippians.

The introduction of the concept of Black Power was debated by the leaders of CORE, SCLC, and SNCC. Martin Luther King and his associates from SCLC disapproved of its use, but the leaders of CORE and SNCC supported its use. A compromise was reached— that the concept was not to be used as the official slogan of the march—but it gained worldwide usage and generated a heated debate among the major black organizations.

Somehow the combination of the words "black" and "power" seemed to offend and frighten white Americans, especially some "liberal" white persons who had contributed time and money to the civil rights movement. To them the concept implied black supremacy (or reverse racism) and black violence. Consequently they resigned from membership and withheld financial support from the more militant organizations. Similarly the more moderate civil rights organizations, such as the NAACP and the National Urban League, expressed their disapproval of Black Power. The organizations which had led the civil rights movement and which had cooperated in the major campaigns and demonstrations in the South were divided along ideological lines.

Those leaders advocating Black Power have attempted to define the concept, but such attempts have usually been lost in the growing debate in the mass media of communications. To Stokely Carmichael of SNCC the concept speaks to the needs of black people at the present time. It is a call to black Americans to liberate themselves from oppression by assuming control over their lives economically, politically, and socially. He has said:

Black Power means black people coming together to form a political force and either electing representatives or forcing their representatives to speak to their needs. It's an economic and phys- ical bloc that can exercise its strength in the black community instead of letting the job go to the Democratic or Republican parties or a white-controlled black man set up as a puppet to

1. Martin Luther King, Jr., *Where Do We Go From Here?* (New York: Harper & Row, 1967), pp. 23–32.

represent black people. We pick the brother and make sure he fulfills our needs. Black Power doesn't mean antiwhite, violence, separatism, or any other racist things the press says it means. It's saying, "Look, buddy, we're not laying a vote on you unless you lay so many schools, hospitals, playgrounds, and jobs on us."[2]

Later he and Charles Hamilton elaborate on the concept of Black Power:

> It is a call for black people in this country to unite, to recognize their heritage, to build a sense of community. It is a call for black people to begin to define their own goals, to lead their own organizations, and to support those organizations. It is a call to reject the racist institutions and values of this society.
>
> The concept of Black Power rests on a fundamental premise: *Before a group can enter the open society, it must first close ranks.* By this we mean that group solidarity is necessary before a group can operate effectively from a bargaining position of strength in a pluralistic society.[3]

Floyd McKissick of CORE sees the following as elements of Black Power: increased political and economic power for Negroes, improved self-image, the development of young, militant black leadership, the development of black consumer power, and strong resistance to police brutality in black communities.[4]

Although Martin Luther King, Jr., opposed the use of the concept of Black Power for a variety of reasons, he acknowledged that it had what he called a "positive meaning."[5] He saw it as a "cry of disappointment" and of despair with the present state of black-white relations. He also interpreted it as "...a call to black people to amass the political and economic strength to achieve their legitimate

2. From "Stokely Carmichael: Young Man Behind an Angry Message," by Gordon Parks, *Life Magazine*, May 19, 1967; copyright © 1967 Time Inc., p. 82.

3. Stokely Carmichael and Charles V. Hamilton, *Black Power: The Politics of Liberation in America* (New York: Random House, Inc., copyright 1967), p. 44. Reprinted with permission.

4. See Fred C. Shapiro, "The Successor to Floyd McKissick May Not Be So Reasonable," *The New York Times Magazine*, October 1, 1967, p. 102.

5. King, *Where Do We Go From Here?*, pp. 32–44.

goals." Finally, he saw Black Power as "a psychological call to manhood." Despite its many positive features, King felt that the concept had too many negative values for it to serve as the basic strategy with which to meet the problems faced by black people at the present time.[6] He believed that it embodied a philosophy of hopelessness about achieving basic changes in the structure of American society. In addition, as an integrationist, King saw the Black Power movement as one based on separation of the races in the United States. He rejected the notion that any group within the larger society could achieve equality through separation. Finally, as a foremost exponent of nonviolence, he felt that the concept was often a call for retaliatory violence, which, he maintained, could only serve to impede progress in race relations.

The more moderate leaders of civil rights organizations have opposed the concept of Black Power from its inception. The leaders of the NAACP and the Urban League joined five other prominent black spokesmen and responded to the militant organizations by placing an advertisement entitled "Crisis and Commitment" in numerous newspapers.[7] In response to the advocates of Black Power they enumerated what they considered to be the "principles upon which the civil rights movement rests." They included four points: (1) a commitment to the principle of racial justice through the democratic process, (2) the repudiation of violence, (3) a commitment to the principle of integration, and (4) a commitment to the principle that the task of bringing about integration is the common responsibility of all Americans, both black and white.

One of the leading critics of Black Power rejects the concept in favor of coalition politics. Bayard Rustin feels that the concept is harmful to the movement for greater civil rights for America's Negroes because "It diverts the movement from a meaningful debate over strategy and tactics, it isolates the Negro community, and it encourages the growth of anti-Negro forces." As an alternative to Black Power, Rustin advocates a "liberal-labor-civil rights coalition which would work to make the Democratic Party truly responsive to the aspirations of the poor, and which would develop support for programs (specifically those outlined in A. Philip Randolph's $100 bil-

6. *Ibid.*, pp. 44–63.
7. *The New York Times*, October 14, 1966, p. 35.

lion Freedom Budget) aimed at the reconstruction of American society in the interests of greater social justice."[8]

Supporters of Black Power reject the notion of forming coalitions with predominantly white liberal, labor, and religious organizations. They insist that those who advocate such coalitions proceed on the basis of three fallacious assumptions: (1) that at the present time the interests of black Americans are identical with the interests of these groups, (2) that a viable coalition can be established between groups with power and powerless Negroes, and (3) that it is possible to sustain political coalitions on a "moral, friendly, sentimental basis; by appeals to conscience."[9]

The debate over Black Power continues. The more militant organizations, CORE and SNCC, are its chief proponents; the more moderate organizations, the NAACP and the Urban League, are strongly opposed, and SCLC takes a middle position. In keeping with their position that Black Power means black consciousness and solidarity, the militant organizations have urged their white supporters to form parallel organizations and to work with the white community to rid it of the racism which is endemic to American life. A coalition between black and white Americans at the present time is seen as unworkable. The major impediment to equality for black people is seen as the resistance of the white community. Consequently, CORE and SNCC have urged their white supporters to work within their own communities.

Less than one year after the concept was first introduced, it had gained widespread prominence. In July 1967 the first National Conference on Black Power was held in Newark, New Jersey. This conference was attended by more than 1,000 black delegates from 42 cities in 36 states. They represented a broad cross section of black leaders, ranging from the militant black nationalists to employees of government agencies. One of the most significant aspects of the conference was its bringing together for the first time a wide assembly of black people who met in workshop sessions to define the concept of Black Power and who agreed to implement its components. When the conference ended, a series of resolutions had been passed, in-

8. Bayard Rustin, " 'Black Power' and Coalition Politics," *Commentary*, Vol. 42 (September 1966), pp. 35–40.

9. Carmichael and Hamilton, *op. cit.*, Chap. 3.

cluding the following: (1) the establishment of black financial institutions such as credit unions and nonprofit cooperatives, (2) the establishment of black universities, (3) selective purchasing and boycotting of white merchants in black communities, (4) the demand for a guaranteed annual income for all people, (5) a boycott by black athletes of international Olympic competition and professional boxing, in response to the stripping of the world heavyweight boxing title from Muhammad Ali, (6) boycotts of Negro churches which are not committed to the "black revolution," (7) boycotts of Negro publications accepting advertisements for hair straighteners and bleaching creams.

Meanwhile, Black Power gained wider acceptance among more radical white Americans. In November 1966 students at Oberlin College, in Oberlin, Ohio, held an intercollegiate conference entitled Black Power in the Urban Ghetto, in an effort to "eliminate the emotionalism which clouds the debate on Black Power and to try to point out the basic issues involved." At its annual meeting in August 1967 the National Student Association, the largest organization of college students in the United States, resolved to support the implementation of the concept of Black Power "through any means necessary." In September the delegates attending the National Conference for New Politics in Chicago voted by a margin of more than two to one to support all resolutions of the Newark Black Power Conference and to support "black control of the political, economic, and social institutions in black communities."

Current interest in the concept of Black Power is perhaps too recent in its origin to gain wide acceptance on its relevance to the problems faced by Negroes. It has emotional implications which white Americans fear, but, stripped of its emotional connotations, it appears to mean the amassing by black people of the economic, political, and social power necessary to deal effectively with the problems they face as a powerless people relegated to a life of poverty in an affluent society. Furthermore, it is a call to black people to reject the social values (especially racism) which are responsible for their low status in the United States and to replace them with an ideology which embraces dignity and pride in blackness. Black solidarity is seen as a precondition to the achievement of these ends. Integration, it is felt, is much more likely to be achieved from a position of strength than from one of weakness.

The concept of ethnic power is not alien to American society. Historically, many ethnic groups have managed to improve their status through the process of organizing themselves into power blocs. Indeed, historically, ethnic solidarity has been a fundamental aspect of American minority relations. One writer has defended Black Power as follows:

> . . . . to the extent that "Black Power" expresses a determination to build a Negro community which would be something more than euphemisms for the ghetto, it is a valid and necessary cry; to the extent that it expresses a despair of the one-by-one absorption of "deserving" Negroes into the general society and puts its faith instead in collective action aimed at dealing with collective fate, it is an intelligent response to the reality of American life.[10]

He sees the attempts to establish group loyalty among Negroes, which is a fundamental aspect of Black Power, as an essential means of dealing with a basically hostile society. Although other minority groups have effectively organized themselves along religious and ethnic lines into political and economic power blocs as a means of improving their status, once this goal has been achieved, they effectively combine forces and join what Negroes call the white power structure, which serves to perpetuate the low status of Negroes. They may be of Irish, Italian, Jewish, or Polish extraction, but in encounters with Negroes, racial homogeneity serves to solidify them. In short, black subordination was achieved and has been maintained by the unabashed use of "white power."

Another writer, who sees Black Power as "the acquisition of power by Negroes for their own use, both offensively and defensively," defends the concept, especially its emphasis on black nationalism and black consciousness, as follows:

> It is important to establish a positive black identity in a great many sectors of the black communities, both North and South, rural and urban, lower and middle class. Indeed, it is both im-

10. "In Defense of 'Black Power'," by David Danzig, *Commentary*, Vol. 42 (September 1966), p. 46. Reprinted from *Commentary*, by permission; copyright © 1966, by the American Jewish Committee.

portant and legitimate to teach black people (or any other ethnic minority) about their history, placing special emphasis upon the positive contributions of other black people. This black consciousness has the potential to create unity and solidarity among black people and to give them hope and self-confidence.[11]

She reports that Black Power has achieved success among Mississippi Negroes because attempts at racial integration in that state have failed.

The use of black political power to achieve Negro rights is not new. In 1941 black leaders effectively forced the President to issue an executive order banning discrimination in employment in industry doing business with the federal government. Such organizations as the Negro American Labor Council of the American Federation of Labor–Congress of Industrial Organizations and the all-Negro organization within the New York City Police Department exist to protect the interests of their members. The idea underlying the concept of Black Power, then, is not a new one. It has, however, gained new strength within the last two years. In 1967 a nationwide organization of elected Negro public officials was formed to develop methods of utilizing their combined power to improve the status of black citizens. A nationwide group of Negro ministers met in November 1967 in an effort to make Black Power a force in American Protestant church policies. They are organizing to serve as a pressure group within the National Council of Churches in an effort to increase the number of Negroes in policy-making positions and to "bring the resources of white churches into urban ghettos in such a way as to enhance Negro leadership."[12]

The civil rights movement was basically reformist, aimed at changing some aspects of the structure of American society insofar as black people were denied some of the rights guaranteed citizens in the Constitution. It was directed toward establishing the principle of legal equality as public policy and toward the responsibility of the federal government in protecting the constitutional rights of citizens. To a degree these goals have been achieved, or, at least, they have

11. Joyce Ladner, "What 'Black Power' Means to Negroes in Mississippi," *Transaction*, Vol. 5 (November 1967), p. 14. Reprinted by permission of the publisher.
12. *The New York Times*, November 2, 1967, p. 52, col. 2.

been accepted as a matter of principle. The Black Power movement, on the other hand, goes beyond social reform. If the demands for political, economic, and social control by black people over the institutions which are responsible to them, along with the other changes necessary for the "liberation" of American Negroes, are achieved, American society will have undergone revolutionary changes. The civil rights movement did not address itself to the complex, deeply rooted problems facing black people in the slums of the United States. The Black Power movement does. In this sense, the Black Power movement might be said to be the logical extension of the civil rights movement. Where the civil rights movement ended, the Black Power movement begins, and it might be said that the death of the civil rights movement gave birth to the black liberation movement. . . .

Joseph L. Love,
"La Raza: Mexican-Americans in Rebellion"

During the 1960s Mexican-Americans displayed a new determination
to acquire legal and civil rights, land, protection of agricultural
workers, and a voice in community and educational activities. Their
increased aggressiveness and sense of unity created a heightened
awareness in the nation of their organizations and leaders. Perhaps
the best known movement was that led by Cesar Chavez and
the National Farm Workers Association, whose successful strike and
boycott of the grape growers in Delano, California, demonstrated
the benefits of organization. Other new and dynamic alliances
included the Political Association of Spanish-Speaking Organizations
(PASO) and the Mexican-American Political Association (MAPA).
In "La Raza: Mexican-Americans in Rebellion," Joseph L. Love
examines the attempts of one of the new militant organizations
to secure land grant rights to millions of acres in New Mexico.

La Raza:
Mexican-Americans in Rebellion

Joseph L. Love

In early June, 1967 a group of Spanish-speaking Americans who call themselves the *Alianza Federal de Mercedes* (Federal Alliance of Land Grants) and claim that they are the legal and rightful owners of millions of acres of land in Central and Northern New Mexico, revolted against the governments of the United States of America, the State of New Mexico, and Rio Arriba (Up River) County, formally proclaiming the Republic of Rio Chama in that area.

On June 5 an armed band of forty or more *Aliancistas* attacked the Tierra Amarilla courthouse, released 11 of their members being held prisoner, and wounded a deputy sheriff and the jailer. They held the sheriff down on the floor with a rifle butt on his neck, searched for the District Attorney (who wasn't there) and for an hour and a half controlled the village (population 500). They took several hostages (later released when the getaway car stuck in the mud).

Despite some of the melodramatic and occasionally comic opera aspects of the affair, both the members of the *Alianza* and the local and state authorities take it very seriously. This is not the first time the Aliancistas have violated federal and state law, attempting to ap-

Abridged from Joseph L. Love, "La Raza: Mexican-Americans in Rebellion," *Transaction*, VI (1969), pp. 35–41. Copyright © 1969 by Transaction, Inc., New Brunswick, New Jersey.

propriate government property (in October, 1966, for instance, their militants tried to take over Kit Carson National Forest, and to expel the rangers found there as trespassers); nor is it the only time their activities have resulted in violence. In this case the state government reacted frantically, sending in armored tanks, 300 National Guardsmen and 200 state police. They rounded up dozens of Spanish-speaking persons, including many women and children, and held them in a detention camp, surrounded with guns and soldiers, for 48 hours. The raiders got away, but in several days all of them—including their fiery leader, former Pentecostal preacher Reies López Tijerina—were captured.

It has become common to associate these actions of the Alianza with other riots or revolts by poor, dark-skinned and disaffected Americans—with Watts, Newark and Detroit. Tijerina himself helps reinforce this impression by occasionally meeting with, and using the rhetoric of, some leaders of the black urban revolt. The fact is, however, that the Alianza movement is really a unique example in the United States of a "primitive revolt" as defined by Eric Hobsbawm, a kind almost always associated with developing nations, rather than advanced industrialized countries—and which includes such diverse phenomena as peasant anarchism, banditry, and millenarianism (the belief that divine justice and retribution is on the side of the rebels and that the millenium is at hand). The attack on the courthouse, in fact, had more in common with the millenarian Sioux Ghost Dance cult of 1889–91 than with Watts.

As the Aliancistas see it, they are not violating any legitimate law. The territory around Rio Arriba belongs to them. They demand the return of lands—primarily common lands—taken from *Hispano* communities, most of which were founded in the Spanish colonial era. Their authority is the famous *Recopilación de leyes de los Reinos de Indias (Compilation of Laws of the Kingdoms of the Indies*, generally shortened to *The Laws of the Indies*) by which the Crown of Castile governed its New World possessions. They claim that according to these laws common lands were inalienable—could not be taken away. Since most of such lands were in existence when the Treaty of Guadalupe Hidalgo was signed in 1848—and since in that treaty the United States government pledged itself to respect property rights established under Mexican rule—the Alianza insists that those land grants remain valid. The members speak primarily of common lands, rather than individual heirs, and define the towns in question as "closed corporations, with membership restricted to the descendants and heirs of the founding fathers and mothers"—that is, themselves.

The Alianza's interpretations of law and history are, of course, selective, and tend to ignore inconvenient facts and other interpretations. It claims that *The Laws of the Indies* were not abrogated when "Mexico invaded and occupied New Mexico," nor when the United States did the same in 1846. The Aliancistas are the early settlers, the legitimate heirs.

The Alianza and its actions cannot really be understood without knowledge of its background and its leader. First, the people from whom it draws its members and its strength—the Mexican-American minority in the U.S.—and specifically New Mexico; second, the rapid economic changes throughout the area since World War II that have so greatly affected their lives; and last but surely not least the dynamism, determination and charisma of Reies Tijerina, without whom the movement would probably never have arisen.

In the 1960 census Mexican-Americans, though they make up only 2.3 percent of the population of the United States, constituted 12 percent of the population of Texas, New Mexico, Arizona, Colorado and California—almost three and a half million persons.

Generally they are a submerged minority that have only lately begun to articulate their demands. They formed "Viva Kennedy" committees in 1960; since then three Mexican-American Congressmen have gone to the House, and New Mexico's Joseph Montoya sits in the Senate. The end of the *bracero* program in 1964 opened the way to a successful unionization drive among agricultural workers; and the celebrated "Huelga" strike in Delano, California in 1965 was a symptom of and stimulus to the new awakening. The federal and state poverty programs, and the example of the Negro revolt, have also undoubtedly had their effects.

New Mexico is a distinctive area of Latin culture. It was the last state in the Southwest to be overwhelmed by Anglo-American civilization, and is the only one with two official languages. The Mexican-American population has been traditionally located along the Rio Grande and its tributaries, and extends into southern Colorado.

Until recent years, the Mexican-Americans of New Mexico have been isolated from other members of *la raza* (the Mexican-American "race"). Texas and California have more than 80 percent of the

Mexican-American population of the Southwest, yet most of these crossed over from Mexico after 1900, or descended from persons who did. But, the New Mexican *Hispanos* (the local name) have resided there for many generations, and some strains go back to the seventeenth century (Santa Fe was founded in 1609). Moreover, large numbers of English-speaking Americans only began to compete seriously for rural property in the 1880's, and appropriation continued into the 1920's.

In the 1960 census New Mexico had a higher percentage of "native born of native parents" than any other Southwestern state (87.4 percent). The mobility of Hispano males between 1955 and 1960 (defined in terms of changing residence) was lower in New Mexico than elsewhere. In 1960 New Mexico had the highest percentage of rural non-farm inhabitants with Spanish surnames.

In absolute numbers New Mexico's Anglo population was for many years roughly in balance with the Hispano. It is now surging ahead as a result of the economic boom which began with the atomic testing program of World War II. In no other Southwestern state was the disparity between the growth of Anglo and Latin populations greater from 1950 to 1960 than in New Mexico, where the former increased by 59.1 percent and the latter by a mere 8.1 percent. Yet in spite of this, New Mexico in 1960 still had a greater proportion of Mexican-Americans than any other state: about two-sevenths of its inhabitants had Spanish surnames, compared to one-seventh of Texans, and one-eleventh of Californians.

The job situation for the Hispanos of New Mexico has also worsened more rapidly than in other states. In 1950 male Mexican-Americans had a greater percentage of jobless in California, Colorado, and Arizona than in New Mexico; but ten years later the Hispanos of New Mexico had the dubious distinction of leading the list.

As some observers have noted, in certain ways New Mexico resembles Quebec: Both are centers of Latin culture founded in the seventeenth century, and both are subject to an increasing degree of Anglo domination. And like the Quebeckers, the New Mexicans have their fringe-group separatists—the *Alianza Federal de Mercedes.*

The Alianza was born in 1963, partly to combat the alienation and isolation of the Hispanos, but specifically to reclaim lands taken from the Spanish-speaking population since 1848. In colonial New Mexico (1598–1821), Spanish officials made land grants of indeterminate size to both individuals and to communities as commons, and the latter were respected through the era of Mexican rule (1821–1848). When Anglo-Americans began to enter New Mexico in significant numbers in the 1880's, they found it possible to wrest lands from the native inhabitants through the legal and financial devices of land taxes, mortgages, and litigation over disputed titles. By 1930, through legal and extralegal means, the Anglos had taken over most of the farming and ranching land in the state, and the state and federal governments appropriated much of the common lands that had previously belonged to the incorporated towns and villages. The Spanish-speaking population ultimately lost 1.7 million acres of community lands and two million acres in private holdings. The Hispanos sporadically reacted to this process by forming secret societies and vigilante groups; but at most this constituted harassment rather than effective resistance.

The Alianza now demands the return of these lands.

Yet in all probability, the Alianza would not exist but for the efforts of a single man, a leader who devotes his life to his cause, and inspires his followers to do likewise. Reies López Tijerina is a man of rare charisma who is most in his element when haranguing a large crowd. Of average height, he seems to have great physical strength as he grasps a microphone with one sinewy arm and gesticulates artfully and furiously with the other. He sometimes shouts violently as he asks rhetorical questions of his audience in Spanish—the language he uses by preference—and gets "Si!" and "No!" bellowed back in appropriate cadences. The author witnessed a Tijerina performance last fall on the steps of the state capitol in Austin, Texas, where the Alianza leader told a group of Mexican-American Labor Day marchers he supported their demand for a state minimum wage of $1.25 an hour, but did so "with shame." Why should Mexican-Americans in Texas ask so little of the Anglos, whose government had repeatedly broken the Treaty of Guadalupe Hidalgo?

Reies Tijerina uses a demagogic style before a crowd, but he holds the tenets of his faith with unshakable conviction: "It's something in me that must come out," Tijerina proclaims. His followers regard him with awe. He is "Caudillo" (leader) of the Alianza, but disclaims any desire to be dictator. He points out that a Supreme Council has ultimate control—though he, clearly, makes the decisions. It seems obvious that no one could step into his shoes, nor has anyone been groomed to do so. In any event Tijerina has no doubt that his followers require strong and able leadership. He justifies this by arguing that the Hispanos are a "young" race. They were "born," he explains, by virtue of a royal decree in 1514 allowing Spaniards to marry Indians; the term "Hispano" or "Spanish American" therefore can generally be equated with "mestizo." This young race is still learning, painfully, how to defend itself and requires strong direction. It is not an ancient and clever people like the Jews, he says.

Recognizing the diverse historical experiences of Texas, New Mexico, and California, the Caudillo realizes that his constituency for the foreseeable future will be limited to New Mexico. He does believe, however, that the land grants to Mexican-Americans in California can still be identified and claimed like those of New Mexico.

It is no coincidence that Tijerina's style and language recall Pentecostal protestantism. He has been a minister in the Assembly of God, and was an itinerant revival preacher for many years to Mexican-Americans throughout the Southwest.

But, unlike the vast majority of his followers, he was not born in New Mexico but in Texas ("A prophet is not without honor save in his own country"). One of seven children of a migrant farm family, once so desperate that they were reduced to eating field rats, he picked crops and preached in Illinois and Michigan as well as in Texas and Arizona. He did not settle in New Mexico until 1960; and, with his five brothers, formed the Alianza three years later.

The quasi-religious fervor of Tijerina has strongly shaped the aspirations and style of the Alianza. However, there is greater emphasis on Old Testament justice than New Testament love. *Justicia* is a word frequently on the Caudillo's lips.

The Alianza now claims to have 30,000 dues-paying members paying at least $2.00 per month. A scholar guesses that 10,000 may be closer to the true figure. It seems clear that Tijerina's computation includes sympathizers or at least persons who have only occasionally contributed funds.

As with some sectors of the American Negro movement, the Alianza's programs began with an emphasis on litigation; and when that failed, frustration and a disposition toward violence emerged.

In April 1966 the "President and Founder" of the Alianza journeyed to Spain in order to gather materials on the registration of

New Mexican land grants in the colonial era; from such documents he hoped to generate a strong legal case to present in federal courts.

In July Tijerina presented a petition to the Governor of New Mexico, Jack Campbell, and stated, "We do not demand anything. We just want a full investigation of the issue." Yet Governor Campbell would do little more than receive Tijerina and hear him out.

In January 1967, the Caudillo, one of his brothers, and a self-styled legal expert in the Alianza named Gerry Noll made a trip to Washington, D.C., where they "limited" their claims to 500,000 acres in the Kit Carson National Forest and to an area around the city of Albuquerque. He only obtained a brief hearing with a State Department attorney and a sympathetic interview with New Mexico's Senator Montoya.

In 1966 the Alianza had already begun to give up hope of legal redress. The Supreme Council of the Alianza "passed a resolution of non-confidence in the Courts of the State of New Mexico and of the United States of America" because of "corruption" and "low standards of knowledge of law."

On October 22, 1966 the Aliancistas proclaimed the existence of the Republic of San Joaquín del Río de Chama (in Rio Arriba County) with Tijerina as "city attorney" (procurador) of the community; they simultaneously attempted to take over Kit Carson Forest, which covers most of the county. They arrested U.S. Forest Rangers for trespassing, decided to print hunting and fishing licenses, and commandeered government vehicles. The rebels were quickly dispersed by local authorities, and Tijerina and four lieutenants were charged on counts of assault, converting government property to private use, and conspiracy.

Demonstrations and protest meetings continued. On January 15, 1967 the Alianza declared it would seek redress in the United Nations if the U.S. Congress failed to act. On April 17 several hundred Aliancistas paraded before the State House in Santa Fe, and Reies Tijerina, out on bond, delivered an ominous message: "We will ... issue to the public and the federal government and the world the last human legal notice exposing the truth.... The government is being warned and advised if anybody is found trespassing on these land grants they will be arrested and punished...."

At the beginning of June the District Attorney of Santa Fe, Alfonso Sánchez, expressed concern about the "communist philosophy" of the Alianza and alleged that Aliancistas were amassing "machine guns, M-1 rifles, and 15,000 rounds" of ammunition. Eleven members of the Alianza were promptly arrested and jailed in Tierra Amarilla, an Alianza stronghold and the seat of Rio Arriba County.

The reaction was swift and violent: On June 5, as noted, the Aliancistas launched their revolt and attacked the Tierra Amarilla courthouse. This time, when caught, the Caudillo and his principal aides were charged with kidnapping, three counts of conspiracy to commit murder, and bombing a public building (the courthouse). Despite the gravity of the charges, Tijerina and some of his men were released on bond after six weeks in prison. The failure of the attack by no means dampened the spirits of the Aliancistas.

In the months following, Tijerina traveled throughout the Southwest to gain backing. He found it, both in radical organizations of Mexican-Americans and Negroes, and in some Mexican-American associations with more traditional reformist leadership.

On October 15, Tijerina was in Los Angeles, linking his cause to the peace movement at an anti-war rally. Labeling the United States' involvement in Vietnam "the most criminal in the history of mankind," he contacted radical Negro and Mexican-American groups in the Los Angeles area. One week later, at a convention of the Alianza de Mercedes on October 21, Tijerina announced that a "Treaty of Peace, Harmony, and Mutual Assistance" had been contracted between his organization and SNCC, CORE, and the Black Panthers. The Caudillo also obtained statements of support from the Crusade for Justice, a Mexican-American organization of slumdwellers in Denver, and from MAPA, an important Mexican-American political action group in California.

While gathering support from non-Anglo groups outside New Mexico in the here and now, Tijerina and his deputies have not discouraged the movement's latent tendencies toward millenarianism[1] and belief in special divine favor back home on the Upper Rio Grande. During the raid at Tierra Amarilla, several Aliancistas witnessed the appearance of a double rainbow, a sure sign of God's grace. According to others, the Caudillo is the prophet of Montezuma who

---

1. Nancie Gonzalez was the first to note millenarian tendencies in the Alianza.

will miraculously return in the imminent future to punish the Anglos for their appropriation of Hispano lands.

Another legend has it that a leader will come "from the east" and expel the foreigners who took the Mexican-Americans' lands. (Tijerina fits, since Texas is east of New Mexico.)

In the "*Corrido de Rio Arriba*," which appeared shortly after the June raid, the balladeer told his audience that when bullets started flying "*Las mujeres y los niños/iban corriendo y llorando,*

Y en este instanite pensamos/Que el mundo se iba acabando."

("Women and children/Ran about in tears

And at that moment we thought/The world was coming to an end.")

Although the "free city-states" which Tijerina hopes to erect are of this world, they clearly represent a sort of secular paradise, a recaptured golden age, somewhat along the lines prescribed in *The Laws of the Indies*. The inhabitants will be able to do any work they please, explains the Caudillo; but most will be herdsmen using the common lands (*ejidos*) of the pueblos. Tijerina himself will simply become City Attorney of the Republic of Chama.

If "la raza" is specially favored and will come into its millenium, why is it suffering so now? This is explained as the result of a "fall from grace" which occurred after the Anglo-American invasion of New Mexico in 1846 and the collusion of certain Hispanos with the alien conquerors. An allegorical mural at Alianza headquarters tells the story: A sacred temple in the center of the mural represents paradise entwined by a serpent, which also clutches three figures symbolizing the oppressed races—the Negro, the Indian, and the Hispano. The snake personifies the "Santa Fe Ring"—the Anglo and upper-class Hispano politicians who appropriated the poor Hispanos' lands in the 1880's and later. Figures on the right side, representing the People, begin to emerge from the Darkness and a reptile-devouring secretary bird, personifying Justice, arrives to attack the snake. At the top of the canvas is a rainbow (a symbol of God's blessing) and the phrase "Justicia." Just below this emblem is the City of Justice, which will once more be reconstituted on earth.

Yet there is a sinister element in the apocalypse which must precede the millenium: Anglos must be driven out. And Hispanos will be judged by whether they aided, stood aside from, or hindered the cause. Those who hindered will be treated harshly. . . .

Helen Wheeler,
"The Puerto Rican Population of New York, New York"

Puerto Ricans have been citizens of the United States since 1917, but denial of statehood limits the influence of their island in national politics as well as its share of national revenues. Poor employment opportunities in their homeland led many Puerto Ricans to migrate to New York City where they numbered about one million by 1970. Cultural and racial barriers impeded employment and acceptance of Puerto Ricans and forced them to occupy the lower rungs of the economic ladder. In Puerto Rico color does not constitute an important social or economic disadvantage, so that prejudice toward darker-skinned islanders on the mainland was an unexpected and perplexing experience for them. Although Helen Wheeler wrote "The Puerto Rican Population of New York, New York" twenty years ago, her observations on the difficulties encountered by the migrants on the mainland are unfortunately descriptive of the situation today.

The Puerto Rican Population of New York, New York

Helen Wheeler

The people who migrate to this country from the Spanish-speaking countries of this hemisphere are frequently grouped together in one category. This is unfortunate, because it hinders an understanding of their motives for coming and their reasons for staying or leaving. Those who migrate from the most economically "underdeveloped" republics do so, obviously, for the purpose of seeking better living standards, and these come in considerable numbers. On the other hand, there probably are not many more Argentinians, Uruguayans, Colombians, and Chileans here than there are Americans in those countries. Their reasons for being here are the same as those of the Americans for being there, namely, study, business, or simply travel.

Although there are no immigration quotas for Latin Americans, as there are for Europeans, American visas are hard to get. A very limited number of persons from each country get a "permanent" visa, and the length of other visas varies according to the purpose of the visit. Therefore, the number of Latin Americans who have arrived in this country during the past ten years, intending to live here permanently, is relatively small. The exception to this is the Puerto Ricans, who,

Abridged from Helen Wheeler, "The Puerto Rican Population of New York, New York," *Sociology and Social Research*, XXXV (1950), pp. 123–127. Reprinted by permission of the publisher.

being American citizens, are free to come and go. They play, therefore, an interesting part in Spanish-American immigration into the city of New York, since they represent the impact of two cultures and its transfer to a great metropolis.

Puerto Rico is more closely associated with United States ways than any other Latin-American country, and the Puerto Ricans are the largest Spanish-speaking group in the city of New York.

Ceded to the United States as a result of the Spanish-American War in 1898, her people were made United States citizens by the Jones Act in 1917. Since that time, Puerto Rico has become the object of interest to many sociologists and historians who see in the island the actual taking place of the impact of two cultures, the tropical and the temperate, and of two races, the Latin and the Saxon. This conflict, together with extreme economic depression in Puerto Rico, has precipitated one of the greatest migrations in New York City's history.

Puerto Rico, with a population of about two million inhabitants, ranks among the most densely populated regions of the world; it is the third most densely populated agricultural spot on the earth, with six hundred people per square mile. More than two thirds of the inhabitants reside in the rural zones, and the population in general depends almost completely on agricultural activities. Seventy-six percent of the population is composed of "whites," and the remaining 24 percent, principally, of Negroes and mulattoes.

On passing into the hands of the United States, a marked increase in the island's population was produced, due in part to the high natality rate, but due principally to the lowering of the mortality rate. The high percentage of unemployed is due to three important factors: the density of population, the scarcity of raw materials, and the almost complete absence of large industrial enterprise. In September 1942 about 37 percent of the active population was jobless.

The workers' movement has not had a great development in Puerto Rico because of the great number of laborers and the relatively poor standard of living of the population. Even during the prosperous years between 1920 and 1927, the number of employable persons always far exceeded the number of vacant jobs. Moreover, the farmers and planters, flattered by the high prices, sold their lands and transferred to the towns.

At the beginning of the [thirties] the island found itself in the midst of the greatest economic crisis in its history, so that the Puerto Ricans by 1931 composed the entire Spanish-speaking group in the city of New York. In August 1933 the Puerto Rico Emergency Relief Administration was established, and dedicated itself to the economic reconstruction of the island; in 1935 this agency was replaced by the Federal Relief Administration. By 1939 this Office had effected a reduction in the number of unemployed, but in that year Congress failed to extend new allocations for it.

The Bureau of Applied Social Research of Columbia University believes that there are about 160,000 Puerto Ricans in New York City at the present time [1950] and that the average age is twenty-four. The main reason these migrants give for coming to New York is their search for economic betterment. In more recent years the Puerto Ricans have come in search of *better* jobs, rather than *just* employment.

Other reasons for migrating refer to their desire to join their families, to attend schools, and to utilize hospitals and other facilities which the city offers. Puerto Rican migration to New York is an example of movement of a people who hope to better their condition. The Puerto Ricans find themselves landless, unemployed, herded into towns, and they look to the United States and New York as means of escape from these economic conditions.

The Puerto Ricans come to New York because of better steamship facilities and rates between Puerto Rico and New York as compared with the Gulf ports. They come to New York to earn the comparatively high money-wages that used to go to the European immigrant groups which are now restricted. The fact that this migration results from population pressure is the greatest difference from the reason for the migration of other Latin-American countries represented in New York. They also come in large numbers by plane.

In addition to the great difference in wages and opportunity which draws the Puerto Rican to this country, he is attracted by the higher standard of living he observes in American movies. Unfortunately, many distorted ideas are also given by these same pictures. Relatives and friends already living in the United States have a strong influence. They draw him here, whether or not they have prospered, for he may simply come to join them, and then too a little appears as a lot. It is customary for Puerto Ricans to share whatever they have with relatives. Ease of movement here is the fifth main motive for the Puerto Rican's migration to New York.

Most of those in the labor force arrive in New York without prior arrangements for a job. Contrary to the recent speculation that Puerto Rican migrants have been brought here by labor contractors, most of them arrive with only great hopes; they do increase their earning power, however, immediately. The migrants consistently earn more money on their first job in New York than they had earned in Puerto Rico.

The New York State Employment Service places Puerto Ricans in industrial and domestic positions. Most of the males find work as assemblers of various products; heavy laborers in the sugar factories; pressers and floor boys in the garment industries; dishwashers, bus boys, pantrymen, and countermen in the hotels; laundry workers, porters, elevator operators and janitors in building maintenance; and many, in shipbuilding, as cleaning, scaling, and painting workers. The International Ladies' Garment Workers Union reports a membership of over five thousand Puerto Rican women workers. In the garment industries they find employment as hand sewers, floor girls, cleaners, and beginning sewing machine operators; in hospitals, as ward aides; in addition, they do piecework at home assembling jewelry and toys, making artificial flowers, and doing hand embroidery and sewing on blouses, underwear, and lampshades.

Most of the Puerto Ricans agree that their greatest handicap in gaining employment is their lack of knowledge of the English language. Other barriers are lack of vocational training, New York City licenses, tools, and local references. Unfamiliarity with New York's streets and with transportation facilities limits the employment of many to the immediate neighborhood in which they live; but, in general, they are quick to become familiar with the city's transportation, hospital, clinic, public welfare, and entertainment facilities. The Puerto Rican encounters a color line which does not exist in Puerto Rico. He is also at a disadvantage because he is not organized with his fellow Puerto Ricans here, and he is subject to sickness, particularly parasitical diseases and tuberculosis. The professional class and business and trades people are practically nonexistent. Almost all fall into the unskilled labor class, depending upon the weekly wage.

The Puerto Ricans in New York are distributed widely throughout the three boroughs of Manhattan, the Bronx, and Brooklyn, with perhaps half of the total population being concentrated in East Harlem and the South Bronx. It is in these neighborhoods, particularly in East Harlem, that the conditions exist which give rise to the articles and photographs which have appeared in the newspapers and magazines. These conditions are part of the whole problem of slum dwellings—a problem of the city as a whole, and not confined to Puerto Ricans. The general characteristic of their housing is that it is bad, but not worse than the way most of them lived in Puerto Rico, or, if in some cases it is, the Puerto Rican feels compensated if he is able to find the position and opportunity he expected. Many do, and a surprisingly small number return to Puerto Rico permanently.

Free to come and go as a United States citizen, the depressed Puerto Rican sees this great city in motion pictures and thinks it is not difficult to make good money here. Moreover, conditions in Puerto Rico at the present time are such that practically any living conditions and rate of pay would be better than those to which he is accustomed. One reads and hears accounts of the unhealthful crowded tenements in the Puerto Rican sections of Harlem, and it is difficult to realize that many of the occupants still consider themselves better off than they were in Puerto Rico. True, most of these people miss home—they long for the tropical climate and scenery, for their families and friends, and, above all, for the slower, more easygoing life—but they do not miss the old standard of living....

John H. Burma,
"The Background of the Current Situation of Filipino-Americans"

The United States' acquisition of the Philippine Islands after
the Spanish-American War paved the way for a new immigration.
Although the movement was minimal at first, by 1930, there
were about thirty thousand and by 1970, seventy thousand Filipinos
living in California where they have concentrated. Employment
opportunities were limited; even today over 50 percent of the men
are either farm laborers or service workers. Writing in 1951, John H.
Burma described "The Background of the Current Situation of
Filipino-Americans," explaining the historical development of
the difficulties of adjustment faced by these immigrants to the
United States. According to Burma, the Filipinos of 1950 considered
themselves white, but the majority society generally viewed them
as nonwhite. On the other hand, today's younger Filipino-Americans
often identify with the Third World, rather than with whites.

The Background of the Current Situation of Filipino-Americans

John H. Burma

The last Asiatic group to migrate in any number to the United States was the Filipino. Prior to 1920 there were not over 5,000 Filipinos in the United States at any one time, although during the previous decade they had begun to immigrate into Hawaii as contract laborers in the sugar and pineapple industries. After 1920 their movement from Hawaii to the mainland increased and was augmented by a stream of direct emigration from the Philippines. During the 1920's well over 50,000 Filipinos came to the mainland from both sources.[1] Possibly one-fourth of this number came via Hawaii. This was a two-way stream, however, the number leaving the United States in any given year being from one-half to one-sixth as great as the number entering. No restrictions were placed on such immigration and emigration as the Filipinos were nationals of the United States (until 1935) and so not subject to any quota restrictions.

The result of this relatively short-time migratory movement was that by 1930 there were some 45,200 Filipinos on the mainland of the

Abridged from John H. Burma, "The Background of the Current Situation of Filipino-Americans," *Social Forces*, XXX (1951), pp. 42–48. Reprinted by permission of the publisher. Some footnotes have been renumbered.

1. See Louis Black, *Facts About Filipino Immigration into California*, California State Department of Industrial Relations, Special Bulletin No. 3, 1930.

United States. This immigration was quite effectively cut off by the exigencies of an immigrant making a living during the depression. Then, when the Philippines were promised their independence in 1935, a formal quota of fifty was set up. This quota was in effect until 1945. At this time the Philippines received their complete independence and were given an immigration quota of one hundred, commensurate with the number of Filipinos then in the United States. Because of the practical and then official limiting of immigration, the number of Filipinos in this country has slightly decreased, so that it is expected that the 1950 census will report 40,000 or less.

The majority of Filipino-Americans are under 55 years of age. Most of them came as young men in their early twenties or later teens, unaccompanied by wives or families.[2] This meant a very disproportionate sex ratio, which in 1930 was 143 to 1. By 1940, because older men had returned to the islands and younger families were having children, this disproportion was down to about 7 to 1 for the group as a whole. For 19 years and under, the sex ratio was about even, but for 20 years of age and up, the sex ratio was approximately 20 to 1.[3] A marriageable Filipina hence is a rare sight.

Most Filipinos did not intend to stay permanently in the United States; they came in order to secure savings large enough to set themselves up in business at home, to get an American education, or just out of a spirit of adventure. More often than not their plans to return have never materialized. Many have never accumulated the desired "nest egg," others have failed to achieve the education they sought; they are failures in their own eyes, and their pride will not permit them to return home until that failure has become success. Because they have intended to return home, most Filipinos have sought acculturation but not assimilation.

The Filipino-Americans landed on the West Coast, and nearly all of them have remained there. Outside this area, only New York City has any appreciable number of Filipinos; Seattle, Portland, and San Francisco have sizeable Filipino-American colonies. Stockton, California, with some 4,000 fairly permanent residents and a "floating"

2. Cf. Grayson Kirk, "Filipinos," *Annals of the American Academy of Political and Social Science*, 223 (Sept. 1942), pp. 45–48.

3. Sixteenth Census of the United States, 1940—*Population: Characteristics of the Non-white Population by Race* (Washington: Government Printing Office [1942]), Table 3, p. 7.

population of about twice as many more, is considered the center of Filipino-American concentration, with its "Little Manila" probably the most highly developed Filipino ethnic area in America. Vying with it is Los Angeles, with 3,000 to 4,000 permanent residents, and a "floating" population of about double that number. Prior to the 1930's, in Los Angeles, they nearly all lived on the outskirts of "Little Tokyo," but during the depression there began a movement away from the First Street area over toward Figuroa and Temple Streets. Japanese relocation accelerated this movement, which is now virtually complete.[4] . . .

On the West Coast the chief occupational opportunity open to the new Filipino immigrant was some form of agricultural labor, and from the beginning to the present, casual, migratory, agricultural labor has been the occupation at which the largest number of Filipino-Americans have been able to find employment. Young, male, and single, they migrate easily, working as a racial group, usually under some variety of the *padrone* system. They are likely to travel in groups of five to fifteen, in battered cars or trucks, and have been found chiefly on the larger ranches. Although widely used in agricultural labor, no special area or crop is actually dependent on Filipino labor, nor are the *Pinoy*[5] dependent on any one crop. . . .

To find a Filipino-American employed in industry has been rare. In Alaska they have worked in rather large numbers in the fish canneries, and occasionally elsewhere in vegetable canning. They have been employed in the Merchant Marine in considerable numbers, and even before World War II some four or five thousand were in the United States Navy, mostly as mess attendants. During the winter months, and sometimes throughout the year, they work in West Coast cities as cooks, dishwashers, bellboys, elevator boys, house boys, or gardeners. Some are engaged in service occupations to their fellows, in barber shops, pool halls, hotels, cafes, taxi service, and the like. During the war many secured employment in shipyards, airplane factories and other war-stimulated industries. A surprising number were hired by movie studios as extras. This, plus the number in the army meant that the war period was the best period economically which the Fili-

---

4. R. T. Feria, "War and the Status of Filipino Immigrants," *Sociology and Social Research*, 31 (Sept. 1946), pp. 48–53.
5. Their own name for themselves.

pinos have experienced since the beginning of their migration to the United States.[6] Unfortunately most so employed were "marginal workers," and were among the first to lose their jobs after the war stimulation ceased.

All those except the disillusioned and disheartened look forward to moving out of the migratory labor, domestic service, etc., to better jobs, but discriminatory hiring plus their own lack of qualification make this a rather unlikely step for most of them. In short, the Filipino-American has filled, in his own way, a function in the economic life of the Pacific Coast similar to that which different waves of migration always have filled on the Atlantic Coast.[7] ...

The living conditions of most Filipino-Americans have been far from satisfactory. They usually do not form permanent ethnic settlements, but live in the cities during the winter and work on farms in the summer. In the city, in order to save money, several will live in one room, usually in an old house which makes no pretext of being anything except a place to sleep. In the rural area they move about week after week, always living in "temporary" housing—poor houses, made-over barns, barracks, or just sheds. Typical furniture includes only cots, a table, and a few chairs. Sanitary facilities may be at an amazing minimum. Hence, winter or summer, urban or rural, the Filipino-American is a slum dweller, with all the problems that such residence entails. ...

As a group, the Filipinos have been subject to a full quota of social problems. The great preponderance of young males, absence of older persons, extensive lack of family life, and living conditions in labor camps promote not only restlessness and migratoriness but also instability of personality and abnormal social life. ...

Most states where Filipinos live have passed laws prohibiting the marriage of "Caucasians" and "Mongolians,"[8] and the court arguments have been over whether the Filipino, who is predominantly Malay, is therefore also a "Mongolian." In California where most Filipinos have lived, such marriage was first considered legal, then

6. Feria, *op. cit.*

7. Bruno Lasker, *Filipino Immigration* (Chicago: University of Chicago Press, 1931), p. 65.

8. *Cf.* N. Foster, "The Legal Status of the Filipino Intermarriages in California," *Sociology and Social Research* (May–June, 1933), pp. 441–54. Also, I. B. Buaken, "You Can't Marry a Filipino," *Commonweal*, 41 (March 16, 1945), pp. 534–37.

374

illegal, with the county clerk of each county serving as judge of race,[9] and then in 1948 California's anti-miscegenation law was declared unconstitutional. That no more Filipina intermarriages have occurred is no doubt chiefly due to the desire of most Filipinos to return home and marry Filipinas, plus the fact that discrimination and social distance prevent intimate friendships which might lead to marriage, and often prevent the acceptance of the husband. Rural intermarriage seems to work somewhat better than urban, probably because there is somewhat less public opposition and discrimination and because the rural environment seems more conducive to stable marriage than the disorganized area of city slums. In either case discrimination, language handicaps, and wide cultural differences are potentially disorganizing factors.[10] . . .

The fact that Filipinos are dark-skinned foreigners (plus living on the West Coast) is sufficient to expose them to discrimination.[11] Such discrimination has followed the usual pattern of social rejection, attitudes of superiority, difficulty in securing housing, difficulty in securing jobs above the labor category, refusal of service in cafes, segregation in movie balconies, being "frozen out" of local or campus social activities, and objections to Filipino-white dating. To these are added the individual slights and injustices which unpremeditatedly occur when one group feels itself superior to another. There are, of course, wide differences in treatment from region to region, from town to town, and from individual to individual. When the Filipinos are few in number they are usually thought of as Latin Americans, because of their color and the fact that they speak Spanish. If few in number and inconspicuous they usually suffer no discrimination. When they arrive suddenly and in large numbers, unfavorable reports are circulated and believed, and discrimination results.[12]

The crux of the most active and bitter discrimination and dislike seems to be the Filipino's refusal to accept his "place" as an inferior.

9. Cf. Emory S. Bogardus, "What Race are Filipinos?" *Sociology and Social Research* (Jan.–Feb. 1932), pp. 274–79.

10. Denicio T. Catapusan, "Filipino Intermarriage Problems in the United States," *Sociology and Social Research* (Jan. 1938), pp. 265–72.

11. Cf. Emory S. Bogardus, "American Attitudes toward Filipinos," *Sociology and Social Research*, 14 (May–June 1930), pp. 469–79.

12. Cf. M. Buaken, "Where is the Heart of America?" *New Republic*, 103 (Sept. 23, 1940), p. 410.

He typically considers himself white, with all the perquisites thereto appertaining in our culture. He has been taught in the Islands that all men are created equal, and his pride and sensitivity will not permit him to passively assume the role of an inferior as did the Chinese coolie a generation or two before him. Most "incidents" seem to stem from the Filipino's conviction that he is as good as any one else, and his consequent behavior.[13] Between 1928 and 1930 there were about a dozen disturbances of significance in Washington and California. Most of these disturbances occurred in small towns and villages and included beatings, dynamitings and near-riots. Although the pattern differed slightly from one to another, the underlying causes were either economic or social. Economically, the Filipinos were often opposed by local labor units or unions on the grounds of lowering wages, and occasionally opposed by employers for striking at a critical time in order to get better wages. Socially, the most prominent difficulty was the attentions paid by Filipinos to white girls, attentions which usually were of alarm to the white men rather than to the white women. In general the vocal objections raised were the same as those voiced against Orientals: they cause low wages by having a low standard of living, they could not become citizens,[14] they could not be assimilated, and contact with them would endanger our racial purity. It is unfortunate that the Filipinos were and are concentrated in an area especially sensitive to the "Oriental Menace," particularly since this concentration prevents the rest of the nation from knowing the facts in the situation.

One result of the above conditions and accusations was the early demand for the exclusion and deportation of Filipinos. In 1924 Congress declared that they were not aliens, but being neither Caucasian nor Negro they were ineligible to citizenship. Hence they possessed the hybrid status of nationals or wards. As nationals, however, their forced deportation was likely to be illegal, and their exclusion was also of doubtful legality. Of those who sought Filipino exclusion and deportation, labor unions and California "Native" organizations were the most prominent. Deportation and exclusion were opposed by

13. Cf. Donald E. Anthony, "Filipino Labor in Central California," *Sociology and Social Research*, 16 (Nov.-Dec. 1931), p. 156.

14. This was true at the time, but Filipinos now may become citizens just as can other immigrants.

those employing Filipino laborers and by the Filipinos themselves. A third suggestion, that Filipino immigration be limited to students and to "better class" Filipinos was supported by intellectual and semi-intellectual groups and hence received less Congressional consideration than either of the other two. The solution came in 1935 with a federal act providing for voluntary repatriation at government expense of any Filipino who would return home.[15] No more than one in forty took advantage of this opportunity, partly from the injury it would do their pride, and partly because such repatriation prohibited their ever returning to the United States. In the same year the granting of partial independence to the Philippines, with the promise of full independence in 1945, helped quiet Filipino complaints and removed their hybrid political position.[16]

The Filipino always doubted whether he would spend the rest of his life in America, yet he did not know when he could return home, for he had to have either money or an education before he could return without disgrace. Then World War II in most instances made him make up his mind to return soon or to stay permanently here; either decision decreased significantly the instability, indecision, and partial goallessness which had been seriously disorganizing factors.[17] . . .

15. Cf. Emory S. Bogardus, "Filipino Repatriation," Sociology and Social Research (Sept.–Oct. 1936), pp. 67–71. Also, "Lovers Departure; Subsidized Exodus," Time, 27 (April 13, 1936), p. 17; Carey McWilliams, "Exit the Filipino," Nation, 141 (Sept. 4, 1935), p. 265.

16. They are now "Aliens eligible to citizenship."

17. Feria, op. cit., p. 52.

Selected Bibliography

A. General Works

Allport, Gordon W. *The Nature of Prejudice*. New York: Anchor, 1954.

Bennett, Lerone. *Before the Mayflower*. New York: Penguin, 1962.

Burma, John H., ed. *Mexican-Americans in the United States*. Cambridge, Mass.: Schenkman, 1970.

Farb, Peter. *Man's Rise to Civilization, As Shown by the Indians of North America From the Primeval Times to the Coming of the Industrial State*. New York: Avon, 1968.

Franklin, John Hope. *From Slavery to Freedom*. New York: Vintage, 1967.

Glazer, Nathan and Daniel Patrick Moynihan. *Beyond the Melting Pot: The Negroes, Puerto Ricans, Jews, Italians, and Irish of New York City*. Cambridge: M.I.T. Press, 1963.

Gordon, Milton M. *Assimilation in American Life*. New York: Oxford University Press, 1964.

Gossett, Thomas F. *Race: The History of an Idea in America*. New York: Schocken, 1963.

Grebler, Leo, Joan W. Moore, and Ralph C. Guzman. *The Mexican-American People: The Nation's Second Largest Minority*. New York: Free Press, 1970.

Hagan, William T. *American Indians*. Chicago: University of Chicago Press, 1961.

Handlin, Oscar. *Race and Nationality in American Life*. New York: Anchor, 1957.

Kitano, Harry H. *The Japanese-Americans: The Evolution of a Subculture*. New York: Prentice-Hall, 1969.

Kovel, Joel. *White Racism: A Psychohistory*. New York: Vintage, 1970.

Lee, Rose Hum. *The Chinese in the United States of America*. Hong Kong: Hong Kong University Press, 1960.

McWilliams, Carey. *North From Mexico: The Spanish-Speaking People of the United States*. Westport, Conn.: Greenwood, 1948.

Meier, August and Elliott M. Rudwick. *From Plantation to Ghetto*. New York: Hill and Wang, 1966.

Myers, Gustavus. *History of Bigotry in the United States*. New York: Capricorn, 1943.

Nash, Gary B. and Richard Weiss, eds. *The Great Fear: Race in the Mind of America*. New York: Holt, 1970.

Schwartz, Barry M. and Robert Disch. *White Racism: Its History, Pathology, and Practice*. New York: Dell, 1970.

Spicer, Edward H. *A Short History of the Indians of the United States*. New York: Anvil, 1969.

B. The Seventeenth and Eighteenth Centuries

Blacks

Greene, Lorenzo. *The Negro in Colonial New England*. New York: Atheneum, 1942.

Jordan, Winthrop. *White Over Black: American Attitudes Toward the Negro, 1550–1812*. New York: Penguin, 1968.

Klingberg, Frank. *An Appraisal of the Negro in Colonial South Carolina*. Toronto: Associated Publishers, 1941.

Mannix, Daniel, and Malcolm Cowley. *Black Cargoes: A History of the Atlantic Slave Trade*. New York: Viking, 1962.

Mellon, Matthew T. *Early American Views on Negro Slavery*. New York: Mentor, 1934, 1969.

Quarles, Benjamin. *The Negro in the American Revolution*. Chapel Hill: University of North Carolina Press, 1961.

Robinson, Donald. *Slavery in the Structure of American Politics, 1765–1820*. New York: Harcourt, 1971.

Tate, Thad W. *The Negro in Eighteenth-Century Williamsburg*. Charlottesville: University of Virginia Press, 1966.

Zilversmit, Arthur. *The First Emancipation: The Abolition of Slavery in the North*. Chicago: University of Chicago Press, 1967.

Indians

Lauber, Almon W. *Indian Slavery in Colonial Times Within the Present Limits of the United States*. New York: Columbia University Press, 1913.

Leach, Douglas E. *Flintlock and Tomahawk: New England in King Philip's War*. New York: Norton, 1958.

Milling, Chapman J. *Red Carolinians*. Chapel Hill: University of North Carolina Press, 1940.

Trelease, Allen W. *Indian Affairs in Colonial New York: Seventeenth Century*. Ithaca, N. Y.: Cornell University Press, 1960.

Vaughan, Alden T. *The New England Frontier: Puritans and Indians, 1620–1675.* Boston: Little, Brown, 1965.

Wallace, Anthony F. C. *King of the Delawares: Teedyuscung.* Philadelphia: University of Pennsylvania Press, 1949.

C. The Nineteenth Century

Blacks

Aptheker, Herbert. *American Negro Slave Revolts.* New York: International Publishers, 1943.

Carroll, Joseph C. *Slave Insurrections in the United States.* Westport, Conn.: Negro Universities Press, 1938.

DuBois, W. E. B. *Black Reconstruction in America.* Cleveland: Meridian, 1935.

Elkins, Stanley. *Slavery: A Problem in American Institutional and Intellectual Life.* Chicago: University of Chicago Press, 1959.

Genovese, Eugene. *The Political Economy of Slavery.* New York: Vintage, 1961.

Litwack, Leon F. *North of Slavery: The Negro in the Free States, 1790–1860.* Chicago: University of Chicago Press, 1961.

Logan, Rayford W. *The Betrayal of the Negro: From Rutherford B. Hayes to Woodrow Wilson.* New York: Collier, 1965.

McPherson, James. *The Negro's Civil War.* New York: Vintage, 1965.

Meier, August. *Negro Thought in America, 1880–1915.* Ann Arbor: University of Michigan Press, 1963.

Quarles, Benjamin. *Black Abolitionists.* New York: Oxford University Press, 1969.

Stampp, Kenneth. *The Peculiar Institution.* New York: Vintage, 1956.

Starobin, Robert S. *Industrial Slavery in the Old South.* New York: Oxford University Press, 1970.

Wade, Richard. *Slavery in the Cities.* New York: Oxford University Press, 1964.

Wood, Forrest G. *Black Scare: The Racist Response to Emancipation and Reconstruction.* Berkeley: University of California Press, 1968.

Woodward, C. Vann. *The Strange Career of Jim Crow.* New York: Oxford University Press, 1955.

Indians

Abel, Annie. *The Slaveholding Indians,* 3 vols. Glendale, Calif.: Arthur H. Clark, 1915–1925.

Andrist, Ralph K. *The Long Death: The Last Days of the Plains Indians.* New York: Collier, 1964.

Brown, Dee. *Bury My Heart at Wounded Knee.* New York: Holt, 1970.

DeRosier, Arthur Jr. *The Removal of the Choctaw Indians.* Knoxville: University of Tennessee Press, 1970.

Downes, Randolph C. *Council Fires On the Upper Ohio.* Pittsburgh: University of Pittsburgh Press, 1940.

Ewers, John C. *The Blackfeet: Raiders on the Northwestern Plains.* Norman: University of Oklahoma Press, 1958.

Foreman, Grant. *Indian Removal: The Emigration of the Five Civilized Tribes of Indians.* Norman: University of Oklahoma Press, 1953.

Fritz, Henry E. *The Movement for Indian Assimilation, 1860–1890.* Philadelphia: University of Pennsylvania Press, 1963.

Hagan, William T. *The Sac and Fox Indians.* Norman: University of Oklahoma Press, 1958.

Horsman, Reginald. *Expansion and American Indian Policy, 1783–1812.* East Lansing: Michigan State University Press, 1967.

Priest, Loring B. *Uncle Sam's Stepchildren: The Reformation of United States Indian Policy, 1865–1887.* New Brunswick: Rutgers University Press, 1942.

Prucha, Francis P. *American Indian Policy in the Formative Years, 1790–1834.* Lincoln: University of Nebraska Press, 1962.

Tucker, Glenn. *Tecumseh.* Indianapolis: Bobbs-Merrill, 1956.

Wallace, Ernest and E. Adamson Hoebel. *The Comanches: Lords of the South Plains.* Norman: University of Oklahoma Press, 1953.

Mexican-Americans

Burns, Walter Noble. *The Robin Hood of El Dorado: The Saga of Joaquin Murietta.* New York: Coward-McCann, 1932.

Greenwood, Robert. *The California Outlaw: Tiburcio Vasquez.* Georgetown, Calif.: Talisman Press, 1960.

Pitt, Leonard. *The Decline of the Californios: A Social History of the Spanish-Speaking Californians, 1846–1890.* Berkeley: University of California Press, 1966.

Chinese-Americans

Barth, Gunther. *Bitter Strength: A History of the Chinese in the United States, 1850–1870.* Cambridge: Harvard University Press, 1964.

Chiu, Ping. *Chinese Labor in California, 1850–1880.* Madison: Historical Society of Wisconsin, 1963.

Coolidge, Mary. *Chinese Immigration.* New York: Henry Holt, 1909.

Miller, Stuart C. *The Unwelcome Immigrant: The American Image of the Chinese, 1785–1882.* Berkeley: University of California Press, 1969.

Sandmeyer, Elmer C. *The Anti-Chinese Movement in California.* Urbana: University of Illinois Press, 1939.

D. The Twentieth Century

Blacks

Cleaver, Eldridge. *Soul On Ice.* New York: McGraw-Hill, 1968.

Cronon, E. David. *Black Moses: The Story of Marcus Garvey.* Madison: University of Wisconsin Press, 1955.

Jackson, Kenneth T. *The Ku Klux Klan in the City, 1915–1930*. New York: Oxford University Press, 1967.

Kellogg, Charles F. *NAACP: A History of the National Association for the Advancement of Colored People*, vol. 1. Baltimore: Johns Hopkins Press, 1967.

Lester, Julius. *Look Out Whitey: Black Power's Gon' Get Your Mama*. New York: Grove, 1968.

Lomax, Louis. *The Negro Revolt*. New York: Signet, 1962.

Malcolm X. *Autobiography of Malcolm X*. New York: Grove, 1964.

Osofsky, Gilbert. *Harlem: The Making of a Ghetto, 1890–1920*. New York: Torchbook, 1966.

Spear, Allan. *Black Chicago: The Making of a Negro Ghetto, 1890–1920*. Chicago: University of Chicago Press, 1967.

White, Walter. *Rope and Faggot: A Biography of Judge Lynch*. New York: Arno, 1928.

Indians

Deloria, Vine, Jr. *Custer Died for Your Sins: An Indian Manifesto*. New York: Macmillan, 1969.

Embry, Carlos B. *America's Concentration Camps*. New York: David McKay, 1956.

Kahn, Edgar, ed. *Our Brother's Keeper: The Indian in White America*. Cleveland: World Publishing, 1969.

Levine, Stuart and Nancy O. Lurie, eds. *The American Indian Today*. Deland, Fla.: Everett-Edwards, 1968.

Steiner, Stan. *The New Indians*. New York: Dell, 1968.

Mexican-Americans

Dunne, John Gregory. *Delano: The Story of the California Grape Strike*. New York: Farrar, Straus, 1967.

Heller, Celia S. *Mexican-American Youth: Forgotten Youth At the Crossroads*. New York: Random, 1966.

Kibbe, Pauline R. *Latin Americans in Texas*. Albuquerque: University of New Mexico Press, 1946.

Matthiesen, Peter. *Sal Si Puedes: Cesar Chavez and the New American Revolution*. New York: Random, 1969.

Nabokov, Peter. *Tijerina and the Courthouse Raid*. Albuquerque: University of New Mexico Press, 1969.

Peattie, Lisa Redfield. *The View From the Barrio*. Ann Arbor: University of Michigan Press, 1968.

Tuck, Ruth D. *Not With the Fist: Mexican-Americans in a Southwest City*. New York: Harcourt, 1946.

Japanese-Americans

Daniels, Roger. *The Politics of Prejudice: The Anti-Japanese Movement in California and the Struggle for Japanese Exclusion.* New York: Atheneum, 1962.

Grodzins, Morton. *Americans Betrayed: Politics and the Japanese Evacuation.* Chicago: University of Chicago Press, 1949.

Hosokawa, Bill. *Nisei: The Quiet Americans.* New York: Morrow, 1969.

Rademaker, John. *These Are Americans: The Japanese-Americans in Hawaii in World War II.* Palo Alto, Calif.: Pacific Books, 1951.

Puerto Ricans

Chenault, Lawrence R. *The Puerto Rican Migrant in New York City.* New York: Russell and Russell, 1938.

Lewis, Oscar. *La Vida: A Puerto Rican Family in the Culture of Poverty—San Juan and New York.* New York: Random, 1966.

Senior, Clarence. *The Puerto Ricans: Strangers—Then Neighbors.* Chicago: Quadrangle, 1961.

Sexton, Patricia Cayo. *Spanish Harlem.* New York: Harper and Row, 1965.

Wakefield, Dan. *Island in the City.* New York: Corinth Books, 1959.

Filipinos

Bulosan, Carlos. *America is in the Heart.* New York: Harcourt, 1946.

Lasker, Bruno. *Filipino Immigration to Continental United States and to Hawaii.* Chicago: University of Chicago Press, 1931.

Index

Index

Index

PRINTED IN U.S.A.